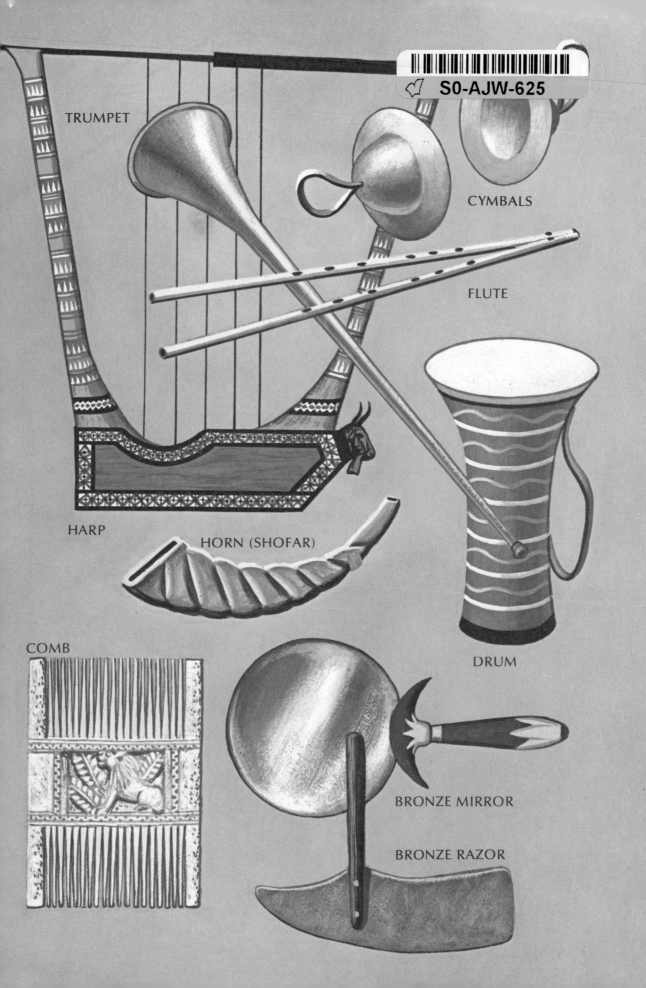

TRUMPET

CYMBALS

FLUTE

HARP

HORN (SHOFAR)

DRUM

COMB

BRONZE MIRROR

BRONZE RAZOR

Presented to

Evan Magers
For Memorizing The Lord's Prayer
Mrs. Neal and
Mrs. Gillman

by

September 28, 1975

date

NELSON'S PICTURE

BIBLE

Text by J. F. Allen, Lane Easterly,
Bernice Rich and Elmer T. Towns
Pictures by Carlo Tora

THOMAS NELSON INCORPORATED

NASHVILLE   *Publishers since 1798*   NEW YORK

This book
is designed for
and dedicated to
the religious education
of all children.

THE OLD TESTAMENT

THE NEW TESTAMENT

THE OLD TESTAMENT

The First People and Their Garden

Genesis 1 to 3

This world is a lovely place. It was not always so. When God made the world, it was like a great ball of land and water mixed together. Great, heavy clouds hung over it. Everything was dark. There were no living things. There were no flowers. There were no birds. There were no animals.

Then God spoke. He said: "Let there be light." For the first time light came to divide the darkness and make Day and Night. This was the first day of Creation. Creation is the name we give to the time when God formed the world into the lovely place we know now. After God made day and night the heavy clouds still hung above. God spoke again. The clouds separated. Now there was a clear division between the sky waters above and the waters on the earth. The second day of Creation came to its end.

Still there was no place for living things. God spoke again. The water that covered the earth separated into rivers and oceans. Now there was dry land where plants and moving creatures could later

15

made on the fifth day. On that day the first bird songs were heard, and the shining silver fish first began to swim in the seas and rivers.

But there were still no animals. God made them on the sixth day. From the smallest to the largest, God made the animals and the crawling creatures, too. On the same day God made His greatest creation, the first man. It is hard to understand how He did it, but the Bible tells us that He made man from the dust of the earth. He shaped him, and then breathed the breath of life into him. Man became a living person. God even gave him a lovely place called Eden. In Eden God planted a special garden. The garden was planted where four great rivers came together—we know only one of them now, the river Euphrates. So that the garden would grow and remain beautiful, God made a mist to rise from the earth to water its surface.

There were two strange and unusual trees in that Garden. There was the tree of life and the tree of the knowledge of good and evil. God had something special to say about the tree of the knowledge of good and evil. He told the man He had made that he could eat as much fruit as he liked from all the trees in the garden except the tree of the knowl-

live. On the same day God made the first grass and bushes and trees grow. Each kind had its own seeds which spread those plants over all the earth. All this happened on the third day.

Then God made the sun and moon and stars. God made the sun to rule in the daytime and the moon to rule at night, with the stars to shine alongside and light up the blackness of the sky. At the end of this fourth day God looked at what He had made. He was pleased.

There were still no birds. There were no fish in the seas. They were edge of good and evil. God told the man he would die if he ate the fruit from that tree.

God called the first man Adam. Adam means, "one made from dust." God gave Adam the right to name all the other animals He had made. God saw that Adam was alone. He knew he must change this. He put Adam into a deep sleep. While Adam slept, God took out one of Adam's ribs and closed up the place. Then from the rib God made the first woman and brought her to Adam. When he saw her, Adam was filled with happiness. He said: "She is bone of my bones, and flesh of my flesh. Because she was taken out of man, she will be called woman." Later Adam gave to her her own special name—Eve.

When God had completed this work, He looked at everything He had made. It was very good. God was pleased. Then on the seventh day He rested. God made that day to be a special day.

Adam and Eve Are Driven out of the Garden

The story of the first people and of the lovely garden God gave them to live in has a sad ending.

We do not know how long they lived in that happy garden—some-times you hear it called Paradise—but for a while they did what God had told them. They talked to Him just as we talk to our own friends. There was nothing ugly or wrong in their lives. Most of all, they remembered what God had said about the fruit of the tree of the knowledge of good and evil.

Then one day a terrible thing happened! The serpent came to Eve when she was near the forbidden tree. The serpent put into Eve's mind the idea that it could really do no harm if she tasted the

fruit from the tree. Eve was shocked. She told him at once that God had forbidden it. But that did not stop the serpent. He said something even worse. He hinted that God had told them they could not eat this fruit because He wanted to keep the best things away from them. He said that it was only because God did not want them to be as He—able to know good and evil.

So Eve took the fruit and ate some of it. She gave some to Adam, who ate it too. They both knew how bad the thing was which they had done.

Then God said to the serpent: "Because you have misled Adam and Eve, in the future you will not be able to walk like other animals, but you will slither in the dust and the dirt. You and the people will be enemies. One will come who will defeat you altogether because you are the devil."

To Eve God promised that she would have pain and sorrow all her life. God told Eve that her husband would have to rule over her because she had done wrong. Adam was told that they would have to leave the garden. By hard work they would have to dig and plant and make the ground grow the food they needed. From dust they had been made, and when they died, their bodies must go back to dust.

The First Brothers and the First Quarrel

Genesis 4

When God turned Adam and Eve out of the Garden of Eden, they went out alone into the world. After a little while God gave them their first son, who was called Cain, and later a second son, Abel. When they grew up, Abel was a shepherd, and Cain was a farmer.

One day Cain and Abel each went to make an altar and offer gifts to God. Abel brought gifts from his flock. God was pleased with his offering. But when Cain brought some of the things he had grown, God was not pleased. Perhaps Cain did not really love God or want to bring God a gift.

But Cain knew that God was not pleased, and Cain was very angry. One day when he and Abel were out in a lonely field together, Cain killed his brother! Then he heard the voice of God saying to him, "Where is your brother Abel?" Terrified, he answered: "I do not know; am I my brother's keeper?" Then God said a most terrible thing: "Cain, your brother's blood cries out to Me from the ground where you have spilt it. From now on my curse shall rest upon you. I will make you a wanderer, fleeing from all men, and the ground will never give you food without a struggle."

Then Cain said to God: "My punishment is too much for me. You have driven me out from my people, and everyone who sees me will do his best to kill me." God had pity on Cain, and He marked him with a special mark so that everyone would know from this that he was under God's protection.

Cain and his wife then took all they had and moved to the land of Nod, sometimes called the land of Wandering.

The Great Flood and the Ship That Saved Lives

Genesis 5 to 9

After the murder of Abel, when Cain had moved away to the land of Nod, Adam and Eve were given another son. His name was Seth.

After some generations there were many people in the world, and many villages and towns.

But the people by that time had become bad-thinking, bad-behaving men and women. God decided that people were so bad they could not go on living. But there was one man who was different. His name was Noah. Noah always tried to obey God. Noah tried to keep away from doing wrong. He had three sons, Shem, Ham, and Japheth.

God decided to speak to Noah. God told him that He was going to destroy all living things by causing a great flood on the earth. But God promised to look after Noah and his family, and keep them alive through it all because they had always done their best to please Him.

To take care of his family, Noah had to make a great ship of wood, called the ark. In that ark there would be room for Noah and his sons and their families. The ark was also like a great stable. Into

20

the ark Noah must take a pair of every unclean animal or bird or creeping thing that human beings do not eat. He was to take seven pairs of every creature that could be eaten so that there would be enough food to last them a whole year.

When all was ready, the great door of the ark was closed and sealed. It began to rain. For forty days and nights it rained without stopping. Outside on the land the water rose higher and higher until there was no place left for the people to hide. Not a mountain top showed. Not a green bush or tree could be seen. The ark just drifted on the water.

Then the rain stopped. But for another one hundred and fifty days the world was under water. The ark had come to rest on the mountains of Ararat. Noah sent birds out from the windows of the ark to see if there was dry land. First he sent out a raven. Then he sent a dove. When the dove came back with an olive leaf in its mouth, Noah knew that the trees were beginning to show again. A week later the dove did not come back at all. Then Noah knew that there was dry land at last.

The first thing Noah did on dry land was to say "thank you" to God. Noah built an altar and brought an offering to God to show that now again he and all

his family would live as God's people, serving Him every day.

At that place God made a wonderful promise that He would never again destroy the world with a flood. God promised that every year there would be seedtime and harvest, and summer and winter, just as it is now. God told Noah that he must go out with his family and that their children would again fill the world. As a sign of His promise God gave the rainbow and said: "This will be the sign of My promise for all the time to come. I put my rainbow in the clouds. When I bring the clouds over the earth and you see the rainbow, I will be looking at it, and I will remember my promise."

The Tower That Was Never Finished

Genesis 10 and 11

When Noah and his family came out of the ark they did what God had told them. They did not all stay in one place. It was not long before they had children and grandchildren. The families grew bigger and bigger. The families grew so large they were called tribes.

Even though all the tribes spoke one language and were really all the same family, they did not all think the same way. Some of the people were beginning again to do wrong.

They settled on a plain in the land of Shinar, about where Persia is today. They had an idea all their own. Since they knew how to make and bake bricks, they decided to build a great tower to reach right into heaven. They decided to build a great city around the tower. Then, they felt, they would be the greatest and the most wonderful of all people.

So they baked their bricks and started building the city. The tower rose higher and higher. But something stopped them, for God was watching. God knew if they stayed together again like they had done before the Flood, those with bad ways would soon rule over

them, especially because they all spoke one language. So God changed their language and what trouble that brought! The brickmakers could not understand the builders, and the builders could not understand the brickmakers, and in a very short time the whole building work stopped. Those who spoke the same languages moved off together, each group in a different direction.

The great tower came to nothing. The place where they had tried to build it was given the name of "Babel," which means "confusion," because there God changed their language.

A Long Journey Through the Desert

Genesis 11 to 13

Not far from Babel, or Babylon as it was called later, was another town, Ur. People who lived in Ur were called the Chaldees. This was the country we now call Iraq.

In Ur was a man called Terah. He had three sons. One of the sons, Abram, became a very great man.

Terah decided to take Abram and his wife, Sarai, and their nephew, Lot, away from Ur. They traveled a long distance through the desert till they came to a place

24

called Haran. There they stayed till Terah died.

From Haran, Abram and his nephew Lot, and their families, with their sheep and cattle, traveled south. They crossed rivers and mountains. Slowly they traveled through the land. Finally they reached the land of Canaan. God wanted them to stay in this land. God came to Abram and told him He would give the land to Abram and his children and children's children.

Because Abram was so grateful to God, he built an altar. On the altar he brought an offering of thanksgiving to God.

During a famine Abram moved his family further south to the land of Egypt, but did not stay there long because the people there did not love God. They went back to the last place where they had stayed in Canaan, near the town of Beth-el.

Abram was a rich man with much silver and gold and a great herd of cattle. Plenty of pasture-land was needed for all the animals. Because there was not enough pasture-land for them all, Lot's shepherds and Abram's shepherds began to fight. So Abram gave Lot the choice of where he would live with his flocks. Lot chose the plain of Jordan with its fertile lands. He went out to the east and settled near the cities of

Sodom and Gomorrah where the people cared nothing at all about God. Soon Lot moved right into Sodom.

God remembered His promise to Abram. As soon as Lot had gone away, God said to Abram: "Stand still and look around you, to the north and the south and the west. All the land you can see I will give to you and all your children and their children forever. And I will make your children after you as many as the grains of dust on the earth."

Abram believed God's promise even though he had no children.

The Angel at the Well

Genesis 16 and 17

Now Abram was an old man, and Sarai his wife was old too. They remembered God's promise to them. They were sad because they had no children. But Sarai had an idea. In those times, long ago, men sometimes married more than one wife. Sarai suggested that Abram marry Hagar, too. Before long Hagar knew she was going to have a baby. She began to laugh at Sarai because Sarai had no children. Sarai and Hagar were unkind to each other. Sarai treated Hagar so harshly that Hagar decided to run away back along the desert pathway that led to Egypt.

At a fountain by the wayside, Hagar stopped to rest. Suddenly with her was an angel from God. The angel asked: "Hagar, Sarai's maid, where do you come from? And where are you going?" She answered: "I am running away from my mistress, Sarai." Then the angel made a wonderful promise to her: "Never mind, Hagar. Your baby will be a son, and God wants you to call him Ishmael. Through him you will become the mother of a great nation. He will be a great hunter and a wanderer and his people will be the same. God will look after you, so do not be afraid. Go back to Sarai, because God's eyes are on you and He will be your helper."

So Hagar went back to the camp. When it was time, she had her baby son. She called him Ishmael, just as God had said. Ishmael means "God shall hear". Every time Hagar looked at her little son she remembered the promise God had sent to her by the angel.

About this time God again spoke to Abram and made the same promise He had made to him before. God told Abram that he would become the father of many nations, and that God would not forget the promise He had made. Although Abram was ninety-nine years old and Sarai was ninety, Abram believed what God said. God changed Abram's name to Abraham, which means "the father of many people". God changed Sarai's name to Sarah.

God told Abraham and Sarah that they would have a baby son. God wanted them to call him Isaac. That was a strange name. It means "someone laughs". God gave that name because when he told Abraham about the little baby who would be born, Abraham laughed. Because he and Sarah were so old, Abraham thought it was impossible to have a son.

A Promise from God, and Fire out of Heaven

Genesis 18 and 19

Abraham's great camp was set up in the plains of Mamre.

One day he looked up and saw three persons coming toward him. He ran to them and bowed down in front of them. Abraham knew these were special men. At once he went to Sarah and had a special meal cooked for them.

Then one of the visitors said to Abraham: "Soon I will come back to you again. Sarah, your wife, will

have a son." Sarah was standing in the tent door. When she heard that she was to have a baby, she laughed to herself—as old as she was, how could she possibly have a baby? The Visitor (who was God himself) said to Abraham: "Why did Sarah laugh? Is anything too hard for the Lord? I will certainly give her a son as I have promised." Sarah was afraid and said that she had not laughed. But the Lord said: "No, you *did* laugh."

As the three men started to leave, the Lord told Abraham what He was going to do next. "There is terrible wickedness in the cities of Sodom and Gomorrah," He said, "and I am going to see whether things are really as bad as they seem and to punish the people." Two of the men went on, but Abraham drew near to the Lord to plead with Him. Abraham's nephew, Lot, still lived with all his family in the city of Sodom. Abraham said to God: "Are You going to destroy the good people with the bad? Perhaps there are fifty good people in the city. Won't You spare it for their sakes?" God said He would. Abraham still kept on asking until God promised that if there were only ten good people in the city, He would not destroy it.

Two of the angels who had been with God to visit Abraham went that evening to Sodom and found

Lot sitting at the city gate. Lot at once got up and invited the strangers to eat at his house and spend the night there. But before they had settled down to sleep, the people of the city found out that there were two strangers in Lot's house. The people began to hammer at the door and try to break it down. The visitors then showed that they were angels by making the people outside blind so that they could not find the door of the house.

The angels spoke to Lot. They asked him to get together quickly all his family and to leave the city. The city was so bad it had to be destroyed. Because Lot was the only good man left, he and his family alone would be saved.

But Lot's sons-in-law would not go. In the early hours of the morning the angels dragged Lot and his wife and his two daughters out of the city to safety. Outside the city they said: "Now run as fast as you can. Don't look back, and don't stop until you reach the mountain, otherwise you will die, too, when the city is destroyed."

Then God poured out fire on the cities of Sodom and Gomorrah. The cities and all that was around them were burned up by the terrible fire. Lot and his two daughters escaped, but his wife turned to look back at the city and at once she was changed into a pillar of salt.

The Ram in the Thorn Bush

Genesis 21 to 23

The Lord had promised to Abraham and Sarah a little son. Just as He had said, when Abraham was

29

a hundred years old, the boy was born. Abraham and Sarah named him Isaac as God asked. When Isaac was about fifteen years old, God spoke to Abraham again. This time He told Abraham to go to a mountain in the land of Moriah and to offer up Isaac to Him on an altar! How sad Abraham was to receive this command from God. But Abraham listened, because it was God who had spoken, and he trusted God.

At the place God had told Abraham about, he and Isaac built the altar. They placed wood on top of it. Then Abraham fastened Isaac's hands and feet and laid him on the wood. After that came the awful moment. Abraham took a knife and lifted it up to kill his only son, Isaac.

But at that very moment a voice cried out to him from heaven, saying: "Abraham, Abraham!" And Abraham stopped and said: "Here I am." Then the angel said—because it was the angel of the Lord calling out to him: "Don't do the boy any harm, don't hurt him at all. Now I know that you fear God and want to serve Him. You have not kept back your only son from Him."

And then Abraham looked up. Right in front of him, caught by its horns in a thorn bush, was a ram! Together Abraham and Isaac used the ram for a sacrifice. They worshiped God there.

How Isaac's Wife Was Chosen

Genesis 24 and 25

When Sarah died, Abraham knew that he would not live much longer. In those days the parents always found wives for their sons. Abraham called his oldest, most trusted servant to tell him how he must go about finding a wife for Isaac.

Abraham send the servant all the way back to Haran to look for a wife for Isaac. Abraham's brother Nahor still lived in Haran. Abra-ham hoped that his servant would be able to find in that tribe a wife for Isaac.

When the servant eventually came to the country of Nahor, near the town of Haran, it was evening, and he stopped beside the well out-side the town. Soon the women would be coming out to get water. Before they came, the servant prayed that God would make the lady who should be Isaac's wife answer him in a special way when he spoke to the women. If he asked one of them to let down her jug into the water and give him water to drink, then the right one must not only give water to him but to his camels as well.

And Rebekah, the daughter of Bethuel, Abraham's nephew, did just that. After the servant had spoken with Rebekah she ran on ahead to tell them at home what had happened.

When he came to Rebekah's house, the servant told her family why he had come. He explained who Abraham was. He gave them the presents Abraham had sent. The servant told how he had prayed to God to show him the lady who was to become Isaac's wife. And then he said he was sure that Rebekah was the right one. Her father, Bethuel, and her brother, Laban, were also sure it was God's will and that Rebekah must go back to be Isaac's wife.

On the evening Rebekah and the servant arrived back near

Abraham's tent, Isaac was out in the field. He saw the servant coming back. He went out to meet them. When he and Rebekah saw each other, they loved each other right away.

Soon they were married. For the first time since his mother died, Isaac was not lonely any more.

A Brother Steals from His Brother

Genesis 25 to 27

When Abraham was one hundred and seventy-five years old he died. His sons Isaac and Ishmael buried him alongside Sarah in the cave of Machpelah. Isaac was now the head of the family. He and Rebekah, like Abraham and Sarah before them, still lived in the land of Canaan. By this time Isaac and Rebekah had two sons. They were twins whose names were Esau and Jacob.

In those times it was the custom that when a father died the oldest son received twice as much of his father's property as the rest of the sons. Esau was just a little older than Jacob, but he was too interested in his hunting to worry at all about his birthright.

One day Jacob had cooked a pot of thick soup. When Esau came home from his hunting, the smell of that soup made him feel very hungry. He asked Jacob to give him some of the soup, but Jacob was very clever. At once he saw what he had to do. "Give me your birthright and I will give you some soup in exchange." And Esau, as careless as ever, said: "You may have it. What good is a birthright to me when I am dying of hunger?"

When Isaac was a very old man, he began to go blind. He knew that he would not live much longer. One day he called Esau to him and said: "My son, I am very old now, and soon I must die. Go out with your bow and arrow and shoot a buck; then roast some of the meat in the way I like it and bring it to me to eat. Then I will give you my blessing before the end of my life comes."

His mother, Rebekah, had heard all that was said. She went quickly to Jacob and told him. Then she sent him to the flock of goats to pick out and kill two kids. She would cook them as Isaac liked. Jacob could take the meat to his father and receive the blessing while Esau was still out hunting.

Jacob did what he was told. He went in to Isaac with the meat. When Isaac asked him who he was, he lied and said he was Esau. Then when Isaac had eaten, he placed his hands on Jacob's head and blessed him, thinking all the time that Jacob was Esau.

Now when Esau heard about what Jacob had done, he was very angry. He decided that when his father Isaac died, he would find Jacob and kill him. Rebekah, his mother, knew of that plan. She told Jacob that as soon as possible he must go away and stay with his uncle Laban, far away in Haran.

After a long journey, Jacob reached Haran. He stopped to rest near a well. As he talked with some men he saw a beautiful girl. The girl was Rachel, the daughter of Laban.

Jacob stayed with Laban and his family. He had fallen in love with Rachel and promised to work seven years for Laban so that he could have Rachel for his wife.

In those times the brides all wore heavy veils until after the wedding service was over. When Jacob lifted the veil from the face of his wife, he found he had married not his beloved Rachel but her sister, Leah.

Laban promised that Jacob could marry Rachel, too, as long as he would work another seven years to pay for her.

In the following years Jacob's wives gave him twelve sons.

A Wrestling Match In the Dark

Genesis 30 to 33

After twenty years in Haran, Jacob was a very rich man. Part of his wages for the work he did for Laban was paid to him in sheep and cattle. Just as God had promised, his herds grew bigger and bigger. Then God spoke to Jacob and told him it was time to begin the journey back to his own home. God promised to take care of him on the long way back.

But Jacob still had something very frightening ahead of him. Jacob had fled from home because Esau, his brother, wanted to kill him. On the way back home he decided to send messengers ahead to find out whether Esau was still angry.

When the messengers returned they brought shocking news. Esau was coming out to meet them with four hundred men!

That night when they set up their camp, Jacob sent Esau five hundred and eighty goats, sheep, camels, cattle and donkeys. Then he took his wives and children across the brook Jabbok. He went back alone to spend the night in prayer.

But suddenly in the darkness he felt a man grasp him and begin to wrestle with him. And that wrestling match went on right through the night until sunrise. It was a terrible struggle, so hard that one of Jacob's legs was hurt so badly he could not walk without limping. He suddenly realized he was not wrestling with a man, but against an angel from heaven. The angel cried out to him: "Let me go, because the sun will soon be rising." But Jacob would not let him go

Esau. Esau ran to meet him and kissed him. The two brothers wept with joy to be together again after all those years. Esau forgave Jacob for the way he had treated him long before.

They Sold Their Brother as a Slave

Genesis 37

When Jacob and Rachel and Leah came into the land of Canaan, they had eleven sons. As far as we know there was only one daughter, Dinah. The sons had these names: Reuben, Simeon, Levi, Judah, Issachar, Zebulun, Joseph, Dan, Naphtali, Gad and Asher. Soon after they came into Canaan, Rachel and Jacob had another son, Benjamin. While Benjamin was still a baby, his mother died.

Now Jacob was very fond of his son Joseph. When Joseph was seventeen years old, Jacob gave him a coat with long sleeves, made of colored cloth. Joseph's brothers became jealous and hated him for it.

One night Joseph had a dream. When he told his brothers about it the next day, they hated him even more. In his dream all the brothers had been cutting wheat in the fields and each one bound what he had cut into a bundle. Then Joseph's sheaf of wheat stood up and all the others bowed down to it.

until the angel had blessed him. Then the angel asked him his name. He answered: "My name is Jacob." Jacob means "deceiver". The angel then said: "Your name will not be Jacob any longer. Now it is Israel, because you have wrestled with God and won."

The next morning when Jacob crossed the river, there was Esau and his men right in front of him. Jacob bowed low before

A few nights later Joseph dreamed again. Once more he told his brothers what he had dreamed. This time he saw the sun and the moon and eleven stars bowing down to him. And then even his father was angry. "What is this?" he said. "Am I and your mother and your brothers all to kneel before you?"

Some time afterward all the brothers except Joseph and Benjamin went out to look after sheep in the district of Shechem. When they had been away several days Jacob sent out Joseph to see them and to find out how they were getting along.

As his brothers saw him coming toward them, but still a long way off, they decided that they would kill him.

The brothers took Joseph's coat from him and then threw him down into a hole. Then they noticed an Ishmaelite camel train on its way to Egypt with all kinds of spices to sell there. Then Judah had a plan. They would sell their brother to the Ishmaelites to be sold again as a slave in Egypt.

So they took Joseph's coat and tore it and dipped it in the blood of a goat they had killed. They sent this blood-stained coat back to Jacob. When Jacob saw it he

all that he did so that Potiphar soon put him in charge of all the other slaves.

But then came trouble. Potiphar's wife tried to make Joseph do something very wrong. But when Potiphar came home she told him that it was Joseph who had wanted to do a wrong thing, and had run away only when she shouted for help.

Potiphar was very angry and immediately had Joseph thrown into prison.

One day two new prisoners arrived. One was Pharaoh's chief butler. The other was his chief baker.

One night each of them had a dream. The butler had seen a vine and the vine had three branches. Then he saw those branches producing bunches of ripe grapes. He took those grapes and pressed out their juice into Pharaoh's cup which he had in his hand. Then he gave the cup to Pharaoh. Joseph explained the dream to him. The three branches were three days. In three days' time Pharaoh would take him out of prison and give him back his work as butler again. Joseph asked the butler, when he received back his high post, to remember him and ask Pharaoh to release him as well, because he had done nothing wrong.

Then came the baker's turn. He had seen himself carrying three white baskets on his head, one on top of the other. In the top basket

mourned terribly because he believed that a wild animal had killed his favorite son.

From a Prison to a Palace!

Genesis 39 to 41

When the Ishmaelite traders arrived in Egypt, they quickly found a buyer for Joseph. He became the slave of Potiphar who was captain of the guard of the Egyptian king Pharaoh. Joseph worked hard and the Lord blessed

there were all kinds of cakes and
baked food, but the birds flew
down and ate them. The meaning
of this dream was not so pleasing.
The answer would come in three
days, but the baker would be
hanged from a tree and the birds
of the air would eat his flesh.

More Dreams

For two more long years Joseph
was in prison. Then it was Pharaoh's turn to dream. He dreamed
that he stood at the riverside.
From the river where they had
been drinking, he saw seven cows
walking up. They were fat and
healthy and they went to feed in
a meadow. Then seven other cattle
came from the river. But these
cattle were thin and scraggy looking. They went to stand alongside
the other cows. The seven thin
cattle ate the seven fat ones.

Then he fell asleep again and
dreamed once more. This time he
saw seven plump ears of wheat
on a stalk. Then seven thin and
miserable ears came up, scorched
by the east wind. The seven thin
ears ate the seven plump ears.

Pharaoh was puzzled. He called
together all his wise men and all
the magicians in Egypt. None of
them could explain his dreams to
him. Then suddenly the butler remembered Joseph and the way
he had told the meanings of the

dreams he and the baker had dreamed in prison. So Joseph was brought to Pharaoh. With God's help he explained the dreams, which both meant the same thing.

The seven fat cows and the seven plump wheat ears were seven good years. The seven lean cows and the seven thin wheat ears were seven bad years. The seven good years would be seven years of plenty with wonderful crops and plenty of food. But then would come seven years of drought and famine. The crops would be poor and there would be so little food and so much starvation that the seven good years would be forgotten.

Then Joseph made a suggestion to Pharaoh. Men should be appointed to put away a fifth of the crops during the plentiful years, so that there would be food for the famine years.

Pharaoh was amazed at what Joseph told him. Pharaoh was so impressed by Joseph's cleverness that he put him in charge of all the food supplies. In fact, he made Joseph the greatest ruler in all Egypt, next to himself in importance.

The Dream That Came True

Genesis 41 and 42

Joseph had his own family now. He had married an Egyptian girl.

Her name was Asenath, daughter of the priest of On. In time, two sons were born, Manasseh and Ephraim.

Very soon the seven years of plenty had passed, and the years of drought and famine arrived. There was famine in all the lands around Egypt, too. Only Egypt had put away enough food for the bad years. But because Joseph had listened to what God said, Egypt had enough to be able to sell even to other countries.

Back in the land of Canaan there was hunger, too. Jacob heard that they could buy food in Egypt. Jacob had great riches, but no food, and what do riches mean when you are dying of hunger? So Jacob sent down ten of Joseph's brothers to Egypt, to buy wheat there. Only Benjamin, the youngest, was kept at home. Jacob was afraid that something might happen to him, too, so that both of the sons Rachel had given him would be taken away.

Jacob's Sons in Egypt

After a long journey through the desert, Joseph's brothers arrived in Egypt. They went straight to the governor in charge of the wheat stores. They did not know this man was their own brother, Joseph. They all bowed down to him—exactly as Joseph's dream had said they would.

They didn't know him, but Joseph knew who they were. Still, he treated them as if they were strangers.

"Where do you come from?" he asked them roughly. "From Canaan, to buy food," they answered. "You are just spies," he said. "You have come to search for the weak places in the land." "No, lord," they pleaded, "all we want is to buy food. We are all the sons of one man. We are all brothers. Our youngest brother is still at home with our father and one—well, one brother has disappeared. We only want to buy food. We are not spies."

But Joseph would not listen to them. "I shall put you to the test. All of you, except one, will be kept in prison. The other brother must go and get your youngest brother. If he is not brought, then all the rest of you will be treated like spies."

For three days they were in prison. Then Joseph had them brought before him. He changed the whole plan. Only one of them would have to stay in prison, while the rest went to get the youngest brother. Simeon was chosen to stay in Egypt and was taken to prison. The rest of the brothers were sent home.

That evening at the inn where they stopped for the night, one of the brothers opened his sack to give a little grain to his donkey. What do you think he found in his sack? The money he had paid for his wheat! And there was money in the sacks of the other brothers as well.

When they arrived at home they told their father Jacob all that had happened and that Simeon had been left behind. Jacob was terribly upset. Two of his sons had been taken from him. Joseph had gone long before. Now Simeon was gone and they wanted to take his little Benjamin away to Egypt as well. He would not allow it. Reuben said he would leave his two little sons with Jacob as hostages. But Jacob refused.

The Lost Brother Found

Genesis 43 to 45

When the food brought from Egypt had nearly all been used, Jacob said one day to his sons: "Go to Egypt again, and buy us more food."

But Judah said to him: "Father, the man who sold us the food said he would have nothing more to do with us unless we brought our youngest brother with us. If you would let Benjamin go with us, then we will go to Egypt for food; otherwise we cannot."

So once more the brothers came to the place in Egypt where food was sold. Joseph saw them arrive, but he did not pay attention to them. Instead he sent his servant to take them to his home and to prepare a great feast.

When Joseph came home, the brothers all bowed low before him —exactly as in the dreams long ago. Then they handed him the presents they had brought. Joseph was very friendly, but he did not say a word about being their brother. All he did was to ask how they were. He asked how their father was. Then he looked across at his own brother Benjamin. He asked if this was the youngest brother they had told him about. He prayed for Benjamin saying: "God be gracious unto you, my son." But then his feelings over-

came him. Quickly he went to his own room and cried. Then he washed his face and went back to his visitors. He gave orders that the feast should begin. Since the Egyptians would not allow the Hebrews to eat with them, Joseph sat at a different table from his brothers. The brothers were surprised by something, they were arranged at the meal according to their ages. They could not understand how the Egyptians knew in order which were older and which younger. Something strange happened too. Joseph sent to Benjamin five times as much of the food as to any of the others.

The Silver Cup

When the meal was over Joseph called his steward. He told the steward to fill the brothers' sacks with wheat, and just as he had done the last time, secretly to put their money back in the bags. "And put my silver cup in the bag of the youngest," Joseph told the steward.

The next morning, as soon as it was light, the brothers started on their way home. They were not far from the city when Joseph sent his steward after them. When the steward caught up with the brothers, he asked them how, after all the kindness that had been shown to them, they could be so ungrateful as to have stolen Joseph's cup. Of course, they denied having stolen anything. They didn't know what was in their bags.

And then the cup was found. Sadly the brothers went back with the steward to face Joseph's anger.

They threw themselves down on the ground in front of him. They promised to become his slaves, Joseph told them to go home to their father, except the one in whose bag the cup had been found. And that one was Benjamin, the favorite of their old father, Jacob. Without him they would not dare go home. They pleaded with Joseph. Judah begged to be allowed to stay as a slave in place of Benjamin.

Joseph could not stand it any longer. He sent all the Egyptians out of the room. When they had gone, he told his brothers who he was.

The brothers were terribly afraid. They remembered what they had done to Joseph. But he comforted them, and said: "Come close to me. Don't be afraid because of what you did long ago. God wanted me to be here. It is because God helped me and showed me what to do that there is food in Egypt, and that you did not die of starvation. I came here as a slave, but God has made me a great man in the land. God told me that there would be seven years of famine. Two years have passed, but there are still five years to come. I still have much work to do. Because there is famine back in our own land, too, you must go back home and get our father, Jacob, and all your families and your flocks and herds. Come to the land of Goshen, the province on the eastern side of Egypt. I shall see to it that Pharaoh gives you a place to stay. There you can live in peace. I will see to it that you always have enough to eat."

Then he hugged and kissed all his brothers, but especially Benjamin, the youngest.

From Poverty to Plenty

Genesis 45 to 50

Joseph's brothers went back to their father in Canaan. They were glad to tell him the wonderful news about their "lost" brother. They told him all about Joseph and of the invitation to go and live in Goshen. Jacob told them to prepare for the journey.

So all the people and their hundreds of animals began the long trip down into Egypt. When they reached Beer-sheba, where Abraham and Isaac had stopped many years before, they stopped too, for a very important reason. Jacob had not forgotten that he owed God the deepest thankfulness for giving him back Joseph once more. At Beer-sheba he built an altar of stones. At a very solemn service an offering of thanksgiving was made to God.

During that night, after the great service, God came to Jacob in a dream and spoke to him: "Jacob, I am the God of your father. Don't be afraid of going down into Egypt because I shall be with you. You will see your son Joseph. There I will make of you a great nation; and when the right time comes I shall bring that nation out of Egypt once more."

When Jacob and all the family came to Egypt, Joseph rode out to meet his father. Joseph took his father and five of his brothers to meet Pharaoh. Pharaoh gave them permission to move into the land of Goshen, the very fertile part on the east of the Nile river.

When Jacob was one hundred and forty-seven years old, he felt that the time of his death was coming near. When Joseph heard this, he took his two sons, Ephraim and Manasseh, and went to see Jacob so that he might bless them. Jacob blessed all his own sons and Joseph's two sons as well. Joseph was surprised to hear Jacob giving a greater blessing to his younger son, Ephraim, than to the older, Manasseh. Manasseh would become a great man and the father of a great tribe, but the greatness of Ephraim and his family would be much more. In time, it happened just as Jacob had said.

An Israelite Baby Becomes an Egyptian Prince

Exodus 1 and 2

When Jacob brought his family to Egypt, there were only seventy of them altogether, including Joseph and his sons. But by the time Joseph and his generation had died, the children of Israel filled the land of Goshen. They were in all the cities of Egypt. They were rich people. They were powerful. But a time came when a new king

ruled in the land. The new king knew nothing about the great Joseph and the wonderful work he had done for the people of Egypt. Because of the numbers and the riches of the Israelites, the Egyptians became jealous. The king began to treat them roughly and to make slaves of them.

There were so many Israelites that the new king was very afraid of them. The Egyptians decided on a really terrible thing. They wanted all the Israelite boy babies to be killed as soon as they were born.

One day a little Hebrew boy was born. His mother did her very best to see he was not killed by the cruel Egyptians. For three whole months she hid him. Then she made an ark or basket of bulrushes, like a little boat. She coated it with pitch inside so that the water could not get in. Inside she laid her little baby. She set the basket in the river between the coarse water grasses near the bank. The baby's sister, Miriam, watched to see what would happen.

After a while one of Pharaoh's daughters, a princess of Egypt, came down to wash in the river. She saw the ark. She sent her maid to bring it to her. When she

opened it, the little baby cried. She knew that it was an Israelite baby, but instead of having him killed she sent the little girl who was watching to find an Israelite woman to look after him. Miriam brought the baby's own mother! Later the princess took the baby to the royal palace and treated him like her own son. She called him Moses, which means "drawn out," because she had taken him out of the river. So a little Israelite baby became an Egyptian prince.

Moses Has to Flee

Exodus 2

One day when Moses had grown into a young man, he was out watching how his own people were being treated badly by the Egyptians. On this day he saw an Egyptian beating an Israelite workman. He killed the Egyptian and buried his body in the sand.

On the next day he came across two Israelites fighting. He asked one man: "Why do you hit your brother-Israelite?" This man said: "Who made you a prince and a judge over us? Do you plan to kill me like you killed the Egyptian?"

Moses was very frightened. He fled away into a land called Midian. There he was invited by Reuel, a priest of Midian, to come and live with his family.

The Voice from the Burning Bush

Exodus 3 and 4

One day Moses was out in the desert with the sheep near to Mount Horeb. Suddenly he saw a little way ahead a thorn bush on fire. He went over to look at this strange sight, but most amazing of all, the fire burned on and yet the bush was not consumed.

Suddenly as he watched, a voice called to him out of the bush:

"Moses! Moses!" Moses answered: "Here I am." The voice was coming straight from the fire where God was speaking. "Do not come near, Moses. Take off your shoes because the ground where you are standing is holy ground." Moses did as he was told. He was afraid.

Then the voice spoke again: "I am the God of your father, the God of Abraham, the God of Isaac, and the God of Jacob." Immediately Moses hid his face. He was afraid to look even at the fire that spoke of God's Presence. Then the Lord spoke again: "I have seen the terrible hardships of My people who are in Egypt. I have come now to free them from the cruel Egyptians and to bring them to a land that is so fertile it flows with milk and honey. I mean the land of Canaan which I promised to their forefathers. Now, Moses, I want you to go to Pharaoh. Get my people away from him and bring the children of Israel out of Egypt."

Then God made a promise to be with Moses and give him all the strength he needed. God told Moses that when the people came out of Egypt they must travel to Mount Horeb. There they must worship God.

But Moses still hesitated. He had another question to ask: "When I go to the children of Israel and tell them that the God of their fathers has sent me to them, they will say to me: 'What is His name?' What shall I answer them?" God's answer was: "I AM THAT I AM. This is what you must say to the children of Israel, I AM has sent me to you."

Moses Is Sent to Egypt

God told Moses to go to his own people still suffering in Egypt. There he must tell them to gather all the elders, or leaders of families, together and explain to them why God had sent him. With the elders he must go to Pharaoh and ask permission to take the Israelites on a three days' journey into the wilderness in order to sacrifice to God. But strangely, God told Moses that He knew Pharaoh would not allow them to go. God told Moses that He would stretch out His hand and punish Egypt by wonderful deeds. In the end the people of Israel would come out of Egypt.

Moses was still afraid, though. He was sure the Israelites would not listen to him. Then God gave him a sign. In his hand Moses had a rod, a walking stick which he used when watching the sheep. God told him to throw it on the ground. Immediately it turned into a snake. Moses jumped back in fright. God told him not to be afraid and to take hold of it by the tail. When Moses did so, the snake turned back into a walking stick again. Then God gave Moses a second sign. Moses put his hand inside his cloak, against his chest. When he pulled his hand out it was snow-white with the terrible sickness of leprosy. And when he put his hand back and pulled it out once more, the leprosy disappeared. Then God said to Moses: "When you go to the people of Israel and they refuse to listen to you, show them these two signs. If they still will not listen, dip some water out of the river and pour it out on the ground. It will turn to blood."

Moses was still afraid. He argued that he was not a good speaker. This time God was angry and said: "Am I not the Lord Who made man's mouth? Do I not make all men? Aaron the Levite is your brother. When you get to Egypt he will come out to meet you. He will go with you and he will be your spokesman. But do not forget your walking stick. You will have to use it to show great signs."

So Moses took his wife and sons and returned to Egypt. As God had said, Aaron came out to meet Moses. Moses told Aaron all that God had said. Then they went and gathered all the elders of Israel and gave them God's message.

God Deals with His Egyptian Enemies

Exodus 5 to 10

Once they had spoken to the elders of their own people, Moses and Aaron made their way to Pharaoh's palace. They went to do as God had said. They asked that the Israelites be allowed to travel out into the desert to worship there.

Pharaoh had something really terrible to say: "Who is the Lord that I should listen to him? I do not know the Lord and I will not let Israel go." He told the overseers of the workmen to make the Israelites work even harder than before.

Moses was discouraged. But God spoke to Moses again and brought him once more the promise that Pharaoh would let the people of Israel go and he would lead them to the Promised Land.

The next morning Moses and Aaron went again to Pharaoh. This time they showed him the miraculous powers God had given them. When Moses told him to, Aaron threw down Moses' stick in front of Pharaoh. It turned into a snake. But Pharaoh was not impressed. He called his own magicians and they, too, turned their sticks into snakes. There was one difference. Aaron's snake ate up all the magicians' snakes. But Pharaoh still would not listen to God's servants.

God Send the Plagues upon Egypt

The next morning God sent Moses and Aaron down to the river Nile to meet Pharaoh. Again they must tell Pharaoh that the Lord God of the Israelite people had sent them to ask him to free God's people so that they could worship Him in the wilderness. This time they added a special warning. Aaron stretched out Moses' stick over the water in the river. The water turned to blood. Aaron stretched

53

the stick over the ponds and the pools and the jars and pots throughout Egypt. All the water in them turned to blood. Pharaoh still would not listen.

A week later God sent Moses and Aaron to Pharaoh once more. They asked again for the Israelites to be freed, otherwise God would send a plague of frogs upon the land. Pharaoh refused once more. Again Moses' stick was stretched out. The land became a hopping, squirming mass of frogs. This time Pharaoh seemed afraid and begged Moses to have the plague taken

away. If this was done, he would certainly let the Israelites go, so Moses prayed to God to take away the frogs. But on the next day Pharaoh changed his mind again.

Once more God had to deal with him. This time Aaron stretched out the stick and hit the dust on the ground. Out of that dust came horrible lice to plague men and animals. But Pharaoh would not let the people go.

The next plague was a plague of flies in all the land except Goshen, where the Israelites lived. God was taking care of His people. This time Pharaoh said: "Go and sacrifice to your God but do not leave the land." Moses explained that this could not be done because the Israelites worshiped differently from the Egyptians. So Pharaoh gave his consent for them to travel a three days' journey into the wilderness. By the next morning in answer to Moses' prayers, God had taken away the flies. Once more, though, Pharaoh refused to keep his promise.

Again Moses and Aaron went in to Pharaoh with a terrible warning. If he would not keep his promise, God would send an awful sickness that would kill the animals in the land. The cattle and sheep and even the camels would die. But Pharaoh again would not listen. Thousands of animals belonging to the Egyptians died, but God protected the animals in Goshen where the Hebrews lived.

Then Moses and Aaron took handfuls of ash and threw it into the air. As the ash was spread by the wind, nasty boils and blisters broke out on the skins of human beings and the few animals still alive. In spite of the pain the Egyptians were all suffering, Pharaoh would not let the people go.

The terrible plagues had not come to an end. This time a fearful hailstorm came across the land. Once again the Israelites in the land of Goshen were protected. Not a single hailstone fell there. Pharaoh was terrified, but as soon as the storm went away, his promise was forgotten again.

Moses' stick was stretched out once more. A great wind from the east blew for a whole day and a night. When the sun rose the next morning, great swarms of locusts came sweeping in on the wind. There were so many of them that they stripped off every green leaf still left on the bushes and trees after the great hail. Pharaoh hurriedly called Moses and Aaron. He asked them to pray for him. But as usual he forgot all about his promises to the people of Israel when God gave a west wind to take away the locusts.

Then a new plague came. It was dark for three days. It was so dark the people could not even see to walk. Again Pharaoh was quick with his promises until the plague was taken away but this time he became very unpleasant. He told

Moses and Aaron to leave the land immediately. If they looked on his face again, he would have them put to death right away. And Moses answered: "You have spoken the truth. I will not see you, nor plead with you again."

When the Oldest Egyptian Boys Died

Exodus 11 to 13

Now there was one plague left, the worst of them all. Pharaoh had broken all his promises before, but this time he would simply have to let the people of Israel leave the land of their slavery.

Moses explained to the Israelites what would happen in the last plague. He warned them they must do very carefully what they were told or else the plague would hurt them, too. He said to them: "Tonight around about midnight God will send an angel to every house in Egypt and in every one of them the eldest son will die. Every Israelite family must prepare itself in a special way. The head of each family must select a year-old lamb. The lamb must be perfect in every way. Then the lamb must be killed and some of its blood smeared on each of the doorposts and across the top of the door. Then the meat of the lamb must be roasted with bitter herbs and eaten with bread made without yeast, unleavened bread. If any of the meat was left over, it must be burned in the fire. No meat must remain until the morning. When you eat it, you must not be sitting down. They were all to stand around the table, dressed ready to leave, with their sandals on. They should even have their walking stick in their hands. This way they would all be ready to move out of the land of Egypt."

The people did just as Moses had said. The angel of death went past all the doors marked with blood. God had promised: "When I see the blood I will pass over you and the plague shall not be upon you to destroy you when I defeat the Egyptians. And in the future, every year you and your children after you must keep this Feast of the Passover to remind you of how I turned death away from you."

That night was one of the bitterest nights Egypt ever went through. There was not a single home where there was not a son dead—even Pharaoh's palace did not escape.

This time Pharaoh sent a message to the Israelites to leave immediately and not leave anything behind. He even begged them to pray that God would be merciful and not punish Egypt any more.

So in the morning all the people of Israel began the journey out of Egypt. They did not move off in a confused way. Tribe by tribe, and family by family, six hundred thousand grownups and a large number of children started the long, long journey. They took no food with them, but only the dough left over from the unleavened bread prepared on the Passover night. They kept this to bake at their first stopping place which was Succoth.

They were going into the desert where there were no marked roads and where it would be very dangerous to get lost. To keep them safe, the Lord Himself became their guide. He went before them by day in a pillar of cloud. By night he gave them a pillar of fire. They knew they were never alone.

God Protects and Feeds
His People

Exodus 14 to 16

Although the people of Israel had been allowed to move out of Goshen, that did not mean that Pharaoh would let them go in peace. They did not go eastward because the warlike Philistines lived there. Instead, they turned toward the southeast, in the direction of Mount Horeb. This was where Moses had seen the burning bush that did not burn away. Ahead of them was the Red Sea—and suddenly behind them were the chariots of Egypt.

Pharaoh had realized that his slaves were leaving the land. So he called together six hundred chariot captains to lead the army of Egypt after the Israelites. Pharaoh wanted to bring them back.

The Hebrew people were caught between Pharaoh's army and the water. Then God commanded Moses to lift up his stick over the sea. The water would divide and the Israelites would be able to pass through on dry land. The pillar of cloud moved away from its usual position and stood behind the

Israelites but in front of the Egyptians. That night the pillar of cloud looked different on the two sides. On the Israelite side it was light but on the Egyptian side it was very dark. The Israelites were hidden from the Egyptians.

In the early morning the Israelites took up all their goods and marched through between the two parts of the sea, which were like walls of water on the two sides.

As they went through, God dealt with the Egyptians out of the pillar of fire and cloud. He made the wheels come off some of the chariots so that they struggled in the deep desert sand. Then as they came into the gap between the two parts of the sea, God told Moses once more to stretch out his stick over the sea. This time the water came rushing back, covering the chariots and drowning every horse and every soldier.

The Journey Begins Through the Wilderness

Goshen had been a fertile land, a land of plenty, in spite of the hardships the Israelites had there. The desert was a different kind of place altogether. There was sand and rock as far as they could see. There were great stormy mountains shimmering in the heat. Hardly a bush was to be seen. Only now and then was it possible to find water in springs near the way they were taking. And sometimes, when they tasted the water, they found it was too bitter to drink.

At Marah the water was like that, but God showed Moses a tree that would help. When Moses threw that tree into the water, immediately the water became sweet enough to drink.

The Israelites traveled on, right into the wilderness of Sin. There, once again, the children of Israel were angry and upset. They wanted to go back again to Egypt.

They thought of the food they had eaten there and blamed Moses for wanting them to starve in the desert. But God knew of the grumbling in their hearts and He had the answer ready. He told Moses what He planned to do. Moses and Aaron passed on the message to the people: "In the evening you will know that it is not Moses, but God, Who has brought you out of Egypt. He will give you meat to eat and in the morning there will be bread too."

That night, just as it became dark, a great swarm of little birds called quail settled in the camp. All the people had to do was to catch them and cook them. In the morning when they woke up all around lay something that looked like frost. It was tiny white balls. They didn't know what it was. They gave it a very strange name, manna. When they first saw it, they asked one another: "What is it? Manhu?" And so it got the name manna, which means "What is it?"

The Mountain That Smoked

Exodus 17 to 31

On all their long journey through the wilderness the people of Israel were always grumblers. It was so easy for them to forget the wonderful help God had given them and to complain about the hardships of the journey. When they came to Rephidim, there was no water. The people were again angry with Moses. "Why did you bring us out of Egypt?" they asked. "There we had water; in this place we will die of thirst. All our animals will die of thirst." They were so angry that Moses was afraid they would attack him. He cried out to God to help him. God told him what to do. Moses took some of the elders and went with them to a rock on the slopes of Mount Horeb. Then he raised his stick and struck the rock. Immediately a stream of water burst out. There was enough for all the people and their cattle. Once again God had shown them that He was with them as He had promised.

Three months after the Israelites had left Egypt, they came to a great mountain called Sinai. At this place God gave His law to His people, so that they would always know how He wanted them to live together. God said to Moses that no one must come near to the mountain or let their cattle graze there. It was a holy place and from the mountain God would speak to His people. When they heard the noise of trumpets sounding, they must draw nearer to the mountain and listen to the voice of the Lord.

On the third morning after that there was a thick cloud around the top of the mountain like smoke. In the cloud the thunder rumbled

continuously. Lightning flamed and flashed. Suddenly the people heard the sound of a great trumpet. They were terrified, but Moses led them out to stand at the foot of the mountain as God had said.

There, as the mountain smoked and flamed, and the earth quivered with the great rumblings, a voice spoke to Moses out of the cloud. God had come down to meet His people. Now God called Moses up into the mountain to give him His message to the people.

Moses climbed the mountain until he disappeared in the smoking cloud. The people were frightened and that was how Moses found them when he came back. The Voice that spoke beyond the clouds was saying,

"I am the Lord your God, Who has brought you out of the land of slavery.

1. You shall have no other gods except Me.
2. You shall not have any carved likeness of anything in heaven or earth, or in the sea, to kneel before it or worship it.
3. You shall not use the Name of the Lord your God in vain. (That means, do not use His Name as a swear word, or without reverence.)
4. Remember to keep holy the Sabbath day.
5. Honour and respect your father and your mother.
6. You must not murder.
7. You must not commit adultery. (That means, a husband and a wife must be true to one another.)
8. You may not steal.
9. You must not bring false witness against your neighbour. (That means, we must not tell lies.)
10. You must not covet. (That means, you must not be greedy for what belongs to someone else.)"

On that mountain top God told Moses many other things He wanted His people to do. But the people were so terrified that they could not listen to God directly. Moses went back to the mountain to receive God's message for the people. There the Law was written or carved out on two tablets of stone, so that God's people would never be able to forget it.

The Golden Calf

Exodus 32 to 34

While Moses was with God up in the dark cloud on the top of Mount Sinai, there was something very unpleasant happening down in the Israelite camp.

The people went to Aaron and said to him: "Make us gods, to lead us. We don't know what has happened to this man Moses who brought us out of Egypt." And then Aaron did a terrible thing. He knew what God had told them in the second Commandment, but he told the Israelites to bring him all the golden ornaments and jewelry they had. He melted the gold down and made from it a golden calf. In front of the calf he had an ăltar built. Then he told the Israelites that on the next day they would make sacrifices and worship before the Lord.

Then God, up on the mountain top, told Moses to go down to the Israelites again. God knew of the terrible things that were happening and He was very angry. He told Moses there was only one thing to be done. The nation must be destroyed. But Moses begged God not to treat them so harshly. God agreed not to destroy the Israelites, but to punish those who did wrong.

Then Moses turned and went down the mountain with the two tablets of the Law in his hands. From a long way off he could hear the noise, but when he saw what was going on he was so angry that he threw down the tablets of stone and they broke into pieces. Then he took the golden calf and burned it. He ground the burned image to powder and threw the powder into water and made the people drink it.

Then Moses called out to them: "Who is on the Lord's side? Let him come to me." All the children of Levi came to him and Moses told them to take their swords and go through the camp and kill everyone who had worshiped before the golden calf. About three thousand men were killed on that day.

Then Moses told the rest of the people to beg God to forgive them. He himself would return to where he had met God in the cloud on Mount Sinai and pray to God for them.

This time Moses stayed away for forty days, but the Israelites did not misbehave while he was away. God told Moses to take again two pieces of stone and He would carve out the Law once more on those slabs. When Moses went back to the people this time, the skin of his face shone like the sun. They were afraid to go near him. He had to cover his face with a veil while he spoke to them. Every time he went to worship God his face shone again just as it had done after the wonderful meeting on the top of Mount Sinai.

The Place Where God Met His People

Exodus 35 to 40; Leviticus 1 to 8

The Israelites needed to be reminded of their duty to God. To make this easy God told the Israelites to build a place of worship where they could bring their offerings to Him and find forgiveness for their sins. God gave them plans for making the place of worship. It was called a Tabernacle or tent.

Inside the walls around the Tabernacle was the altar for burnt offerings. The altar was made of hard wood covered with a thick layer of brass. It was like a box with a grate on the top. It had rings at the sides. The rings made it easier to carry the altar when the Tabernacle was moved to a different place. The altar was big. It was about seven-and-a-half feet square and four-and-a-half feet high. Every evening and every morning a special offering was made on the altar for the sins of the people. In the Tabernacle, there was a room called the Holy of Holies. The Ark of the Covenant was in this special room. The Ark of the Covenant was a large box made of wood covered with gold. Inside it were the two tablets upon which God had written the law for Moses on Mount Sinai. On the top of the box were two golden statues of angels. The angels were called cherubs. Their wings stretched out to meet above the Ark.

Aaron was in charge of all that was done in the Tabernacle. He was called the High Priest. His sons helped him. God had arranged for Aaron to be the High Priest and lead the Israelites in their worship.

What happened each day in the Tabernacle? Every morning when the sun came up a fire was made on the great brass altar. That fire was never allowed to die out completely.

At about nine o'clock the first burnt offering was made. Either

an ox or a lamb was killed in the courtyard. Its blood was caught in a big bowl. The animal was cut up in a special way. The meat was laid on the altar and the blood was sprinkled all over it. Then the altar fire was fanned to make it very hot. The hot fire burned away the whole sacrifice. The sacrifice helped God's people remember to give their lives to be completely His. At three o'clock in the afternoon another sacrifice was made in the same way.

The Terrible Result of Disobedience

Leviticus 10

Aaron and his sons were given very important positions in the service of God. No others were allowed to be near to God in the way Aaron and his sons were. They had to carry out very carefully the instructions God had given for His worship in the Tabernacle.

over their disobedience that immediately He made a great flame burst out and burn them both to death.

When Moses was told of this awful tragedy, he said to Aaron: "Now the people will understand what the Lord meant when He said that all who come near Him must do so with reverence, and with respect for His glory."

Moses would not let Aaron come near the bodies of his sons. He called two relatives, Mishael and Elzaphan, to take them out of the camp to be buried. Aaron and two of his other sons, Eleazar and Ithamar, were not even allowed to go to the funeral. They had to stay in the Tabernacle and see to it that God's instructions for worship were followed.

The Lord had a special message for Aaron, too. He warned him that neither he nor his sons must ever drink wine or other strong drink when they were on duty in the Tabernacle. If they did, the same thing would happen to them as had happened to Nadab and Abihu.

The Scapegoat

Leviticus 16

A person who has to suffer for what another person has done is sometimes called a scapegoat. Did

The fire on the great brass altar was never allowed to go out and the fire on the golden incense altar had to be kept going with embers from the brass altar.

Nadab and Abihu were two of Aaron's sons. They did not think it was very important to follow God's instructions. One day they used what the Bible calls "strange fire". This means that embers which were not from the brass altar were used to set the incense altar burning. God was so angry

you know that the word "scape-goat" came from the Bible?

In one of the most solemn services in the Tabernacle on the Day of Atonement, two goats were used. One of them was called the scapegoat. The Day of Atonement was a very special day. It was the only day of the year when the High Priest was allowed to go into the Holy of Holies. Then he could stand in front of the Ark of the Covenant with the golden cherubs on its lid. The service on the Day of Atonement was to show that all men are sinners and only God can take away and forgive sin.

For a whole day before the Day of Atonement the children of Israel fasted to show they were sorry for their sins. No one, not even the children, ate anything. On the day of the service no one except the High Priest could even go into the Tabernacle. Everyone had to stay outside. The High Priest had to take off all the beautiful robes he wore at other times

and then wash himself very carefully. Nothing unclean could go into God's Presence. Then the priest dressed himself from head to foot in white linen clothing.

Early in the morning a special sin offering was made on the big brass altar. A young ox was killed and sacrificed for Aaron's sins and the sins of his family. He could not ask God to forgive the sins of the people unless his own sins were forgiven first. Aaron took a censer, an incense burner, full of glowing coals from the incense altar and a handful of sweet smelling incense. He then went into the Holy of Holies with a bowl of the blood of the sacrifice. He sprinkled some of the blood on top of the Ark between the two cherubs. This place was called the Mercy Seat. He also sprinkled some of the blood on the ground in front of the Ark. All the time, he made sure that a cloud of smoke was rising from the censer, so that the glory of God's

Presence would not strike him down. The blood had to be sprinkled to show he knew he owed his life to God and because of his sins he deserved to be punished with death. This special sin offering showed that Aaron had come to ask God to forgive him.

Then the High Priest would go out of the Holy Place again and stand beside the brass altar of judgment. Two goats would then be brought to him and he would cast lots to decide which of them was to become the sacrifice. The one chosen by lot would be sacrificed. The other would become the scapegoat. Then Aaron would place both his hands on the head of the scapegoat and confess all the sins of the children of Israel just as if he were transferring all their guilt to the goat. This scapegoat would then be led out by one of the men into the wilderness to a place where no one lived. The scapegoat would not be able again to find his way back. That was to show that the sins of the people had been taken away and would not come back again.

When this solemn service was over, Aaron would go into the Tabernacle and take off his white linen clothes and leave them there. Then he would wash himself again and put on the beautiful blue robe and the linen apron called an ephod. By then it would be time for the evening sacrifice. After that the people would return to their tents. They would be happy because they would know in their hearts that their sins were forgiven.

And one day the blood of God's Son would have to be shed for the forgiveness of the sins of all His people.

Grapes from the Promised Land

Numbers 13 and 14

The people of Israel spent a whole year living at the foot of Mount Sinai. During this time they were building the Tabernacle according to God's plan and learning from Moses the laws God had given. Then they moved to the wilderness of Paran. There something happened which must have excited the people very much, because it meant they were coming close to the Land of Promise. God gave instructions to Moses. Moses chose a leading man from each tribe. There were twelve men in all. They were to go ahead to spy out the land of Canaan. They were to find out about its riches and to see how strong the enemy was. Someday they would have to fight in the land of Canaan. Moses made Joshua, the son of Nun, the leader of the twelve spies. This was dangerous work, but Joshua was a brave man.

The spies slipped into the land of Canaan. They searched through it from south to north. On their way they passed through the land of the tall people, the giants, the sons of Anak. This was a frightening experience for most of them. On their way back they came to the brook of Eshcol. There they found a wonderful grapevine. They cut off one branch of grapes from the vine. It was so heavy that two men were needed to carry it on a pole between them. They also took pomegranates and figs to show Moses and the rest of the Israelites. For forty long days they searched through the land of Canaan. Then they went back to the Israelite camp at Kadesh-barnea in the wilderness of Paran.

There they reported that the land was truly a rich land. But most of them were afraid of the people that lived there. All they could think of were the towns they had seen with high walls and the war-like tribes who lived in them. Only Caleb and Joshua felt that they should move into the land at once.

As usual the Israelites began to cry and to complain. If they had only stayed in Egypt and died there, or even out in the desert, then they would never have had to face these terrible people. They lost heart so easily. They even wanted to choose another leader and struggle all the way back through the desert to Egypt.

about the Tabernacle. This was to warn the people He knew what was happening and to remind them of His promises. To Moses God said that He was so angry with the people that He wanted to destroy all except Moses and his family. Moses begged God to be merciful and not to destroy the people. Then God said that He would not do as He had said but all the people who had rebelled would not be allowed to go into the land. Of all the grownups, only Joshua and Caleb would be allowed to go into the Land of Promise together with the children of the rest of the people. For every day the spies had spent in

When they heard this, Moses and Aaron threw themselves down on the ground and prayed to God for their people. Caleb and Joshua were so upset that they tore their clothes as they pleaded with the people. They begged them to trust in God. Canaan was a good land and rich and if they were obedient, God would lead them in safely. But the people tried to kill Joshua and Caleb.

Then God stepped in. He let the people see His glory shining the land, the Israelites would have to spend a whole year in the desert, forty years altogether.

God would not listen to their cry. They must go back into the desert as He had told them. If they did not, He would not be with them to protect them.

The End of the Long Journey Draws Near

Numbers 20 to 22

For forty long years the Israelites wandered in the wilderness. Their disobedience had cost them much. But God still saw to it that they had food to eat. The older Israelites died, the young ones grew up, till when the forty years of punishment were nearly over, they arrived once more in the wilderness of Paran. Shortly after they reached Kadesh-barnea, Miriam, the sister of Aaron and Moses, died.

But there was another reason for unhappiness. The fountain had dried up and there was no water. The Israelites were upset and angry and they began their usual complaint, "If we had only died with the others in the desert or stayed in Egypt. Moses, why did you bring us out of Egypt into this terrible place?" When they heard this, Moses and Aaron went to the Tabernacle to pray to God.

God told them what to do. Moses must take the walking stick which he had used in Egypt and go to the great rock in front of the camp. With all the people watching, he must speak to the rock. Moses called the people together and as they watched he struck the rock twice. This was not quite what God had told him to do. Still, in a wonderful way, a stream of water burst out of the rock and there was enough for the people and all their flocks and herds. Because Moses and Aaron did not do exactly what God had said, they, too, were not allowed to go into the Land of Promise.

When they came to Mount Hor, east of Edom, God told Moses to take Aaron and Aaron's son, Eleazar, up into the mountain. There the High Priest's clothes were taken from Aaron and put on Eleazar, and Aaron died. When Moses and Eleazar came back from the mountain without Aaron the whole Israelite nation mourned for him for thirty days.

By this time the Israelites were near to the land of Canaan, and the king of the Canaanites, Arad, heard that they were moving toward his land. He sent out an army. The army attacked the Israelites and some of them were taken prisoner. The Israelites asked God for strength. They defeated the Canaanites and destroyed their towns. The name of that place was Hormah.

the people went to Moses and asked him to pray for them. When he did, God told him to do a very strange thing. He must make a snake out of brass and hang it up on a pole. If any Israelite was bitten, and then looked toward the brass snake, the bite would be healed and he would not die. What a strange way to be healed. But it was God's way.

After this the Israelites moved on until they came to the border of the kingdom of the Amorites. There Sihon was king. Sihon

Although God had helped them, and kept all his promises to them, the Israelites were still a people who grumbled easily. When they found the way around the land of Edom very rough and unpleasant, they began to complain again. They talked about the time their fathers had lived in Egypt. They even grumbled about the food God gave them every day. This food was called manna. God was so angry at this that He sent poisonous snakes. Many of the people were bitten and died. Then

would not allow them to pass through his kingdom. He gathered his people together and fought against the Israelites at a place called Jahaz. God was with the Israelites. The Amorites were heavily defeated. Several of their towns were captured. The Israelites occupied all the land between the rivers Arnon and Jabbok. They took over the Amorite towns. From that stretch of land the Israelite warriors moved forward and defeated the army of Og, king of Bashan, and took over his land, too.

Before long the children of Israel were camped near Jericho. They were within sight of the land of Canaan on the other side of the river Jordan. Their long wanderings were nearly over.

A Clever Man Learns from a Donkey

Numbers 22 to 25, and 31

After the small tribes along the edge of the land of Canaan had seen what happened to the Amorites and the people of Bashan they were afraid of what might happen to them.

At that time Balak the son of Zippor was king of the people of Moab. He was very worried about the Israelites who were camped not far away. Balak thought of a plan. Nearby there lived a man named Balaam, the son of Beor. Balaam was looked upon as a prophet. A prophet was a man who could speak to God and to whom God told what He planned to do.

Balak sent messengers to Balaam, and asked him to curse the Israelites. But God told Balaam not to curse the children of Israel because He had blessed them. So Balaam told the messengers from Balak that God would not allow him to do what they wanted.

Then Balak sent other men to Balaam and promised him great rewards if only he would do as Balak asked. This time God told him to go back to Balak with the messengers but to do only what God told him to do. But deep in his heart Balaam wanted the riches Balak promised.

Balaam went out, riding on a donkey with his two servants alongside. Suddenly the donkey saw what Balaam could not see. An angel of the Lord was standing in the way with a drawn sword in his hand. The donkey immediately jumped out of the road and began to run into the field. Balaam beat the donkey back onto the road. This time the angel chose a place where the road ran between two stone walls. When the angel appeared before the donkey the second time, the donkey jumped to the side and crushed Balaam's foot against the

wall. He beat the donkey again. Then the angel disappeared for a moment, only to appear a little further on. When the donkey was frightened this time, Balaam beat the donkey again very hard.

Then an amazing thing happened. God opened the mouth of that donkey so that she could speak, and she said to Balaam: "What have I done to you that you should beat me three times like this?" Balaam was so angry he didn't realize what a marvelous thing was happening, and he answered the donkey: "I hit you because you wouldn't listen to me." The donkey answered: "Have I not always served you faithfully? Have I ever given you trouble before?" Balaam had to admit that the donkey had served him well.

Then God opened Balaam's eyes to see the angel standing in the road with the drawn sword in his hand. Balaam threw himself down in deep reverence. The angel asked him why he had beaten the donkey so terribly. The donkey had really saved Balaam by being frightened at the sight of the angel. Otherwise the angel would have used his sword on Balaam. He was very sorry then that he had beaten the donkey, and offered to turn back home again if the angel was angry about the way he was going. The angel told him to go with the messengers of King Balak. But he must not say anything except what the Lord had told him.

On the next morning Balak took Balaam up into a high mountain so that he could look down on the camp of the children of Israel in the valley below. There Balaam told the servants of Balak to build seven altars. They were to catch seven young oxen and seven rams to be offered up to God on the altars. When they had done this, Balaam told Balak to stay near the altars while he went further up the mountain to pray to God. When he came back Balak wanted to know immediately what God had said. He was angry when Balaam told him: "He has told me

to bless the children of Israel, and I cannot change that."

Then Balak tried again to persuade Balaam to curse the children of Israel. But Balaam reminded the king that he had already told him that he had to do what God wanted. So Balak got Balaam to climb another mountain and to build seven more altars and ask once more for God's word. This time the message was even less what Balak wanted. As Balaam looked at the Israelite camps, God's Spirit told him what those people would be like in the future. They would increase just like gardens growing by the riverside. Their kingdom would be great, and they would destroy all their enemies.

Balak was so angry he told Balaam to go back to his own home immediately. But the prophet had another message to give from God. It had to do with what God was going to do later with Balak's people. A Star would come out of the people of Jacob, and a Scepter out of the people of Israel, to stretch out over the land of Moab as her ruler. And the lands of Edom and Moab and Ammon would one day be under the control of Israel.

Now Balaam thought of a plan to get Balak's reward. He suggested that Balak have his people marry the Israelites and lead them astray to worship the idols of the Moabites. That is exactly

the way it worked out. Then everything began to go wrong. It seemed that all the Israelites were turning away from God. Then God sent a plague to remind the Israelites that He was their God. Thousands died. Moses had the ringleaders put to death.

Then the Israelite armies, strong and depending on God, turned against the Moabites and their neighbors, the Midianites. The Moabites and Midianites were defeated heavily in battle. Their towns were destroyed. Their kings and princes were killed. One of those killed was Balaam. God had spoken to Balaam and he was able to find out what God was going to do. But Balaam was greedy. The price of that greed was death among the enemies of God's people.

Just a Look at the Promised Land

Numbers 26 and 32 and Deuteronomy 31

While the Israelites were camped east of the river Jordan on the plains of Moab, Moses and Eleazar counted all the people who were twenty years old or more. When they added together the numbers in all the tribes, they found that there were over six hundred thousand men, not counting the women and children. No wonder the Moabites and the other nations were so afraid of them. Of all those men only three were over sixty years old, Moses and Caleb and Joshua.

Moses was a very old man, already one hundred and twenty years old. He, too, would not cross into the Promised Land, but God would let him see that land before He took him into heaven.

At this time the Israelites controlled all the land east of the Jordan between the rivers Arnon and Jabbok. There was good grazing there, especially in the part called Gilead. Just before the Israelites began to cross the Jordan, the leaders of the tribes of Reuben and Gad and of half of the tribe of Manasseh went to Moses. They asked permission to stay in these grazing lands. They owned great herds of cattle and felt that this was a good place for them. They would build houses for their wives and children and pens for their cattle and sheep. Then the men would go with the rest of the Israelites and fight with them against the enemies until all the tribes were settled in their own lands. Moses was satisfied with their promise. Soon they were busy setting up homes for their families.

When the men of Gad and Reuben and Manasseh had taken their place again with the rest of the Israelites, Moses gathered all the leaders together in front of his tent. First, he told them that his work was nearly over. He would not be able to go with them into Canaan, but before he was taken away from them he wanted to remind them of all God had done for them and for their fathers since they left Egypt. He told them again all the laws which God had given them. Moses told the people how God had asked them to teach those laws to their children, too, so that they could all live as the obedient servants of God. "Go the way he sends you," Moses said. "Always remember that God is forever, and his strong, everlasting arms will hold you safe, keeping you from danger."

During that very important speech Moses placed his hands on Joshua's head and appointed him to lead the Israelites in his place.

Then Moses blessed all the tribes, and greeted their leaders, and walked through the camp and out across the plains of Moab until he reached Mount Nebo. There he slowly climbed the peak called Pisgah. When he reached the top, God showed him all the southern part of the land in which his people would live, right across to the Mediterranean Sea. After he had seen the Land of Promise,

Moses died. God buried him up in the mountains in a place no one has ever found.

Job, the Man God Trusted

Job 1, 2 and 42

A long time ago a good man called Job lived in the land of Uz, on the edge of the desert. Job was a very rich man with thousands of sheep, camels and cattle. He had many servants. He also had a large family. There were seven sons and three daughters. Job loved and served God very much. Whenever his sons held feasts in their homes, Job made special offerings for them. The special offerings were just in case they had sinned against God and let wrong thoughts creep into their minds.

One day the angels gathered in heaven to bring their reports to God and the devil slipped in with them. God asked him: "Did you notice my servant Job? There is no one like him in all the world, he is honest and upright, and avoids all that is wrong." Then the devil sneered, and said: "Yes, but doesn't it pay Job to serve God? Is he not blessed in every possible way? Take away his riches and see what happens then. He will curse God, I am sure." God said: "Everything Job has is in your power. You may do what you wish with his possessions or his family, but Job himself you may not touch."

With that the devil went back again to the world and began to trouble Job. One day Job's eldest son held a great feast. All his brothers and sisters were enjoying the feast with him. Job was at

80

home, when suddenly a messenger came rushing in and said: "The Sabeans have attacked us. We were plowing, and the Sabeans have stolen all the oxen. They have also stolen the donkeys which were grazing nearby. They have killed all the servants who were working there. I am the only one to escape." He hadn't finished speaking when another man rushed in with more bad news: "The lightning has struck and killed all the sheep and the shepherds who were looking after them." Then another messenger came running in: "The Chaldeans attacked us in three bands, took away all the camels and killed all the herdsmen except me." And then came the worst news of all. While Job's sons and daughters were enjoying their feast, a whirlwind swept in from the desert, and brought the house tumbling down, and all the young people were killed.

So in one day Job lost everything he had. He threw himself down on the ground, and with his face on his arms he cried out: "When I came into this world I had nothing; when I go from it I will not have anything either. The Lord gave, and the Lord has taken away. Blessed be His Name." Even though Job had lost everything, he did not sin against the Lord.

A little while later the angels gathered again in heaven. Once more the devil slipped in with them. God challenged him the same way as before: "Have you seen my servant Job? There isn't another man like him in all the world. Even though I let you harm him so terribly, he has still not turned against Me." But the devil mocked God and Job horribly: "A man will give all that he has for his life. If Job's health is taken away from him, I am certain he will curse God." And God took up the challenge: "I give Job into your hands. You can do with him what you will, only spare his life." The devil went back and made Job very sick. He gave him very painful boils all over his body, even on his feet and in his hair. Job felt so bad he went and sat among the ashes. His wife came and stood in front of him,

and said bitterly: "What has it helped you to serve God? You might as well curse Him, and die". But Job answered: "You speak like a person with no understanding. We have received many good things from God; how can we now refuse to receive bad things?" Once again Job had not sinned. The devil had failed to snatch him away from God.

By this time the news had spread around of all Job's hardships. Three of his friends came to see him. Their names were Eliphaz, Bildad and Zophar. But these men were no help to Job at all. They were sure that Job must have done something wrong. Poor Job tried to explain to them that he had always done his best to keep God's commandments, but his friends were sure he must have sinned. How miserable he must have felt as they made long speeches about the terrible sin they were sure he had committed.

In spite of all they said, Job stood firm. He could not understand why God was treating him in this way, but he still trusted God.

Then God Himself spoke and told the friends that they had not spoken the truth about Him, as Job had done. They must bring a sacrifice. Then Job would pray for them and God would forgive them.

Job prayed for his friends and when he had done that, God made

him well again. Then God gave Job twice as many sheep and cattle as he had had before. There was no richer man in all the land. God also gave him seven sons and three daughters.

The Sign of the Red Cord

Joshua 1 and 2

Moses, the great leader of the Israelites in the wilderness, was not allowed to enter the Promised Land. From the peak called Pisgah of Mount Nebo he was allowed to look across the river Jordan and see the land spread out westward, but then he died.

In Moses' place God appointed Joshua, the son of Nun. You can imagine how nervous Joshua was, leading his people into a land strange to them, and against fierce enemies. But Joshua trusted God, and God had a special message of encouragement for him: "Lead this whole nation across the river into the land which I shall give to them, just as I promised Moses. As I guided and strengthened him, so I shall be with you: I will not fail you nor forsake you. Do not be afraid."

Then Joshua told the people to prepare themselves for crossing the river Jordan into the land which the Lord had given to be theirs. Not far away, at the foot of a

mountain range, stood the city of Jericho. The people who lived there were called Canaanites.

Before they crossed the river, Joshua sent out two men to go into Jericho and spy out the land. These two spies crossed the river, and slipped into the city. In the evening they found a room in the house of a woman called Rahab, whose house was built right on the wall of the city. The next day some of the people of the city went to the king and told him that there were strangers in the

of God's wonderful works for the Israelites and of His promise to them about the land of Canaan. Then she asked them to promise that when the Israelites took Jericho, they would spare her life.

They promised to see to her safety as long as she did not give them away.

When it was dark, Rahab let the two spies down on a rope out of the window of her house, and down the city wall. Before they left, they told her that when the Israelite army came up to take the city, she should hang a red cord from the window from which she had let them down. All who stayed in the house would be safe.

So the two men went back across the Jordan. When they brought their report, the Israelites were much encouraged because now they knew that the Canaanites were afraid of them.

city, and that they were staying in Rahab's house. The king sent to Rahab and demanded that she should hand over the men, but she had hidden them under stalks of flax which were drying on the roof of her house. Then she told the king's men that the two spies had left the house and gone toward the Jordan, so they went away to search for the spies. When all was safe, Rahab went to the two Israelites. She told them that the people of Jericho knew

How the People Walked through a River; and How a Great City Was Taken

Joshua 3 to 6

When the spies had brought back their report, Joshua felt that it was time to cross the river. The whole Israelite camp was moved right to the banks of the river.

For three days they stayed there getting ready for the crossing.

Joshua knew that God was going to do something wonderful. He told the people to be ready for it.

Early in the morning Joshua gave the word, and at the head of the long column of people the priests took up the Ark of the Covenant. Down into the river they marched, till all the priests bearing the ark were standing right in the water. And then a wonderful thing happened. The river stopped flowing. It had been flooding and overflowing its banks. But suddenly upstream the water gathered in a great mass and did not flow down. Downstream it flowed away toward the Dead Sea. The riverbed in front of the Israelites was dry. Then the priests carrying the Ark of the Covenant took up their position right in the middle of the riverbed and around them the rest of the people crossed into Canaan.

Because of the marvelous thing God had made to happen, Joshua decided that a monument should be put up where they had crossed. One man from each of the twelve tribes went down into the riverbed and picked up a large stone from the place where the priests had stood. These stones were carried across to the other side, to the place where they had had their last camp outside Canaan. There they were placed in a heap to be always a reminder to the children of Israel of the amazing way God had let them pass into the Promised Land. Another twelve stones were taken and placed where the priests had stood, right in the middle of the riverbed.

Only after all this had been done did the priests move out of the riverbed. Then the river flowed once again as it had done before.

It was just before the Passover that the people crossed the river. When they came into Canaan, they found that there was corn in the fields. They were no longer in a barren desert. From the corn the women made flour and baked unleavened cakes. On the day after

the Passover they first ate those cakes. When they did, God stopped giving them the manna from heaven. From then on they must eat the food of Canaan.

How the Israelites Took Jericho

The Canaanite kings were very much afraid of the Israelites, especially when the news reached them of the dry crossing of the river Jordan. But the city of Jericho was still a danger to God's people. One day Joshua walked across to inspect the city and to see what they would have to do to overcome it. Near the city he suddenly saw a man standing, a soldier with a sword in his hand. Joshua challenged him: "Are you for us or for our enemies?" And the answer came: "No, I am the prince of the Lord's armies, and I have come to help." Joshua threw himself to the ground, and worshiped and said: "What has the Lord to say to His servant?" Joshua knew this was not a man, nor even an angel, but the Lord Himself. The Lord told Joshua to take off his shoes because he was standing in a holy place. Then He told him all that the Israelites must do to capture the city of Jericho.

During the next seven days Joshua made the Israelite soldiers do as the Lord had said. Each day, led by the priests carrying the Ark of the Covenant and blowing trumpets made of ram's horns, the soldiers marched around the city. They did not shout or raise any warcry, but simply followed the priests. On the seventh day, early in the morning, the priests and soldiers marched again. This time they circled the city seven times. At the end of the seven circuits Joshua told them all to raise a mighty shout. And when they did, the walls of the city fell down flat, except the part on which Rahab's house was built. Into the city poured the Israelite soldiers, and killed all the people of Jericho except Rahab and her family.

There were great treasures in the city. There was gold, and silver, and copper, and iron, but the Israelite soldiers took nothing for themselves. All was taken for the treasure of God's Tabernacle.

From that time Rahab became an Israelite and married one of the princes of Judah. One of her descendants many years later was David, the great king of Israel.

The Piece of Gold That Wiped Out a Family

Joshua 7 and 8

After the victory at Jericho, the Israelites turned toward the stronghold of Ai. This time their spies felt that two or three thousand men would be enough to overrun this city, but disaster followed. The men of Ai defeated them badly.

Joshua was terribly upset that the Israelites had run away from their enemies. He knew it would make them fearful in future battles, and he felt that when the other Canaanite kings heard of the defeat they would all turn against the Israelites. He humbled himself before God and mourned because of what had happened. Then God told him why this terrible thing had happened. The Israelites had sinned in Jericho. They had taken some of the forbidden treasure and hidden it with their own things. God had cursed them for their sin. God would turn away from them and let them be destroyed altogether if they did not punish the wrongdoer.

The next day Joshua called all the tribes together to a great parade. When the men of Judah passed by, God told Joshua that the wrongdoer was in that tribe. Then as the families of Judah passed, God pointed out the particular family. In the end only one man was left, and all Israel saw that the guilty one was Achan.

Then Joshua said to him: "My son, honor God and confess your sin to Him. Tell me what you have done. Do not try to hide it any longer." Achan confessed. He had taken a Babylonian garment and two hundred shekels of silver, and a piece of gold weighing fifty shekels and he had buried them in his tent.

The sin of Achan had caused harm to many of the Israelite families. Achan and his family and all their animals were taken out of the valley of Achor and stoned to death. All their property was burned. Then a great heap of stones was made over them all. Every time the rest of the Israelites saw the great heap of stones, it was as a warning to them to listen to the commandments of the Lord.

When this had been done, the Israelites turned back again to Ai. This time the city was taken.

The Israelites moved on then to Mount Ebal. There they took stones and made an altar and offered up offerings of thanksgiving to God. After the service Joshua arranged half the people on the slopes of Mount Ebal and half over the ravine on the slopes of Mount Gerizim. From the ravine in between he read to them all the laws God had given through Moses.

How "General" Joshua Captured the Land of Canaan

Joshua 9 to 11

After the victories at Jericho and Ai it did not take long for the news to spread to all the tribes in the land of Canaan. What strange names those tribes had. There were the Hittites, and the Amorites, and the Canaanites, and the Perizzites, and the Hivites, and the Jebusites. They saw that each tribe on its own would not be able to fight against the Israelites, so

they joined together to fight in one army.

Not far from the Israelite camp there lived a small tribe called the Gibeonites. These people were afraid after what had happened to Jericho and Ai, so they worked out a clever scheme. They dressed themselves in old clothes, put on old patched shoes, saddled their donkeys with old sacks and even took dry and moldy bread with them. Then they straggled into the Israelite camp just as if they were from a country very far away. They begged the Israelites to make an alliance with them. These visitors were so clever that the Israelites forgot that God had told them to drive out all the Canaanites and destroy their cities.

Three days later the Israelites discovered how they had been tricked, and that these people were really their near neighbors. At first they were very angry, and wanted immediately to go to war against the Gibeonites, but they remembered the alliance that had been made with solemn promises. They decided to leave them in peace. However, in the future they would have to serve the Israelites by getting wood and water for them. The Gibeonites would have to carry out all the heavy work connected with the Tabernacle. So, wherever the Israelite camp stood, some of the Gibeonites always had to be there to do this work.

and try to separate that tribe from the Israelites.

When the Gibeonites saw what was happening, they sent quickly to Joshua. They asked him to remember their alliance, and to come and help them. God gave Joshua a special message not to be afraid, for He would see to it that the enemies fell into the hands of the Israelites. During the night Joshua moved his forces from Gilgal to Gibeon. In the morning the enemies were terribly defeated at a place called Beth-horon. The enemy fled in all directions. There was even a hailstorm which killed more of the fleeing soldiers than the Israelites had.

On that day Joshua did a strange thing. He called out to the sun to stand still in the heavens, so that the Israelites could deal with all their enemies before it became dark. "Sun, stand still over Gibeon; and Moon, over the valley of Ajalon," he cried. And the sun and the moon did stand still. There never was such a day, before or since, when God listened in that way to the voice of a man.

In that day the power of the Canaanites was broken in the southern part of the land. The Israelites could move in safely and turn northward as well, right up to Mount Hermon. All the kings of the Canaanites were put to death, their cities destroyed, and their people scattered in all directions.

The Sun Stands Still

While the Israelite camp was at Gilgal, close to where they had crossed the river Jordan, the nearest big city was Jerusalem. The king of Jerusalem, Adoni-zedec, was getting very worried. He sent men to the kings of Hebron and Jarmuth, and Lachish, and Eglon. They made an agreement to go together with all their forces, to Gibeon, the city of the Gibeonites,

The Old Man Who Fought Against the Giants

Joshua 14 to 19

Now that the War of Conquest was over—though a few cities had not yet been taken from the Canaanites—Joshua decided to allow Reuben, Gad and the half-tribe of Manasseh to take over the land they had chosen east of the Jordan. One day an old man came to Joshua where he still had his own camp at Gilgal. The name of this old man was Caleb. Caleb, like Joshua, had been one of the spies Moses sent into Canaan from the wilderness to spy out the land. Then he had been forty years old. Now he was eighty-five. But as old as he was, he was still strong. He felt he was still just as strong as he had been when he went into Canaan as a spy. Now he wanted land on which to farm. He had chosen Hebron where the Anakims, the giants, still had control. Moses had promised him a place of his own when he agreed to go into Canaan as a spy, and now he wanted to take over that land.

When Joshua gave him the permission he wanted, Caleb led his soldiers up to Hebron, drove out the Anakims and took over the city and district.

The Rest of the Land Is Divided

After this God told Joshua to divide up the rest of the conquered land of Canaan between the remaining tribes. Nine and a half tribes still had to know where they would stay. The names of these tribes were Asher, Simeon, Judah, Benjamin, Issachar, Zebulun, Dan, Ephraim, Naphtali, and the half-tribe of Manasseh.

Judah, one of the biggest of the tribes, was given the mountainous districts on the west side of the Dead Sea between Hebron and Jerusalem. Simeon lay southward toward the desert. Benjamin lay north of Judah, and eastward to the Jordan; Dan again north of Judah, but westward to the Great Sea which we call the Mediterranean. Ephraim would have the area in the middle of the land around the city of Shechem and the mountains of Ebal and Gerizim, where Joshua read the Law to the people. This is where Joshua himself went to live, because he was an Ephraimite. And here, near Mount Ebal they buried the body of Joseph, which they had kept in its coffin of stone, unburied ever since they left Egypt.

North of Ephraim again, right across the country from the Jordan to the Great Sea, lay the portion of the remaining half-tribe of Manasseh. Manasseh and Ephraim had both been the sons of Joseph, so that the descendants of Joseph were now two tribes instead of one.

The northern part of Canaan was divided between four tribes. Issachar was the southernmost of them, Asher was in the west along the coast of the Great Sea, Zebulun lay in the middle, and Naphtali was in the east, up to the western shore of the sea that afterward was called Galilee.

It seemed that the Israelites had come at last to peaceful occupation of their land. But they had not obeyed God completely. Many Canaanites were still in the land. Several of the cities were still their strongholds, and in the south the Philistines still lived in an area around Gaza.

Cities of Safety

Joshua 20 and 21

The Israelites had many interesting laws. One of the laws had to do with the person who had accidentally killed another person.

Back in those times when anyone was killed, the man who was his closest relative became the "avenger of blood". It was his duty to seek out the killer and avenge his relative's death, usually by killing him, too. The death could have been completely an accident but the "avenger of blood" would still hunt the one responsible, perhaps for years, and kill him. There did not seem any way out for the man who had accidently killed another person.

Now Joshua was told to apply one of the laws that had been given to Moses. He appointed certain cities to be "cities of safety". If a hunted man came to the elders of such a city where they sat at the city gate, and they were satisfied with his story, they could let him in. No one had any right to touch him while he stayed in that city. He could stay there in safety until the death of the High Priest. When that happened he could return to his own home, and no one was allowed to hurt him. There were six of these cities, three west of the Jordan, and three beyond the river. They were Kedesh, Shechem and Hebron in the west, Bezer, Ramoth and Golan in the east. Every Israelite was within one day's or, at the most, two days' journey of such a city of safety.

The Levites

When the tribes of Israel were given land in Canaan, the Levites were left out. It was the duty of the Levites to act as priests and interpreters of God's Law to the people. It would not be good for them to live as a tribe all in one place. They must live among all the tribes.

Joshua called together the heads of the Levites, and the heads of the fathers of families in all the tribes. Certain cities and lands were set aside for the Levites throughout the country. In these places they lived, and went up to the Tabernacle at certain times in the year to take their turn there.

Since the tribes were no longer on the move, it was necessary to decide where the Tabernacle would stand. Joshua chose a hill called Shiloh, about in the middle of the country. There the Tabernacle stood for nearly four hundred years. Three times every year all the people of Israel gathered there for important festivals. There was the Passover, when they remembered how God had led their people out of Egypt. Then there was the Feast of Tabernacles, when they made little huts of branches to live in during the feast. This was to remind them of their wanderings in the wilderness. And then there was the Feast of Pentecost, when they brought the first of the crops from their gardens as a gift to God.

Those were the main festivals, but every day offerings were made for sin and people came especially to bring sacrifices to God and to pray for forgiveness and blessing.

One People Serving One Lord

Joshua 22 to 24

When the war against the Canaanites had come to an end and the tribes were ready to move off to their own parts of the land, Joshua first called to him those who were going to live on the other side of the Jordan. He thanked them for the way they had kept their promise and stood by their brothers in all the battles against the Canaanites. Now the time had come for them to go home, back to their wives and children, their flocks and their herds. But Joshua warned them that when they came to their own lands and settled down there, they must not forget God. Then Joshua blessed them and allowed them to go from the Tabernacle at Shiloh toward the river Jordan and their own families east of the river. The country they were going to was called Gilead.

By this time Joshua was very old and he knew he would soon die. He decided that he must now give his last message to the people of Israel. He called all the leaders of the tribes together. All the princes and judges and other officers met with Joshua at Shechem. There he reminded them of all the wonderful things God had done for them and for their fathers before them. He talked

in sincerity and truth. Do not turn to worshiping idols but serve the Lord faithfully." Then Joshua challenged them to make their choice: "Choose this day whom you are going to serve, either the gods your fathers worshiped beyond the Euphrates and in Egypt, or the gods of the Canaanites. But as for me and my family, we will serve the Lord."

The people answered with one voice: "We will do so, too. The Lord Who brought our fathers out of slavery in Egypt, we will follow Him." But Joshua reminded them that this would be no light matter. God had given them His laws. They must keep those laws. Otherwise they would be punished and their way would be hard and unhappy. The God Who had blessed them, would punish them severely. But the people said: "No, we will serve the Lord."

So Joshua wrote down their promise in the book of the Law. He then placed a great memorial stone under a tree near the Tabernacle to be a continual reminder to the people of their great promise. The princes and people then went off to their own parts of the country.

Not long afterward Joshua died. He was one hundred and ten years of age. As long as the elders lived who had followed him, the Israelites faithfully served God, but after that they began to be disobedient.

about their history from the time of Abraham until finally they came safely into Canaan, and now lived there in peace, just as God had promised. Then Joshua said something very important to his people: "God has given you a land for which you did not work, and cities which you did not build and you are living in them. You eat the fruit of vineyards and olive trees which you did not plant. He has given you these good gifts, and now you must honor Him and serve Him

Jael's Great Victory

Judges 4 and 5

After the death of Joshua it was still necessary for the Israelites to fight against the Canaanites. They had not all been driven out of the land as God had commanded. Until that was done there would be no lasting peace.

As soon as the elders died who had known Joshua, the people began to turn to the ways of the heathen and worshiped the false gods of Baal and Ashtaroth. In His anger, God left them to the mercies of the Canaanites. In spite of their disobedience, though, God still loved them, and He raised up from among them, judges, leaders who could help them escape from their enemies.

The Israelites in the north fell into the hands of Jabin, king of Canaan, and his general, Sisera. For twenty years they did not know what freedom meant. But while they were under the rule of the Canaanites they still had a judge of their own ruling in the south. The judge was a woman, the prophetess Deborah. A prophetess was a woman who lived in close touch with God and was able to pass on God's message to the people. A man who was called to do the same work was called a prophet. Deborah lived between Ramah and Bethel in the land of Ephraim. The people went to her whenever they needed advice because they could see she had been given wisdom from God.

Deborah was very sad about the unhappy condition of the Israelites in the north. She sent for a man called Barak and told him to gather together ten thousand men from the tribes of Zebulun and Naphtali. She told him to move his army in the direction of Mount Tabor, where they would meet Sisera, the Canaanite, with his chariots and all the rest of his

army. But Barak would not go unless Deborah herself went with him. Deborah promised to go with him but the honor in this battle would not be to Barak, but to a woman into whose hands God would give Sisera, the Canaanite.

Barak and Deborah then gathered together their army of ten thousand men and moved up toward Mount Habor. Sisera, in the meantime, had been told of their plans by a traitor called Heber, the Kenite. Sisera gathered together his nine hundred iron chariots and the rest of his army. But on this day the armored chariots did not help him. Barak's little army defeated the Canaanites very heavily, and even Sisera himself had to run away on foot. After he had run some distance he came to a tent which happened to belong to Heber, the Kenite. Heber's wife, Jael, invited him in to hide there awhile. She covered him with a coat and gave him some milk to drink from a leather bottle. He asked her to stand guard in the door of the tent, and then fell fast asleep. While he lay asleep Jael took a tent peg and hammered it through Sisera's head, and he died.

Then Jael went out and found the Israelite general, Barak, coming across the valley. To him she said: "Come, and I will show you the man you are looking for." So, in that day Jabin the Canaanite king and his army and all his people were subdued before the Israelites—all through the deed of Jael, the wife of Heber. The war between Canaan and Israel was so bitter that the Israelites thought highly of Jael for what she had done. Deborah and Barak even composed a victory song to remind the people of what had happened. Here are a few of the verses of that song.

"Praise ye the Lord for the avenging of Israel. . . . Hear, O ye kings; give ear, O ye princes; I, even I, will sing unto the Lord; I will sing praise to the God of Israel.

My heart is toward the governors of Israel, that offered themselves willingly among the people. Bless ye the Lord.

The kings came and fought; then fought the kings of Canaan in Taanach by the waters of Megiddo. . . .
They fought from heaven; the stars in their courses fought against Sisera. ... .

Blessed above women shall Jael the wife of Heber, the Kenite, be; blessed shall she be above women in the tent. . . .

She put her hand to the nail and her right hand to the workmen's hammer; and with the hammer she smote Sisera, she smote off his head, when she had pierced and stricken through his temples."

And after that great battle the land of Israel had peace for forty years.

they had to suffer the attacks of the Midianites for seven long years. The Midianites were desert-dwellers coming in from east of the Jordan. Every year when the Israelites' crops were ready for reaping, the Midianites swept in and stole everything.

God made it clear to the Israelites why these things were happening to them. He sent a prophet to them to remind them of all He had done for their people in bringing them out of Egypt and into the land of Canaan. He reminded them, too, of the warning He had given them not to worship the false gods of the heathen nations in Canaan, but they had not obeyed.

One day one of the Israelites, Gideon the son of Joash, was threshing wheat in a hole in a rock which was normally used as a wine press. Suddenly, sitting under an oak tree next to where he worked, there was an angel from God. The angel spoke to him: "The Lord is with you, you brave man." But Gideon replied: "Oh, my Lord, if the Lord is with us, why has all this happened to us? Where are the miracles the Lord once did to help our fathers when He brought them out of Egypt? But now the Lord God has turned away from us, and let us fall into the hands of the Midianites." But in mercy the Lord answered: "Do not be afraid! Go out in strength to help your people, and you will

Gideon and the Gallant Three Hundred

Judges 6 to 8

It seems as if the Israelites would never learn that disobedience of God's commandments always caused them trouble and sorrow. When the forty years of peace ended they were once again misbehaving themselves and God had to punish them again. This time save them from the Midianites. Do not think you are alone in the fight. I shall be with you."

Then Gideon went and prepared some cakes of unleavened bread, some goat's meat, and a pot of broth. He took this food out to where the angel was still waiting under the oak tree. But the angel did a strange thing. He told Gideon to lay the meat and the cakes of bread on the rock in front of him, and to pour out the broth over the meat and the bread. When Gideon had done that, the angel reached out and touched with his staff the food on the rock. At once fire burst out of the rock, and the offering of food was burned up. And as this happened, the angel disappeared from sight. Terrified, Gideon cried out to God: "What shall I do? Because I have seen an angel face to face."

But God knew how he felt, and comforted him: "Let peace be in your heart. Do not be afraid. You will not die."

The very same night the Lord told Gideon what he had to do. His first task was not to fight against the Midianites but to free his own people from their idol worship which made God so angry with them. So with ten men Gideon went out and cut down the worship pole where false worship was paid to Ashtaroth. They broke down the altar to Baal. On the same spot Gideon set up an altar to God, and using the wood

of the pole they had chopped down, a young bullock was offered as a burnt offering to God.

When morning came and the people of the little town awoke, they were shocked to see what had happened. They did not know who had done it, but quickly one of them guessed it must have been Gideon. They rushed off to his father Joash and told him they wanted to kill Gideon for what he had done. But Joash was not afraid. "If Baal is really a god," he said, "he is able to take care of himself. He will himself punish the person who broke down his altar." When the people saw that Gideon was not harmed they began to turn back to the true God.

After this Gideon sent out messengers to the people of Manasseh, Asher, Zebulun and Naphtali, asking their men to come and meet him. The gathering place was around the fountain at Harod, on the slopes of Mount Gilboa.

Gideon turned again to God. He believed in God, and he wanted to be certain that it really was God's will for him to lead his people against the Midianites. He prayed and said: "If it is Thy plan to use me to save Israel, then give me a sign. I shall put a piece of woolly sheepskin on the floor. If in the morning there is dew on the fleece only, and not on the ground round about, then I shall know it is right for me to lead the people." In the morning that was exactly what had happened, and Gideon was able to wring a whole bowlful of water out of the fleece.

But Gideon wanted to be very sure, so he asked for another sign. This time the fleece only must be dry, and all the ground around, wet. In the morning God had again proved He would help Gideon to save his people.

By now men from the other tribes had gathered at Harod. The Midianite army was camped near them. Something really surprising happened. God told Gideon there were too many Israelite soldiers. If they defeated the Midianites they would think it was by their own

strength they had done it, and they would forget all about God again. So Gideon had to tell them that everyone who was the slightest bit nervous must go back home. Of the original thirty-two thousand, only ten thousand stayed for the fight. But God said there were still too many of them. Gideon must bring the soldiers down to the riverbank. There God would tell Gideon what to do. God told Gideon he should tell the soldiers to drink water from the stream. Almost every one of them knelt down to drink. Only three hundred scooped up water with their hands. Those were the men God chose, because they kept themselves ready to fight, even while they were drinking. They remembered even as they drank that the Midianites were nearby. All the rest of the men were sent back to their tents while Gideon prepared the three hundred for the battle.

Gideon's Victory

That night God told Gideon to call his servant Phurah. Gideon and the servant were to creep down into the Midianite camp to spy out the land and listen to what the enemy had to say. Gideon heard one of the enemy soldiers telling his friend of a

dream he had had. He had seen a little cake of barley come tumbling down the mountainside, right against the side of a tent. It knocked the tent over. His friend said: "That cake of barley is Gideon, that man of Israel, because God has given us, all the army of Midian, into his hands." When Gideon heard this he was very pleased. God had made the Midianites afraid, and the victory would be much easier for the Israelites. He slipped back to the three hundred and made them ready for battle. They were divided into three companies.

Every man was given a trumpet, an empty jar and a lamp to put in the jar. Then the lamps were lit inside the jars so that their light could not be seen. The soldiers then crept down until they were close to the Midianite camp. Each of the three companies moved around to a different side of the camp. Then suddenly, at a signal from Gideon, they all blew their trumpets and smashed the jars and rushed into the camp with their lights showing, and shouting: "The sword of the Lord and of Gideon." The Midianites were so terrified they did not even fight but ran eastward as fast as they could, to try to cross the Jordan into safety. But Gideon sent messengers to the tribe of Ephraim, and they attacked the Midianites as they fled. Two of the Midianite princes, Oreb and Zeeb, were killed in the flight, and most of their people were killed by the Israelites as well. That was the end of the power of Midian.

From then on Gideon remained a judge of Israel until he died. The Israelites loved him so much they wanted him to be their king. They wanted his family to become the royal family of the nation. But Gideon would not hear of it. God only must be King of Israel, and the people must always serve Him faithfully.

Never Promise Without Thinking First

Judges 8 to 11

Gideon was a humble man. He did not want to be king of Israel. He did not want his family to become the royal family. But one of his sons did not think the same way. That son was Abimelech. Soon after Gideon died, Abimelech murdered all his brothers except one who managed to get away. Then Abimelech went to Shechem and declared himself to be king, but only Shechem would have him. He did not really become king of Israel, although he called himself that. Three years later Abimelech was killed during a battle at Thebez, when a woman threw a heavy stone from the city wall onto his head.

Again the people of Israel turned away from God and were worshiping heathen idols. So God gave them into the hands of the Philistines and the children of Ammon. The Israelites humbled themselves before God and once again a great leader was given to save them from their enemies. This time it was Jephthah, the son of Gilead.

The Ammonites came from east of the river Jordan, so Jephthah sent to all the tribes living on that side and called on them to follow him against the enemy. Then he

did a very foolish thing. He made a promise to God without thinking carefully what he was saying and what it might mean. Jephthah promised that if God gave him the victory over the Ammonites, when he returned home, whatever met him first of his possessions he would give to God as his thank-offering.

The Ammonites were defeated and driven out of the land. The Israelites returned home in peace. But when Jephthah arrived home, it was his only child, his beloved daughter, who came out to him first. He was upset when he remembered his promise to God. But his daughter was very brave and she said: "Father, God has given you the victory over our enemies. You must keep your promise to Him. Only let me spend two months in the mountains with my friends to sorrow over what has to happen to me."

After the two months she returned, and her father did to her what he had promised the Lord. It became a custom in the land that every year the young girls went apart into the mountains for four days to mourn for Jephthah's daughter.

The Life and Death of Samson the Strong

Judges 12 to 16

Though the Israelites had turned to God in the time of Jephthah, it was only for a while. Before long they were again worshiping idols. Three judges followed Jephthah: Ibzan, Elon and Abdon, but they could make no difference to the wrong, heathenish ways of the

people. The Philistines began to spread across the land, oppressing the Israelites. The Philistines lived on the coastal plain near the Mediterranean Sea. Their soldiers moved into the mountains to attack the Israelites. For forty long years this went on.

As so often when they were in trouble, the Israelites turned back to God for help. This time God again sent an angel.

In the land of Dan, alongside the country of the Philistines, lived a man called Manoah who had no children. One day an angel appeared to Manoah's wife and told her that she would have a son, and that son would begin to save his people from the Philistines. But as long as he lived his hair must never be cut.

When the little baby was born, he was given the name of Samson. As he grew up he became an extremely strong man.

When he was a young man, one day he went down to a village called Timnath. There he fell in love with a Philistine girl.

As he walked through the vineyards outside the village, suddenly a young lion jumped out at him with a frightful roar. Samson had no weapon but he tore the lion in pieces with his bare hands.

Some time later he went down to Timnath again. On the way he went to look at the skeleton of the lion he had killed before. When he came to it, he found that a swarm of bees had made their home inside and there was honey there which he could eat and enjoy.

Samson married the Philistine girl, and there was a great feast that lasted a whole week. During this feast Samson had as his close companions, thirty young Philistine men. One day Samson asked them a riddle. He promised thirty shirts and thirty suits to them if they could answer. But if not, they must give him the shirts and suits.

The young men asked him to tell them his riddle. It was: "Out of the eater came forth meat, and out of the strong came forth sweetness." They tried and tried, but they could not find the answer. On the seventh day they went to Samson's wife and said: "Persuade your husband to tell us the answer or we shall burn your father's house down, and burn you as well." Then she went weeping to her husband and begged him to tell her the answer. At first he would not, but she cried and carried on so much that in the end he told her. Of course, she went straight to the young men and told them. On the seventh day, just before the end of the feast, they went and gave Samson the answer: "What is sweeter than honey? And what is stronger than a lion?" Samson knew immediately what had happened, and he said to them: "If you had not plowed with my heifer, you would not have found out my riddle."

Samson Sets Fire to the Philistines' Wheat

When harvest time came along, Samson's anger had cooled off and he decided to go back to his wife. By then her father had given her to another man to be his wife, so he offered Samson his younger daughter. But Samson was furious. He went out and caught all the foxes he could find, until he had three hundred altogether. He tied them together two-by-two by their tails, and fastened behind each pair a burning stump of wood. Then he drove them into the fields of the Philistines, and very quickly the fire was roaring through the cornfields.

When the Philistines realized who had done this, and why Samson had been so angry, they went and burned down his father-in-law's house with the old man and his daughter inside.

When Samson heard what had happened, he was angry all over again. He went back to the village and killed everyone he could get hold of.

The Philistines were now so furious they were ready for war against all the Israelites. They

of an ass, and with it he attacked the Philistines. With that bone he killed one thousand Philistines.

After that amazing victory Samson was the judge of Israel for twenty years.

Samson and Delilah

After this Samson again fell in love with a Philistine woman. Her name was Delilah. She lived in the valley of Sorek. When they heard what was happening, the Philistine leaders went to Delilah and promised to give her a large sum of money if she found out how Samson got his great strength, and how they could overcome him.

Three times she asked Samson about it. Each time he gave her a different answer. But each time when the Philistines came, he easily broke away from them. Finally he became so tired of Delilah's questions that he told her the real secret. If his hair was cut off he would no longer be a Nazarite, and God would take away the gift of strength from him.

That night the end came. While Samson slept with his head on Delilah's lap she called a man to come and shave off all his hair. This time when she shouted out that the Philistines were on him he jumped up as usual, but he did not know that the Lord was not with him. The Philistines took him

moved their army up to attack the men of the tribe of Judah, but Judah was without any weapons and wanted only to be left alone. They were so afraid of war that they bound Samson tight with two new cords and carried him off to hand him over to the Philistines at a place called Lehi.

When they reached this place the Philistines shouted at him and mocked him. Then God gave him great strength. He snapped the cords as if they were cotton threads. He snatched up a jawbone

prisoner. They put out both his eyes. Then they took him to prison and fastened him up with chains of brass. In the prison they made him work grinding corn. What they did not notice was that his hair was growing again. And his strength, too.

Samson's End

A while after Samson had been handed over to the Philistines, they called together their people to make a great sacrifice to their god, Dagon. They thought he had handed Samson over to them.

When all the people had gathered in the great temple of Dagon, they dragged Samson in to jeer at him in his helplessness. The temple was packed with people. On the roof balcony there were three thousand watching. While the sacrifice was being made, Samson asked the little boy who was his guide to lead him to the great pillars that held up the roof. When he felt them with his hands, Samson prayed that God would give him strength for this last time.

Then Samson pressed the pillars with all his might. Down they tumbled, and with them the roof as well. In the ruins more Philistines died than Samson had killed in all the rest of his life—but he died with them.

The Story of a Wonderful Woman

Ruth 1 to 4

During the time of the judges, there once was a terrible famine in the land of Canaan. Many people moved away into other lands where there was still some food left. One of these was a man called Elimelech from Bethlehem-judah, who took his wife, Naomi, and their two sons, Mahlon and Chilion, and went to live in Moab. In time Elimelech died, leaving Naomi and her sons still living in the land of Moab. The two sons took Moabite wives, Orpah and Ruth.

For ten years they lived happily together, but then Mahlon and Chilion both fell ill and died. Because Naomi now felt she was a stranger alone in a foreign land, she decided she must go back to Judah in Canaan, to her own people. She asked Orpah and Ruth each to go back to their own mothers.

But Ruth would not go. She threw her arms around Naomi and said: "Please do not ask me to leave you; wherever you go, I will go, and where you stay, I will stay. Your people will be my people, and your God my God. I want to be buried where you are buried when

113

you die. May God punish me if anything other than death parts us."

So the two women walked the long way back from Moab to Bethlehem in Judah, back to Naomi's own people.

Naomi and Ruth were terribly poor, and because they needed food so badly, Naomi sent Ruth out after the harvesters in the wheat fields of Boaz, who was a distant relative of Naomi.

Ruth went down to the fields right away. It happened that on that very day Boaz himself came out from Bethlehem to see how the harvesters were progressing. He made Ruth a very kind promise. She could gather wheat in his fields as long as she wanted to, and no one would drive her away. She could also drink water from the harvesters' vessels if she was thirsty.

At the end of the harvest season Naomi was very sorry for Ruth, who had worked so hard to find food for them. She told Ruth to go to Boaz at the time of the great harvest feast and explain that she was the widow of Elimelech, who had been a relative of Boaz. Perhaps Boaz would be willing to help them without Ruth having to work so hard finding food for them.

But when Boaz saw Ruth again he at once fell in love with her. Before very long a marriage was arranged between the great Boaz and Ruth, the little widow from Moab. Naomi went to live with Boaz and Ruth in their great house.

After a time God gave to Ruth and Boaz a little son whom they called Obed.

When Obed grew up and was married, he and his wife had a son, too. That son was called Jesse. Jesse was the father of David who first was a shepherd boy but then became the greatest king that Israel ever had.

The Boy Who Was Given to God

I Samuel 1 to 3

After the death of Samson, the strong man, the next judge of Israel was Eli. He was also the high priest in the Tabernacle at Shiloh. Eli was an old man and was helped by his two sons, Hophni and Phinehas.

At that time there was also a

rich man called Elkanah who had, like many men in those days, two wives. His favorite wife was Hannah, but she had no children.

Each year they went up especially to the Tabernacle at Shiloh to bring an offering to God and to beg Him to bless them with a son. One year when they were staying near the Tabernacle, Hannah slipped away quietly to the Tabernacle to pray on her own. As she prayed, she wept, because she longed so much for a baby. And her longing was so great that she made a special promise to God: "Dear God, please give me a little son. If You give me a son, as soon as he is old enough I will give him back to You to serve You."

Hannah prayed so hard, and wept so bitterly that Eli, the high priest, noticed it. He prayed with her that God would give her the son she longed for so dearly. Hannah went away happily because now she believed that God would really answer her prayer.

That was exactly what happened. Not many months afterward a little boy was born. Hannah called him Samuel, which means "asked of God".

Hannah did not forget her promise to God, either. As soon as the little boy was old enough, she took him up with her to the Tabernacle at Shiloh. There she handed Samuel over to Eli so that he could be taught to serve the Lord there.

One night Eli had gone to bed in his little tent at the side of the Tabernacle. Samuel was not asleep yet. Suddenly the Lord Himself called Samuel. The little boy did not know whose voice it was, but he answered: "Here I am." Then he ran to Eli because he thought that the old man had called him. But Eli answered: "I did not call you. Go and lie down." So Samuel went back to his sleeping mat. He had hardly laid down when the voice called once more. Again Samuel ran to Eli, and again the old man told him to go back to his

bed. When it happened a third time, Eli realized that it was the Lord calling Samuel. He told the boy that if he heard the voice again, he must answer: "Speak, Lord, for Thy servant is listening."

God did call again and Samuel answered. God gave Samuel this very important message: "I have seen how badly the sons of Eli behave, and I have seen that Eli has done nothing to stop them. I will punish them greatly. The priesthood will be taken away from them, and none of their descendants will have the right to act as priests ever again."

After hearing that awful message Samuel lay on his bed until morning, without sleeping. He was afraid to tell Eli what God had said, because he loved the old man so much. But in the morning Eli called him and made him tell what God had said. Eli was sad, but he knew that what God had said was right.

It was not long before all the people knew that God had spoken directly to Samuel. That meant he was a prophet, God's spokesman to His people. The people respected Samuel greatly. From then on God spoke often to Samuel, and in the Tabernacle at Shiloh he passed on to the people of Israel God's message to them.

How a Great Idol Fell Down

1 Samuel 4 to 7

When Eli, the priest, was a very old man, the people of Israel were greatly troubled by the Philistines who lived along the coast of the Mediterranean Sea. There was a great battle near a place called Eben-ezer. The Israelites were very badly beaten.

When they heard the terrible news, the elders of Israel gathered to consider what must be done to prevent the whole nation from being destroyed. They decided that the Ark of the Covenant must be brought out of the Tabernacle in Shiloh and taken with the army, and then all would be well. So up they went to Shiloh, right into the Holy of Holies. No one was supposed to go into the Holy of Holies at all, except the High Priest. The High Priest could go in only on the Day of Atonement. What made it worse was that the two bad sons of Eli, Hophni and Phinehas, helped to take away the Ark, and went with it to the army camp. When the Ark arrived in the camp the soldiers gave a great shout.

When the Philistines heard the shout, they were afraid, and were sure that now the Israelites would defeat them. But when the battle took place, the Israelites were beaten again. Worst of all, the Ark was captured. Eli's two sons were killed in the battle.

On that day the old man, Eli, was sitting on a seat beside the road, waiting fearfully for news. At the end of the battle a man came running into Shiloh with his clothes all torn and dirty to tell what had happened. When Eli heard of the death of his sons, and especially of the capture of the Ark, the poor old man—he was ninety-eight years old—fell from his seat, broke his neck and died.

The Philistines were overjoyed because they had taken the Ark. They rushed it back to one of their great cities, Ashdod. They set the Ark up alongside their great idol, Dagon, in his temple. But when they came into the temple the next morning the idol was lying on its face on the ground. Very carefully they set the idol up again, but the next morning they found that it had fallen down again. But this time the head and both hands had broken off. A worse thing happened, too. The people of Ashdod and all the people around were afflicted with a terrible disease which brought up painful boils on them. The Philistines were sure that all this had happened because they had taken away the Ark from the Israelites. They decided that it should be moved to the city of Gath. But that brought terrible hardship to the people of Gath, too. When the Ark was sent on from Gath to Ekron,

the sickness came to them, too.

For seven whole months the Philistines suffered because they kept the Ark. Finally they decided to send it back. They loaded the Ark onto a newly made cart, with two cows harnessed in front. On the cart with the Ark they placed offerings of gold, to be a sacrifice to the God of Israel. No men led the cows, but as soon as they were let go, they pulled the

117

cart away in the direction of the hills where the Israelites lived. The cows pulled the cart right into the valley of Beth-shemesh, where some of the people were harvesting wheat. When they saw what was on the cart, these people were very glad. Some of them who were Levites immediately built an altar and, using the wood of the cart to make the fire, they offered up the two cows to God as their sacrifice of thanksgiving.

But some of the people of Beth-shemesh were more inquisitive than they ought to have been. They wanted to see what was inside the Ark. They opened it, although they knew this was wrong. The result was that God sent a great plague on them, and a very large number died.

When that happened the people who were left were afraid. They sent a message to the inhabitants of Kirjath-jearim, asking them to come and get the Ark. This was done, and for twenty years that was where the Ark remained, in the house of Abinadab.

The Last of the Judges

1 Samuel 7

Now when Eli died, Samuel was too young to judge over Israel. But after a few years, when the Ark had been brought to Kirjath-jearim, Samuel began to tell the Israelites what they must do if they wanted to overcome the Philistines. The Philistines were still raiding their villages and stealing their crops, and making life very unhappy for the Israelites.

Samuel told the Israelites they must stop worshiping the false gods of the Canaanites. He told them they must destroy their ugly idols and turn back to the Lord, the only true God. When they did that, He would help them to drive out the Philistines.

The Israelites listened to what Samuel said. On a certain day many of them gathered at a place called Mizpah to fast and to pray that God would deliver them. There Samuel was appointed judge over the nation and there they all promised to serve God faithfully.

Before long the Israelites were able to take back all the cities the Philistines had captured from them, from Ekron right up to Gath. From then on, during all the time that Samuel was judge over Israel, the Philistines were not able to trouble them again. Samuel set up his home in Ramah. From Ramah he went out from town to town to judge and to settle all the disputes between the people.

Israel Demands a King

1 Samuel 8 to 10

There were two other judges in Israel when Samuel was a very old man. These were his two sons, Joel and Abiah. But just like Eli's sons long before, they were bad men. They were greedy, and instead of judging honestly they took bribes. The people were very unhappy about this, so one day the elders went to see Samuel and said to him: "You are an old man now, and your sons arc not judging in the way you did. All the nations around about have kings. Appoint a king to rule over us, too."

Samuel was very sad about this, so he went to talk to God about it in prayer. God answered his faithful old servant and explained to him that the people were not really turning against Samuel, but against God Himself. Finally God told him to choose them a king. Samuel sent all the elders back to their own cities, and set out to find a king for them.

At this time there lived in the district of the tribe of Benjamin a man named Kish. Kish had a strong and handsome son. The son was a tall man, head and shoulders above other people, and his name was Saul. Kish owned a number of donkeys, and these donkeys strayed away. Saul took a servant and went to look for them. They had traveled a very long way without catching sight of the missing animals. When they reached as far as the land of Zuph, Saul decided they must turn back home in case his father began to worry about them. The servant, however, remembered that in a town nearby lived a wise man, a prophet of God. That wise man was Samuel. He suggested that Saul should go to see Samuel and ask him for help in finding the donkeys.

When Saul arrived at the city gate near which Samuel was standing, God told the prophet in his heart that this was the man that must rule over His people. Saul knew nothing at all about this. He did not know who Samuel was. He went up to him and asked him politely how to find his way to the prophet's house. How amazed he must have been at the answer he received. Samuel said: "I am the man you want. Come and eat with me today, and tomorrow you may leave again. Do not worry about the donkeys. They are found already. And for whom is all Israel longing? Is it not for you and for all your family?"

Saul hardly knew how to answer: "Am I not a Benjamite, belonging to one of the smallest tribes of Israel? And is my family not one of the least important in Benjamin? How can you speak to me in this way?"

Samued gave him no answer, but took Saul and his servant into the dining hall in the high place of the town, and made Saul sit in the chief seat between all the important people round about.

Early the next morning, before Saul left to go back home, Samuel called him aside. The old man took a horn of oil and poured it out on Saul's head and kissed him and said: "It is the Lord Himself who has anointed you to be king over His people. Now go on your way. When you come to Rachel's grave, just as you enter the land of Benjamin, you will see two men who will tell you that the donkeys are found and that your father is worrying in case you are now lost. Go on from there and on the plain of Tabor you will meet three men going up to sacrifice at Beth-el. One of them will be carrying three kids. One will have three loaves. The third will carry a bottle of wine. They will greet you and give you two loaves of bread, which you will accept from them. After that you will meet a group of prophets playing on musical instruments and prophesying in the Name of God. You will see that they are filled with the Spirit of God. The Spirit will come on you, too, and you will be made a new man. All this will happen to prove to you that it is God Who is calling you to be the king. Wait for me in Gilgal, and

in seven days' time I will meet you there."

Everything happened exactly as Samuel had said. When the Spirit of the Lord came upon Saul, he became a changed man. Now he was no longer just a farmer's son, but a king.

Jonathan the Brave

1 Samuel 13 and 14

When Saul had reigned for two years, he decided that the Israelites must put an end to the at-

121

tacks of the Philistines. He chose for himself three thousand men for the campaign. Two thousand of them were under Saul's command in Michmash and around Mount Beth-el. The other thousand were under the command of Jonathan around Gibeah in Benjamin. Jonathan, who was Saul's eldest son, led an attack against the Philistines in Geba and defeated them.

This was the signal for Saul. He sent messengers throughout the land to call the people for an all-out war against the Philistines. By now the Philistines had gathered many soldiers. The Israelites were terrified. They hid themselves wherever they could find places. Some even fled across the river Jordan into the lands of Gad and Gilead.

Saul unhappily gathered his little company of men, now only about six hundred, and went to join forces with Jonathan.

Jonathan was a brave man. He was determined that the Philistines should be driven away. One morning, without saying anything to his father, he called his armor-bearer, and the two of them quietly slipped away to spy out the Philistine positions between Michmash and Gibeah.

Together they climbed up to the top of a rocky hill. There they stood up in full view of the enemy garrison on another hill close by. When the Philistines saw this they were amazed and shouted: "Look, the Hebrews are crawling out of their holes in the ground. Come over where we are, and we will show you a thing or two!" Jonathan and the armor-bearer rushed across and beat down the Philistines in front of them. There was such confusion that in the first attack they killed about twenty men. So fierce was the fight that panic took hold of the whole Philistine army. They even began to fight among themselves.

When Saul and his soldiers saw what was happening they rushed to join in the battle, and so did some of the Israelites who had been hiding in the hills and bushes round about. One group of Israelites which had been caught up by the Philistines to be their servants broke out in revolt. Soon the mighty Philistine army was running away.

The Sin of Saul the Selfish

1 Samuel 14 and 15

After the great victory against the Philistines Saul took courage and led his men against the enemy nations on all sides. He led his army against the Moabites and the Ammonites, and the Edomites, and the kings of Zobah, and again against the Philistines. In every battle his men defeated their enemies.

South of the country of the Israelites there lived the tribe of the Amalekites who were a great problem to Saul's people. They raided all the farms and villages on the edge of the desert and stole and killed. One day the prophet Samuel came to Saul with a special message from God. The king must lead his people against the Amalekites to destroy everything they possessed. The Amalekites had been enemies of the Israelites since they attacked them on their way through the wilderness from Egypt, and had kept on tormenting them.

Saul's armies attacked the Amalekites and defeated them, killing all they found. But Saul did not altogether keep the commandment of the Lord which Samuel had brought to him. He preserved the life of Agag, king of the Amalekites. Saul preserved also the best of the sheep and the cattle. It was only the worthless animals that he had destroyed.

Now Samuel was not with the armies. Being an old man, he was going to follow them later. The Lord spoke to Samuel and said: "I regret that Saul was ever made king, because he has not kept My commandments." That night Samuel prayed all night long for Saul.

In the morning Samuel went out to meet Saul. When Saul met the prophet, he was very proud of the victory they had won. "May the blessing of the Lord be upon you," he said. "I have done what the Lord commanded." But Samuel answered: "What then is this bleating of sheep and lowing of cattle that I hear?" And Saul said: "We have brought them from the Amalekites. The people have spared the best cattle and sheep to offer them as a sacrifice to God. The rest we have destroyed altogether."

Then Samuel said: "Let me tell you what the Lord told me last night. When you thought nothing of yourself He made you king over all Israel. Then He sent you on a journey and told you to destroy altogether the Amalekites. Why did you not obey? Why did you try to gather riches for yourself instead of destroying everything as God said? You speak of sacrifices. Do you think God is willing to receive them from you if you refuse to obey Him? To rebel against God is as bad as serving idols. Because you have refused to listen to God's Word, God has rejected you from being king."

Saul felt very bad when he heard Samuel's words. He begged Samuel to forgive him and to go with him to worship God, but the prophet would not because the king had refused to heed God's commands. Then Saul took hold of Samuel's cloak and held on so tightly that the cloak tore. When that happened, Samuel said: "Just as you have torn away part of my cloak, so God has torn away the kingdom from you and has given it to a neighbor of yours who is better than you. God does not lie. What He has said, He will do, be sure of that."

Because Saul continued to plead with him not to shame him before all the people, Samuel did go up to worship with him. After that he returned to his home in Ramah and never went to see Saul again. From that day forward, Samuel mourned for Saul.

Only a Shepherd Boy —But God Chose Him to be King

1 Samuel 16

Samuel, the prophet, mourned daily for king Saul who had proved so faithless. One day God called upon Samuel to go out and look for the new king who would take the place of Saul. He must go to the house of Jesse, the Bethlehemite, because the new king would be one of his sons. Samuel must take with him a horn of oil to anoint the man.

The Lord told him to take a heifer and to go to sacrifice it in Bethlehem. There he must call upon Jesse to come and worship with him. God would Himself point out the son of Jesse who was to be anointed.

So Samuel went off with the heifer to Bethlehem. When he arrived there the elders of the town were terrified. They thought that the prophet had come to punish them for some wrong they might have done. But instead Samuel told them he had come in peace, and Jesse and his sons must go to sacrifice with him. When the young men and their father prepared themselves for worship, and came to the altar of sacrifice, Samuel looked them over very carefully to try and pick out the new king. He looked first at the eldest son, Eliab, and was sure that he was the one God wanted. But God said to him: "Do not look at a man's height or his appearance. God does not see as man sees. Man looks on the outward appearance, but God sees the

heart." One by one the sons passed by Samuel. Abinadab and Shammah and all the rest, but God did not point out a single one of them. Samuel was puzzled and asked Jesse if there were no other sons. There was another, but he was still young and out looking after the sheep. He had to be sent for. Samuel would not sit down to eat until the youngest son had come.

When David, that was the name of the youngest son, came into the house, the Lord said to Samuel: "Stand up and anoint him. This is the one I have chosen to be king." So Samuel anointed David and the Spirit of the Lord came upon the boy from that day on. Still, he went back to his work of caring for his father's sheep, out in the hills around Bethlehem. There he became not only strong in body, but strong in spirit, too, a young man who learned to know the Lord as his own special friend. More than once he had to fight off and kill the lions and bears that attacked his sheep. He became an expert in the use of the sling with which he hurled stones at the animals that troubled the flock.

He became a good musician, playing on his harp. But because David loved God so much, he made hymns to God's praise and sang them to the music of his harp. We still have many of those songs of praise today. We call them the Psalms. One of the most

beautiful of them is the Shepherd Psalm, Psalm 23:

"The Lord is my shepherd: I shall not want.

He maketh me to lie down in green pastures:

He leadeth me beside the still waters.

He restoreth my soul: He leadeth me in the paths of righteousness for His name's sake.

Yea, though I walk through the valley of the shadow of death, I will fear no evil: for Thou art with me;

Thy rod and Thy staff they comfort me.

126

Thou preparest a table before
me in the presence of mine
enemies:
Thou anointest my head with
oil; my cup runneth over.
Surely goodness and mercy
shall follow me all the days
of my life: and I will dwell in
the house of the Lord for
ever."

Out in the hills David drew
closer and closer to the Lord and
the Spirit of God taught him. But
in the royal palace things were
not going so well with king Saul.
The Spirit of the Lord had with-
drawn from him, and he was becoming moody and unhappy.
Sometimes he behaved completely
like a madman. His servants were
afraid of him. After a while they
discovered that if someone quietly
played the harp when Saul was in
a bad mood, he soon felt better.

One of the servants remembered
that he had seen a young man, a
son of Jesse the Bethlehemite,
who was not only a clever harp
player, but also an expert with the
weapons of war and a shrewd
businessman. That young man
was David.

Soon David was brought to
Saul, and Saul grew to love him
very much. He made him his
arrow-bearer.

David's harp music must have
been very beautiful and soothing.
After a while Saul was so much
calmer that David could go back
again to Bethlehem to be his
father's shepherd as he had been
before. No one knew that this
young man had been anointed to
become king in Saul's place.

The End of a Giant

1 Samuel 17

Although Saul defeated the Philistines in several great battles, the
war against them went on to the
end of his reign.

On one occasion they gathered
their men together near Shochoh
in the land of Judah. The Israelites drew up their army near the
valley of Elah, not far away. The
two armies were drawn up on
facing mountains with a valley
between.

The Philistines had with them
a giant from the city of Gath. This
man, whose name was Goliath,
came out into the valley each day
and jeered at the Israelite soldiers
and taunted them to come out
and fight with him.

Among the soldiers of king Saul
were three of the oldest sons of
Jesse. David was at home at this
time, looking after the sheep. One
day his father sent him off to take
food to his soldier brothers and to
find how they were. While David
stood in Saul's camp, talking to
his brothers, the Philistine giant
came stalking out into the valley
and mocked the Israelites and
their God. The Israelites told

David that if any man fought and
killed Goliath then the king would
reward him with great riches. The
king would also give him his
daughter to be his wife, and make
his family a noble family in the
land.

David asked his brothers why
no one dared to go out and stop
this man from speaking so terribly against God. That made his
eldest brother, Eliab, very angry.
He felt David was insulting them
for their cowardice. David did feel
very strongly about it. When he
found that none of the Israelites

dared to go out against Goliath, he decided to ask Saul for permission to fight the giant himself. At first the king did not want him to. David was only a youth, but Goliath had been a man for many years. David, however, could not bear that this giant was able to keep on mocking the Name of God. David begged to be allowed to fight him. Finally Saul agreed. "Go," he said, "and the Lord be with you." Then he gave David his own helmet and metal coat and sword. But David was not used to them, and they were too heavy for him. Instead, he took his own stick and his own shepherd's sling and in his little skin bag he carried five smooth stones from the stream. Out he went to face the greatest warrior in the Philistine army.

When Goliath saw the slender youth and the strange weapons he was carrying, he roared out in rage: "Am I a dog for you to come out against me with sticks?" Then he cursed David by all his heathen gods. "Fight against me," he said, "and I will give your flesh to the birds of the air and the beasts of the field."

But David was not the slightest bit afraid. "You come out against me with a sword and a spear and a shield," he said, "but I come against you in the Name of the Lord of hosts, the God of the armies of Israel, Whom you have defied. Today God will give you into my hands. I will defeat you and cut off your head. The birds will feast on your body, so that all the world may know who is the Lord God, and that He has other ways of winning the victory than with spears and swords. This battle is the Lord's."

In anger Goliath lumbered forward. David fitted a stone to his sling and ran out and hurled it right at Goliath. The stone hit the giant in the middle of the forehead and down he fell, dead. Then David snatched Goliath's own sword and chopped off his head, just as he had said he would.

When they saw that, the rest of the Philistine army fled. The Israelites went after them, driving them right back to their own city of Gath, and killed tens of thousands of them during the battle.

David had won the battle, but not really in his own strength. He won because he had fought in the Name of the Lord. All Israel knew how God had used the young David to free them from the hands of their enemies.

Arrows Shot into the Air

1 Samuel 17 to 20

Saul was a strange man. Though David had played the harp for him in his palace, when the young man came to him and asked to be allowed to fight against Goliath, Saul did not recognize David at all. After the victory Saul sent his general, Abner, to find out who the man was, and to bring him to the royal tent. There David told him he was the son of Jesse, the Bethlehemite. He was taken again into the royal household, but this time as a leader among the warriors.

Of course the king was very glad about the victory over the Philistines. But when the soldiers returned home again, his whole mood changed. The news of the killing of Goliath had spread throughout the land. In village after village the women came out, singing and dancing and praising David for what he had done. "Saul has slain his thousands, and David his ten thousands," they sang, and Saul was very jealous.

The very next day Saul was in one of his black moods again. Once more David played on the harp to soothe him as he had done in the days before the war. But this time Saul was holding a javelin in his hand. So great was his jealousy that he threw it at David and tried to pin him to the wall. Twice it happened, and each time David managed to jump aside.

Saul had promised to give his daughter to be the wife of the man who killed Goliath. When the time came, Saul deceived David and gave his daughter, Merab, to Adriel the Meholathite. David had been sent away to fight once more against the Philistines. Saul hoped secretly that they would kill him. When David came back he found that Merab was already married. But Michal, Saul's second daughter, loved David, and this was reported to the king. Once again he sent David off to fight against the Philistines. This time when

David came back the marriage had to be held. David became Saul's son-in-law.

David and Jonathan

Saul's hatred for David was so great that he told all his servants, and even his son Jonathan, to look for a chance to kill the young man. Jonathan was most upset, because he loved David. He went at once to tell his friend to hide himself.

One day David met Jonathan,

and asked him what he had done that Saul should hate him enough to kill him. Jonathan tried his best to tell David that this was not true. But David explained to him that Saul was hiding his evil plans from his son, because he knew how much Jonathan loved David.

The two young men made a plan together. Jonathan would go back to the palace and see how Saul felt about David. David should be there to feast with the king at the festival of the new moon, but he would stay away. If Saul missed him, then Jonathan should say that David had asked permission to be at Bethlehem for a family feast.

Out in the field that day they made a special promise to each other, too. If it happened that Saul was still angry with David it would not be allowed to make any difference to their friendship.

Jonathan worked out a plan for telling David how Saul felt about him. On the third day of the feast he would come to the place where they were now talking, and bring his bow and arrows. He would also bring a little boy to run and get the arrows. He would shoot three arrows and send the boy after them. David should be hidden in the bushes nearby. If he heard Jonathan shout to the boy that the arrows were on this side of him, then all was well. But if he shouted that they were further away, then David should get away as quickly as possible.

So Jonathan went to his father's feast. On the first day, Saul said nothing about David's absence. On the second day, though, he asked Jonathan why David had not come to the feast. Then Jonathan did as had been arranged. He told Saul that David had asked to be excused so that he could attend the family festival at Bethlehem. Saul was fearfully angry with David, and with Jonathan, too, for being David's friend. He told Jonathan that as long as David remained alive he could never become king himself. He must get David immediately so that they could kill him. But Jonathan asked: "Why should he be killed? What wrong has he done?" That made Saul so angry that he threw his javelin at his own son, just as he had done before at David.

Jonathan immediately got up from the table and went away, because his father was behaving so shamefully. Early the next morning he went out to the agreed place with his bow and arrows. He gave David the sign he had promised; however, he loved his friend so much that he could not let him go without saying goodby. He sent the boy back into the city with his bow and arrows. Then David came out of hiding. The two young men wept together and kissed one another. Before they parted, Jonathan blessed David with these beautiful words: "Go in peace; and the Lord see that we keep the promise we have made to be friends together, and our children after us, forever."

Where David Found Goliath's Sword

1 Samuel 21 to 22

When David turned away from Jonathan, he became a wanderer. In the course of his wanderings he arrived at the little town of Nob where the priest named Ahimelech lived.

When David arrived, Ahimelech was surprised to see him all alone, but David told him that the king had sent him on a special secret mission and his men would join him later. Then David asked him for a few loaves of bread. Ahimelech answered that he had no bread except the holy bread out of the house of prayer. David then said to him: "Give us some of the holy bread. Under the circumstances we have a right to eat some of it." So Ahimelech gave him five loaves of the bread.

When David had eaten and was ready to leave, he asked another favor of Ahimelech. He had left home in such a hurry, he said, that he hadn't time to take a spear or a sword. Did the priest not have any weapons he could give him? Ahimelech answered: "I have nothing here except the sword of Goliath the Philistine, whom you killed. You may have that sword if you wish." So David took the sword and went off into the wilderness.

On one of the mountains David found a cave which the people called the Cave of Adullam. David made that cave his home. Many men that were in trouble with king Saul, or discontented with the way Saul was governing the land came to David. In the end he was captain over about four hundred men.

Now David was worried about the safety of his father and mother. He went to the king of Moab and asked him to allow his father and mother to stay there. They went to live in Moab in safety.

David was warned by a prophet named Gad to move away from his cave in case Saul should discover where he was. David then moved into Judah, and hid in the forest of Hareth.

Saul's Life Is Spared

1 Samuel 23 to 27

Although Saul had driven David out into the hills, that didn't mean that David sided with Saul's enemies. The Philistines were still the enemies of the people of Israel. When David heard that they were attacking the village of Keilah, he and his soldiers went to Keilah. There they defeated the Philistines very heavily, killing many of them, and capturing their cattle.

Once again David and his men were wanderers. But now there were about six hundred of them. They moved about in a mountainous part in the wilderness of Ziph. One day a surprise meeting took place. Jonathan met David in a forest. What a wonderful meeting it was! The two friends sealed their bond of faithfulness again. After this they never saw one another again.

While Saul was away, David found new caves in which his men could live. These were around

Engedi, on the rocky shores of the Dead Sea.

Saul very soon discovered where they were. He collected three thousand of his best men. They hunted David and his little group of men. They searched the mountain strongholds where they were hiding. One evening, just at dark, Saul and his party reached a cave where the king planned to spend the night. Little did he realize that David and his own best soldiers were hidden in cracks in the rocks, and in smaller caves leading off the main one. Saul lay down to sleep. Some of David's men whispered to him that now was his chance.

But David had no wish to kill Saul. Instead, he crept into the main cave and secretly cut off the skirt of Saul's robe while he slept.

In the morning, Saul got up and went on his way. David ran to the entrance and shouted after him. Then he asked Saul why he kept on listening to men and believing that David wanted to harm him. If he had wished to hurt Saul,

could he not have killed him there in the cave? But all he had done was to cut off the skirt from Saul's robe.

When Saul heard David's words he was upset, and wept, saying: "Is that your voice, David, my son? You are more righteous than I am. You have behaved well toward me, but I have treated you badly. Today, when you could have killed me, you spared my life. May the Lord reward you greatly for the way you have dealt with me. But please promise me that when you become king, which I am sure will happen, you will not be unkind to my family, and will spare their lives."

David gave his word, and then Saul went home. But it was not very long before Saul led out another army of three thousand men to look for David and his little band in the wilderness of Ziph. From his hiding place David watched their great camp being set up near the hill of Hachilah. That night he and Abishai, one of his warriors, slipped away in the dark to Saul's camp. Right through the ranks of sleeping soldiers they crept, until they came to the very middle of the camp. There they found that Saul was sleeping in the middle of a ring of his carriages and chariots. Abner, his general, and a number of men of the royal bodyguard were with him. The two brave

men slipped to Saul's side. When they reached him, Abishai whispered to David: "Now God has delivered him to you. Just let me pin him to the earth with my spear. It will not need doing a second time!" But David answered: "On no account! We have no right to touch the Lord's anointed. Just take his spear and the water bottle lying next to him, and we will carry them away."

As quietly as they had come they slipped away again between the sleeping soldiers.

Early in the morning David stood on a hilltop quite a way from Saul's camp. David shouted across to the soldiers, and to Abner their general: "Abner, why don't you do your duty to look after the king? In the night two of the king's enemies were right at his side. If they wished, they could have killed him. See, we have Saul's spear and water bottle."

King Saul recognized David's voice, and he cried out: "Is that you, my son, David?" And David answered: "Why do you hunt me, my lord? What have I done? If others have set you against me, may God deal with them." Saul was sorry once more for what he had done, and confessed that he had sinned.

Saul's Sad End

1 Samuel 28 to 31

Although David and his men were allowed to live in the Philistine city of Ziklag, the Philistines continued to hate Israel and to send armies to attack the Israelites. After David had settled in Ziklag, the Philistines decided to make an all-out attack against Israel. So they gathered their armies from all parts of the land.

In the meantime king Saul had drawn his Israelite armies together in the plain of Jezreel, at the foot of Mount Gilboa. When he saw the great number of Philistines, Saul was afraid.

Samuel, who had given them such encouragement, was dead. Saul himself was old and sickly and he had driven David away. To whom could he turn? He had caused all the priests to be killed so that there were none who could bring him a message from the Lord.

139

up?'' she asked. And he answered: "Samuel's.''

When Samuel suddenly appeared, the woman was terrified, and cried out. In that moment she realized who her visitor was. "Why have you deceived me?'' she asked, in fright. "You are Saul.'' Saul told her not to be afraid, and asked her what she had seen. Her reply was that it had been an old man, like a god in appearance, with a long white beard, and wearing a mantle. A mantle was a sleeveless coat worn by prophets and kings. Saul then knew that it was Samuel, and he bowed himself down.

Then Saul showed what he was really like in his heart. Although he had commanded that all wizards and witches should be driven away, he sent out his servants to find a witch whose advice he could ask. They knew of one. She lived not far from the camp, at a place called Endor.

That night Saul disguised himself and put on other clothes. With two of his servants he went to visit the witch. The witch was afraid. But her mysterious visitor promised, in the name of the Lord, that no harm would come to her for what she did, and she was satisfied. "Whose spirit shall I call

Then suddenly out of the darkness came the voice of Samuel: "Why have you disturbed my rest?" Fearfully Saul explained: "I am in great trouble. The Philistines are making war against me. I can get no answer to my prayers, and no promise of help from God. That is why I have called you, to ask you what I must do." Then the spirit of Samuel answered: "Why, then, are you troubling me if the Lord has turned from you and become your enemy? Did I not warn you about this? Did I not tell you that because of your disobedience the Lord would take the kingdom away from you, and give it to your neighbor, David? I tell you now, that tomorrow the Philistines will defeat Israel. By this time tomorrow night you and your sons will be with me."

When Saul heard that, he collapsed to the ground. After a while his servants and the witch picked him up and placed him on the bed. They gave him food to strengthen him. Then he and his men returned to the camp, but all the courage had gone from them.

Early the next morning the battle began. The Philistines stormed the Israelite camp in Mount Gilboa, and defeated them terribly. Soon the Israelites were running away, with Saul's three sons, Jonathan, Abinadab and Melchi-shua, lying dead. Saul himself was hit by several arrows.

When he saw how badly the fight was going against him, he asked his own armor-bearer to kill him with his sword. Then because the armor-bearer would not, Saul threw himself on his own sword and died.

So the reign of Saul came to an end. It was a reign which began with great promise but, because of Saul's disobedience to God, ended in tragedy.

"The beauty of Israel is slain upon thy high places: how are the mighty fallen!

Tell it not in Gath, publish it not in the streets of Ashkelon; lest the daughters of the Philistines rejoice!

Saul and Jonathan were lovely and pleasant in their lives, and in their death they were not divided.

I am distressed for thee, my brother Jonathan: very pleasant hast thou been unto me.

How are the mighty fallen, and the weapons of war perished!"

The Shepherd King

2 Samuel 1 to 5

When Saul was killed and the Israelites so badly defeated by the Philistines, David and his people had been back in Ziklag for two days. David was very sad about the death of Saul and Jonathan. He composed a lament, a song of sorrow, which he called "The Song of the Bow." Here are a few verses from the song:

After this David decided to move away from Ziklag. With all his people he settled in the cities of Hebron. There the men of Judah came to him, and anointed him king over their tribe. For seven years and six months David reigned in Hebron as king of Judah. In the meantime, the uncle of Saul, who had been the commander of his army, made one of Saul's sons king over all the tribes of Israel in the north. This man was called Ishbosheth, which means "man of shame." Under Abner's influence a very unhappy civil war broke out between David's people and the people of Ishbosheth. That meant there were two kingdoms in the land, but David's kingdom became stronger and stronger, while Ishbosheth's kingdom weakened.

Later the northern kingdom collapsed.

Two of Ishbosheth's men, seeing the way things were going, decided that they would earn themselves the favor of David. One hot day, as Ishbosheth lay on his bed, they crept in and stabbed him to death. Then they went to David to boast about what they had done. But David did not deal with them as they expected. He had them put to death at once.

After the death of Ishbosheth, the leaders of all the tribes came to see David in Hebron and asked him to be their king.

And that day, David made an agreement with them. He became king of Israel and reigned for thirty-three years over the whole land.

The Mysterious Wind in the Treetops

2 Samuel 5 to 7
David did not become king over a happy and peaceful nation. The people were recovering from a civil war, and the Philistines were still their enemy—and a very strong enemy, too. In the land there were also small areas still occupied by heathen tribes who had never been driven out as God had commanded. One of these groups, the Jebusites, lived in Jerusalem.

The Israelites stormed Mount Zion and the walls of the fort on the top and drove out the Jebusites. From that day on Jerusalem was the capital of the land. David set about building a great city there. Hiram, king of Tyre, sent cedar wood to David, as well as men to help build a palace for him.

When the Philistines heard that David had become king of Israel, they decided that they should make an end of him quickly. Their warriors poured into the valley of Rephaim, a little way to the south of Jerusalem. There David and his men met them and defeated them very heavily. They fled in such a

panic-stricken way that they even left behind their wooden idols. David burned the idols.

But that was not the end of the struggle. The Philistines came again into the valley of Rephaim. Once again David went first to pray and to hear whether God wanted him to attack the Philistines. This time he received a strange answer. He must not attack the Philistines directly. He was to lead his army around behind them, until he came to a thick wood of mulberry trees. There the army must wait until they heard a rustling in the tops of the trees. Then they must move quickly to attack the Philistines, because that sound would mean that the Lord Himself was going ahead of them.

David did exactly as God had said. That day the Philistines were not only defeated, but also driven right back into their own land along the coast.

The Ark of the Covenant Is Brought Back

For a long time the Ark of the Covenant had not been honored in Israel as it should have been. David decided that it should be brought from Kirjath-jearim to Mount Zion, to a new tent or Tabernacle of worship which would be set up there.

After this there was a time of peace for all Israel. David lived quietly in his palace, and God was worshiped in the Tabernacle. But David was not altogether happy. It seemed to him wrong that he should live in a palace lined with cedar wood, while the Ark of the Lord stood in a tent. When he told this to Nathan the prophet, Nathan said to him that he should go on with his plan to build a better home for the Ark, and the Lord would bless him.

That night God spoke to Nathan, giving him a message for David. He said: "From the days that I led My people out of Egypt, the Ark of My presence has stood only in a tent, and I have never told My people that they should build Me a house of cedar wood. But in David's heart I have such honor that he wants to do this for Me. David, I took you from herding sheep, and made you king over My people, and cut down your enemies before you. Now, because you have obeyed Me, I shall establish your family as the royal family of Israel. When you die, your son will become king, and he will build Me a house. To you and your children, and your seed after you, I shall give the throne and the kingdom forever."

In this promise God was telling beforehand of the coming of Jesus, Who would be a Son, a descendant of David.

A Place for the Cripple at the King's Table

2 Samuel 8 and 9

When David became king over the united people of Israel, all the small nations round about, and their kings, were afraid. Instead, however, of making alliances with David, they raided his towns and villages. He had to make war against them. David defeated several tribes and the kings of other nations made alliances with him.

When peace came to the land, David had the chance to think of the promise he had made to his friend Jonathan—to care for Jonathan's children and all his family. David sent to find out if there were any of the descendants of Saul to whom he could show kindness for Jonathan's sake. His men discovered that an old servant of Saul's, Ziba, was still living. They brought him to David. The king asked him if he knew of any of Saul's family to whom he could be kind out of memory for Jonathan. Ziba answered that there was a son of Jonathan, who very much needed help. His name was Mephibosheth, and he was a cripple. When the terrible battle had taken place with the Philistines, in which Saul and Jonathan were killed, Mephibosheth was a little boy. As the Philistines came pouring into the land, his nurse had tried to run away with the boy and hide him. But as they fled, Mephibosheth fell and hurt his legs. After that he was a cripple because his legs never healed properly.

When David heard this he sent for Mephibosheth. The young man was afraid. When he came to David he threw himself down before the king. But David said: "Do not be afraid, I will not harm you. For the sake of your father, Jonathan, who was my dear friend, I will be kind to you. All

the land which belonged to your grandfather, Saul, I give to you. You will always have an honored place at the royal table in my palace." Then David called Ziba and told him what he had given to Mephibosheth. Because Mephibosheth was a cripple, Ziba and his family must take care of his land. Mephibosheth himself would live, and be looked after, in the king's palace all his days.

In this way King David kept the promise he had made to his good friend Jonathan.

Only a Poor Man's Lamb

2 Samuel 11 and 12; Psalm 51

King David had been a great general, but when his kingdom became larger, and his power increased, he no longer led his armies in battle. Instead, he sent out Joab to be their leader, while he remained at home to take care of the affairs of the kingdom.

One evening David went to the flat, walled roof of his palace to enjoy the cool evening breezes. As he strolled there, he looked across to a nearby house. There he saw a beautiful woman washing herself. As soon as he saw her, he longed for her to be one of his wives. But when he asked his servants, they told him that she was Bathsheba, the wife of one of his soldiers, Uriah the Hittite, now out with Joab's army. David sent for her, and loved her.

Then David had a terrible idea. If Bathsheba were a widow, he could take her for his wife. Somehow he must get rid of her husband, Uriah. So David sat down and wrote a letter to Joab. David sent the letter to Joab with Uriah himself, for Uriah had come back to the palace with a message.

In the letter David wrote that Joab must set Uriah in the front rank in the most dangerous part of the battle, and then draw back the other soldiers from him, so that the enemy would kill him. That is exactly what happened. Through the letter he wrote, David became the murderer of Uriah!

When her time of mourning for Uriah was over, Bathsheba came to live in the palace, and became David's wife. But David's deed displeased the Lord, and He sent Nathan the prophet to David to explain how He felt about David's awful sin.

Nathan told the king a story. "There were two men in a certain town, one of them rich, and the other very poor. The rich man had great flocks and herds. The poor man had nothing except one little ewe lamb, which he had bought and cared for. One day a traveler came to visit the rich man, but instead of taking one of his own sheep for their meal, he stole the poor man's only lamb and killed it and made its meat ready for the visitor."

When David heard the story, he was very angry about that rich man and said: "The person who does such an awful thing deserves to die!"

Then Nathan pointed to David and said: "*You* are the man! This is God's word to you: 'I made you king over Israel, and I rescued you from the attacks of Saul. I gave you all the riches you could wish for, and a palace full of wives. Why did you do this horrible thing? You have murdered Uriah and stolen his wife. Because of this you will be punished. You will suffer, and know hardship and sorrow all your days. The child which Bathsheba bore to you will die.'"

Not long afterward, David's son by Bathsheba became very sick and on the seventh day died.

After this time of sorrow, God gave to David and Bathsheba another son, and his name was Solomon. God loved Solomon and blessed him, and he grew up to be a wise man and a great king.

David never forgot his sin, and how God had forgiven him. He wrote a Psalm, the fifty-first, to tell the people of the greatness of his sin, and the greatness of God's mercy. Here are some verses of that Psalm:

"Have mercy upon me, O God, according to Thy loving-kindness: according unto the multitude of Thy tender mercies blot out my transgressions.

Wash me thoroughly from mine iniquity, and cleanse me from my sin.

For I acknowledge my transgressions: and my sin is ever before me . . .

Create in me a clean heart, O God; and renew a right spirit within me . . . "

David's Son Steals the Kingdom

2 Samuel 13 to 17

God had told David that he must suffer for his sin. It was not long before those sufferings began. David had many sons by his other wives. Not all David's sons were good men. Some of them were really wicked, and at times there was such hatred among them that they even murdered.

One of the sons was called Absalom. He was the handsomest man in all the land, and very proud of his looks, too.

But in his heart, Absalom was an evil and unthankful man, and cruel. He was planning all the time to take the throne away from King David.

He began with a very clever scheme, too. Each morning he got up early and waited beside the city gates for any men who might come from different parts of the country to discuss their problems with the king. There he would treat them like real friends, and because he was a king's son, they felt highly honored. When they told him their problems, he would say: "Oh dear, but there is no one who will listen to you, from the king downward. If only I were king, I would see to it that there was justice for all, and all could come freely to me."

So gradually Absalom turned the people of Israel against his father.

Before long it seemed that the whole nation was turning against David to follow Absalom. The terrible news reached David and he told his servants they must all flee. So they fled from Jerusalem, just a little party of servants, with David's wives, and especially Bathsheba and her young son, Solomon.

When the sad little party left the city gates, they found, moving with them, six hundred soldiers under the command of Ittai, one of David's generals. So David's party crossed the river Kidron and went toward the desert.

By the Wayside

When David reached the crest of the Mount of Olives, he met Hushai, one of his best friends. Hushai was bitterly grieved over what had happened. As a sign of his sorrow he had torn his coat and rubbed ashes in his hair. He was ready to go with David into the desert. But instead, the king sent him back to Jerusalem, to mingle with Absalom's men and to pass on all he heard to Zadok and Abiathar, the priests.

A little further on, the king met Ziba, the servant of Mephibosheth. Mephibosheth was the

crippled son of Jonathan, to whom David was so very kind. Ziba had brought with him two donkeys for the king, two hundred loaves of bread, a hundred bunches of raisins and a large amount of fruit for the rest of the men. But he had also brought sad news for the king.

After all David had done for him, Mephibosheth had gone over to Absalom's side, thinking that the throne might be given to him. When he heard this, David gave to Ziba the servant all the property and land that had belonged to Mephibosheth. What David did not know was that this was all a terrible lie. Ziba was the traitor, not Mephibosheth. The crippled prince was loyal to David.

By now Zadok and Abiathar, the priests, had sent out the news to David of Absalom's plans. David established himself at Mahanaim in the land of Gad, east of Jordan. He called his supporters there from all parts of the country. Before long he was ready for any attack Absalom might make against him.

David Returns to the Throne

2 Samuel 17 to 20

In the land of the tribe of Gad David experienced great kindness. The very first to help him in-cluded people who did not belong to the nation of Israel at all. They brought bedding and crockery and food to help the poor people who had had to flee from their own country. Soon everyone felt much better, and soon, too, warriors were streaming in from all parts to come and fight for the king.

Although his army was not as large as Absalom's, he was able to split it into three divisions, each commanded by one of his trusty generals, Joab, Abishai and Ittai. It was David's plan to fight with his armies, but the people would not allow him to go. They knew that Absalom's men would try most of all to kill David, for then his people would lose heart and his throne would be Absalom's without any further struggle.

So David remained back in the town of Mahanaim. From there, he directed the great battle between his forces and Absalom's, in the woods of Ephraim. On that day twenty thousand of Absalom's men were killed. Absalom died, too.

Absalom was very proud of his good looks. He was also very proud of his long hair, and it was his long hair that cost him his life. During the battle he rode on a mule. When he met a party of David's warriors, he charged under the overhanging branches of a big oak tree. His hair caught in the branches, and as the mule galloped away he was left hanging from the tree. One of David's

men saw this and rushed away to tell Joab, the general. When Joab heard this he asked him why he had not killed Absalom. The man replied that they had all heard David tell the three generals that no one was to harm his son Absalom.

But Joab said: "I have no time to stand and argue with you." Joab rushed off and drove three spears into the heart of Absalom while he hung there helpless from the branches of the tree. After that, Joab had the trumpet blown to call back David's men from chasing those who had followed Absalom. Then he had Absalom's body put in a pit in the woods, and a great heap of stones was piled up over it.

The news of his son's death was taken to David. When the man who carried the news came in sight of the city the watchman on the wall saw him and announced his approach. The man who carried the news was a Cushite, a stranger, and he did not understand how David would feel about Absalom's death. He simply blurted out the whole story, and David was very upset. "Oh, my son Absalom! My son, my son Ab-

salom!" he cried. "Would God I had died for thee, O Absalom, my son, my son!"

Though Absalom had rebelled against David, and treated him terribly, the young man was still his son.

When it was reported to Joab how David was mourning and weeping, he had the victory celebrations turned into a time of mourning for the prince who had died.

Joab went to David, and said: "My king, you are doing a strange thing. Instead of praising the soldiers for what they have done for you, you weep just as if you were on Absalom's side, and your own men have done you a terrible harm. Stand up now, and behave in a manly way, and let your soldiers know how pleased you are over the victory they have won; or else they will leave you, and the land will be worse off than it was when Absalom lived."

David very wisely stood up and went to sit in the city gate, as was proper for a king. After that he led his men back to the Jordan. There the tribe of Judah was waiting for him. They had a ferry-boat ready to carry the king and his household across the river. When David got back across Jordan, the very first man to meet him was Shimei, the member of Saul's family who had mocked him so frightfully and thrown stones at him when he was fleeing from Absalom. Now Shimei had come to beg his pardon. Abishai, who had wanted to kill him the first time, wanted to kill him now. But David said: "Today no one will die in Israel. I am king again, and it is not necessary to kill."

The next to come to David was Mephibosheth, the crippled son of Jonathan. David had been told that Mephibosheth had gone with Absalom, but it was not true. When Mephibosheth arrived his hair was long, his beard ragged, and his clothes dirty and tattered. He had been mourning ever since Absalom had driven David out.

He explained how his servant, Ziba, had deceived him by promising to go with the king in his place because he was a cripple, and might be a nuisance in the desert. But he was not angry with Ziba now, because the king had come back. David then said that Mephibosheth and Ziba would have to divide between them the property that had been Saul's, but Mephibosheth said that Ziba could have all.

At the crossing of Jordan, it was the men of the tribe of Judah who took care of David. They welcomed him back into his own land, but the rest of the tribes of Israel were angry about this. "You behave as if you are the king's only friends," they said. "We also have a right to David." The men of Judah answered that David belonged to their tribe, and they

loved him. This did not please the rest of the Israelites, and the men of Ephraim were especially angry. They let a man named Sheba persuade them not to listen to David. Soon it looked as if there might be another civil war.

David sent out one of his warriors, Amasa, to stop Sheba. But Amasa was so slow and so unfaithful, that Joab, the general, went out after him and killed him. Then he went on until he had cornered Sheba in the town of Abel. After several days of siege, someone inside the town killed Sheba and threw his head over

153

the wall. Then Joab's army went back to Jerusalem. Once again there was peace in the land.

The Angel with the Drawn Sword

2 Samuel 24; 1 Chronicles 21

After the rebellion of Absalom, David reigned undisturbed to the end of his days. There was not always peace in the land. The Israelites had to fight several times against the Philistines. Neither was there always prosperity. For three years there was a terrible famine. But no one tried to take David's throne from him.

After a time David decided that he must carry out a census, a numbering, of all the people in the land. Joab warned David that a census was against the commandment of God. God did not want His people to be filled with a feeling of their own greatness, and

turn from trusting in Him. However, David was stubborn and would not listen to Joab or the other captains of the army. They had to carry out his orders to number the people of all the tribes. At the end of nine months and twenty days they went back to report to David. They told him that in the whole land there were eight hundred thousand men able to bear arms, and of them five hundred thousand belonged to Judah. The tribes of Levi and Benjamin were not included.

Once the numbering was over, David began to worry. Now, when it was too late, he admitted that he had broken God's commandment, and pleaded to be forgiven for behaving so foolishly. But it was too late. Joab had warned him, and he would not listen.

Early one morning God sent Gad the prophet to David, saying: "The Lord offers you three things: choose one of them. Either seven years of famine will come to the

threshing floor that belonged to Araunah the Jebusite. At the time, King David was there. He saw the angel of the Lord standing between heaven and earth, with his sword drawn and stretched out over Jerusalem. Then David and the elders who were with him threw themselves down on their faces and begged God to take away the plague and spare Jerusalem. David prayed: "O God, I have sinned, and not my people. Let Thy punishment come upon me and upon my family, but spare my people, who have done no wrong themselves."

land, or else for three months your enemies will overrun the land, or else for three days there will be pestilence and terrible disease, in the land." David was very worried, but was afraid to fall into the hands of men. He chose the three days of pestilence.

When it came it was terrible. In the three days, seventy thousand people died. In the end, the angel of death arrived at the gates of Jerusalem, and came to the

Then the angel passed on God's message to Gad the prophet, who told it to David. The king must go in and build an altar on the threshing floor of Araunah the Jebusite. David immediately obeyed, but Araunah and his sons had seen the angel, too, and hidden themselves in fear. As David came in, the angel disappeared, and then Araunah and his sons ran and bowed themselves down in front of their king.

David asked Araunah to name the price of the threshing floor, so that he could buy it and build the altar. At first Araunah wanted to give the place to him, together with the oxen for burnt offerings, and the threshing instruments for firewood, and the wheat for a food offering. But David refused to take it without paying. This was his reason: "I must pay the full price, because I will not take somebody else's property for the Lord, nor offer Him burnt offerings without them costing me anything." So David paid six hundred shekels of gold for the place, and built his altar there. On the altar he arranged the firewood, and on top he placed special peace offerings and burnt offerings. Then God answered by sending fire from heaven to set the wood and the offerings alight. From that moment on, the pestilence stopped spreading, and David's punishment was over.

Solomon Succeeds David

1 Kings 1

When David was an old man, he had gathered great treasures together. He wanted very much to build a great temple to the glory of God. But this was not allowed. God honored him for his wish, but because he had been a man of war and blood, he could not build the temple. That work would have to be done by his son, Solomon, after him.

In his last years, David was very weak and nearly blind, and spent much of his time in bed. This gave some of his enemies the chance they were looking for. His greatest enemy was once again one of his sons, Adonijah, the brother of Absalom who had rebelled before. Adonijah plotted with Joab and with Abiathar, one of the priests, to make Adonijah king even before David died.

But Zadok, the other priest, and Nathan the prophet, and Shimei and others heard of this evil scheme. They went to Bathsheba, David's wife and the mother of his son Solomon, and explained to her what was happening. If she wanted to be sure of their safety she must go at once to David, and have David make it clear to all the people that Solomon was to become king.

Bathsheba went to David, and

while she was still explaining to the old and sick king what Adonijah was doing, the prophet Nathan came in with the same report. Then David was so stirred up that he raised himself up on his elbow, and said: "As surely as the Lord God lives, it is Solomon my son who is to follow me. This is my wish, and the will of the Lord God."

Then he had them send for Zadok the priest and Benaiah the counselor. He told them to get the royal mule, on which no one could ride except the king. They must place Solomon on its back. Down to the part of Jerusalem called Gihon they must go. There Zadok must anoint Solomon the king.

Then the trumpets must be sounded, and in full view of all the people they must cry out: "God save the King!" That is exactly what they did.

They caught Adonijah and his band completely unprepared. They were still feasting, when from the city outside they heard shouting and the sound of great excitement. Then they realized what was happening. Solomon had already been proclaimed king. When the followers of Adonijah heard this they were afraid, and slipped away quietly to their homes.

Adonijah himself fled to the temple and took hold of the horns of the altar so that he would be safe from any of Solomon's men who might want to kill him. Then he sent a message to the new king, asking for pardon. But Solomon was a wise man: "Yes," he said, "I pardon you. But if in time to come you make one move against me, I shall kill you."

Not long after this David called Solomon to his bedside to give him good advice about ruling the country. The most important part of that advice is one we should all listen to: "Keep the charge of the Lord thy God, to walk in His ways, to keep His statutes, and His commandments, and His judgments, and His testimonies, as it is written in the law of Moses, that thou mayest prosper in all that thou doest, and

whithersoever thou turnest thyself. . . ."

A while afterward David died,
after reigning over the people of
Israel for forty years. The young
King Solomon took the throne in
his place.

The Wise Young King

1 Kings 3 and 4; 2 Chronicles 1
When Solomon came to the
throne, the kingdom of Israel ex-
tended from the river Euphrates
to the border of Egypt, and from
the Mediterranean Sea in the
west to the great desert beyond
Jordan in the east. There were not
only Israelites living in the kingdom, but also people belonging to
the desert tribes, such as the Edomites and Ammonites, and much
of Syria as well.

To rule over a kingdom like that
the young king needed great wisdom. He was only twenty years
old when he came to the throne.
He needed the help of God.

A little while after he took over
the kingdom, Solomon went to

159

good and bad. For who can in his own strength rule such a great nation?" Solomon did not ask for riches, but for wisdom, and that pleased God very much. He gave Solomon what he wished for. "Because you have asked for this thing, and have not asked for long life, nor riches, nor victory over your enemies, I shall give you your wish. But I shall give you also the things you did not ask for, riches and honor, so that to the end of your days there will be no king to compare with you. And if you keep My commandments as David did, I shall grant you a long life, too."

Gibeon to worship God. He offered up a thousand burnt offerings on the altar. That night God spoke to Solomon in a dream and told him to ask for some special gift. Then Solomon showed his real greatness. He remembered God's goodness to his father, David, and how David had walked honestly and righteously with God. Then he thought about how difficult was his own task, with such a great kingdom and so many different people in it.

Then he asked for this gift: "Give therefore Thy servant an understanding heart to judge Thy people, that I may tell between

It was not long before Solomon had the chance to show the wisdom God had given to him. Two women came to him with their tiny babies, but one baby was dead. Each woman said that the living baby belonged to her, and they were very angry with one another. Now they wanted the king to decide to which of them the living baby belonged. The king was very wise. He called for a sword, and told one of his guards to cut the living baby in two so that each mother could have half. He knew that the real mother would be horrified at the idea. And that's exactly what happened. The real mother cried out: "O, my lord the king, don't do it, please! Rather let her have the baby. Do not kill it, please."

But the false mother said: "Cut the baby in two, then it won't be mine, but it won't be hers either."

The king said: "Give the child to the mother who did not want it killed. It really belongs to her."

Everyone in the palace was amazed at the clever way Solomon had found out to which woman the baby belonged.

King Solomon very wisely at this time chose for himself a number of able leaders to help him govern the country. There were twelve main officers, and under them served many other officers. Part of their work was to see that the army was kept up to strength, for Solomon had forty thousand horses for his chariots, and twelve thousand horsemen. Beside this there were men mounted on camels, and foot soldiers, too.

There was much feasting in Solomon's palace. There he passed on his wisdom to the people who feasted with him. He taught them three thousand proverbs and one thousand and five songs. The fame of Israel was greater than it had ever been before.

The Building of the Temple

1 Kings 5 to 9; 2 Chronicles 3 to 7
Now the time had come for the building of the Temple in Jerusalem. It was built on Mount Moriah, and was Solomon's great work.

Hiram, king of Tyre in Syria had sent gifts of cedar wood to his friend, David, for the building of the palace. Now he sent servants to Solomon to promise his help once more. The new king told them what he planned to do.

Great quantities of cedar trees and fir trees were chopped on the mountain and taken down to the sea and then floated down the coast in great rafts till they reached the place where they must be taken overland to Jerusalem. That seaport was called Joppa.

Although the men of King Hiram were in charge of the work on Mount Lebanon, Solomon also sent some of his own men.

The walls of the great Temple were made of stone. All the blocks were shaped completely in the quarries. On Mount Moriah they were simply fitted together. No sound at all of hammer or chisel was heard there. All the walls were lined with cedar wood, and the beams and roof were of cedar, too.

The Temple was designed in the same way as the old Tabernacle in the wilderness, except now it was not movable any more, but a fixed building. And it was much bigger. The Tabernacle had only one forecourt, but the Temple had two.

One court was for the people of Israel. Men from strange nations, even though they worshiped the God of Israel, were not allowed there. The court behind it was for the priests only. Beyond the fore-court, just inside the gate to the Holy Courtyard, stood the great altar of burnt offering. The altar was made of rough stones which had never been shaped with a hammer or a chisel. Nearby was a great basin, or bowl, made of brass. This was made by King Hiram himself.

The basin stood on the backs of twelve brass oxen. It was used for washing the offerings before they were laid on the altar. There were also ten other brass basins for washing.

Inside this courtyard also stood the Holy Place, the House of the Lord, which was the real Temple. This was all of marble and cedar wood. At the front of it was a tower in which were special rooms for the High Priest and his sons.

Behind this was a long hall. In the hall was a table made of cedar wood, covered with gold, on which were placed the twelve loaves of showbread. There was also a golden altar for incense. In different places in the Temple hung ten golden lamps burning the purest olive oil.

Between this Holy Place and the much smaller Holy of Holies behind it, hung a great heavy curtain embroidered with beautiful designs. Inside the Holy of Holies stood the Ark of the Covenant, which still contained the two stone tablets on which Moses had written the Law God gave him on Mount Sinai. At the two ends of the Ark stood two beautifully carved cherubim overlaid with gold, and their wings stretched out over the Ark.

At the entrance to the Temple building were two great carved pillars, which were called by the names Jachin and Boaz. This Temple took seven whole years to build. Many thousands of people worked there. When it was finished, King Solomon held a great festival and service. A platform was built in front of the altar of burnt offering. There Solomon prayed for himself and his people.

Not long afterward, one night

162

he had a dream, and in his dream God brought him a warning: "I have heard your prayer, and I have made holy the Temple you built. It will be My house, and I shall live there. As long as you follow in the footsteps of your father David and keep My laws, your throne will continue safely. But if you turn away and no longer follow Me, then I shall go from this house, and the enemies of Israel will come and take away all its glory."

Solomon's Last Days

1 Kings 10 and 11

The kingdom of Solomon was very rich and very powerful. It was so rich, and the fame of Solomon's wisdom was so great, that the rulers of all the nations round about came to see. One of them was the queen of Sheba, who came to him with many questions with which to test his wisdom. She brought camel loads of treasures to make Solomon richer still. And, although she was a great queen, she was amazed to see the splendor of Solomon's court and the city of Jerusalem.

When she had seen all, she said: "All that I was told in my land, a thousand miles away, about your riches and about your wisdom, was true. However, I did not believe, but came to see for myself. Now I know that the half was not told to me. Happy are your servants who have the privilege of serving you daily, and blessed be the Lord your God Who has delighted in you, and raised you up to be such a great king."

But all was not well. Solomon was ignoring the commandments of God. He had married many wives. Some of them were heathen women. Solomon had built for them places where they could worship their heathen idols. Worst of all, he began to worship with them. He still went to the Temple to worship, but he also went with his wives to bow down before idols of wood and stone, and to worship the sun and the moon and the stars.

One day God spoke His final word to Solomon, whom He had blessed so greatly: "Because you have not kept My commandments, and have turned to worshiping false gods, I am angry with you. I will take the kingdom away and give it to your servant. However, for David's sake, who was My faithful servant, I shall not take away the kingdom in your lifetime. And when I do take it away, I shall leave one tribe, the tribe of Judah, in your son's control, for the sake of David, and for the sake of Jerusalem, the place I have chosen."

So God stirred up an opponent for the king of Israel. He was a young man named Jeroboam, the son of Nebat, of the tribe of Ephraim.

One day Jeroboam was traveling down from Jerusalem, when the prophet Ahijah, the Shilonite, met him. Jeroboam was wearing a new cloak, and Ahijah did a strange thing. He snatched the cloak off Jeroboam's back, and tore it into twelve pieces. Then he took ten of the pieces and gave them to Jeroboam, and said: "This is what God says to you: 'I will take the kingdom from the control of Solomon's family and

will give ten of the tribes to you. One tribe will be left with them, for the sake of David, and of Jerusalem. Solomon will remain ruler until the end of his life and then you, Jeroboam, will take his place. You will be blessed, if you obey My laws and do My will, and your kingdom will be great. Because of their disobedience, the family of David will be punished, but not for ever.'"

The news of this soon got about, and when he heard, King Solomon was very angry. He wanted to kill

Jeroboam. But the young man fled to Egypt and lived there under the protection of Shishak, the king.

For forty years Solomon reigned in Jerusalem, and the kingdom of Israel was at its greatest. But Solomon was preparing the land for a terrible fall, because he did not serve the Lord his God, and Him alone.

The Break-up of a Great Kingdom

1 Kings 12; 2 Chronicles 10

When Solomon died, Jerusalem was a place of splendor, but the people of Israel were very tired of

the heavy taxes they had to pay to keep up the glory of the royal court. Rehoboam, Solomon's son, who was to take the throne after his father, was a weak man and a silly man.

All the elders of Israel gathered at Shechem to crown the new king. Jeroboam, the son of Nebat, came all the way from Egypt to be there, too. Before the crowning, they challenged the young prince: "Your father taxed us until it hurt. Now make the burden of taxation lighter, and we will serve you." Rehoboam sent them away for three days, and when they had gone he asked for help from his trusted advisers.

The old men warned him to be wise and promise to make the load of taxation less. But Rehoboam was too silly to listen. When the rest of the elders came back on the third day, this is what he said to them: "My father beat you with whips; I shall beat you with scorpions." By that he meant that he would be even harder to them than his father had been.

When they heard that answer, the people said: "What have we to do with David's family any more? To your tents, Israel. Let David's family take care of themselves!" All that were left to Rehoboam were the men of his own tribe, the tribe of Judah.

There had once been a great kingdom. Now Rehoboam reigned over Judah only, with Benjamin their ally. Jeroboam was made king over all the rest of the land. In Solomon's time Syria and Moab and Ammon and Edom had all been part of Israel. Now they all fell away, so that altogether there were six kingdoms instead of one.

Rehoboam tried to draw together an army to force Israel, the kingdom of ten tribes, to join with Judah again, but God sent Shemaiah the prophet to forbid him to make war against his own brethren, and Rehoboam listened.

So now the tribes of Israel were divided into two kingdoms: ten of Israel in the north, under Jeroboam, with their capital at Shechem, and the kingdom of Judah in the south with its capital at Jerusalem.

The King Who Misled Israel

1 Kings 12 to 15

What wonderful opportunities God gave to Jeroboam when He made him king over the ten tribes of Israel. But Jeroboam thought he was too clever to listen to God's warning to obey His commandments.

Jeroboam was afraid that if his people went to Jerusalem to sacrifice in the Temple there, they might turn away from him, and accept Rehoboam as their king. He worked out a plan to keep them from going to Jerusalem. He had two golden calves made. One of them he set up in Beth-el and the other in Dan. Then he made a strange announcement to his people: "It is too much trouble for you to have to go to Jerusalem. These are your gods, O Israel, which brought you up out of the land of Egypt."

Jeroboam even arranged for a number of priests to serve in the temples of the golden calves in Dan and Beth-el. But they were not really priests at all, but people of the lowest kind. Then Jeroboam

called a great feast to be held at the same time as the great feast in Jerusalem.

At the great feast, Jeroboam decided that he would act as priest. That was against God's law, because no king was allowed to do the work of a priest.

When Jeroboam stood in front of the altar, a young man, a prophet from Judah, came to the Temple and spoke in God's name against this disobedient king. He foretold that a child would be born in David's family, Josiah by name, and he would offer up Jeroboam's false priests on the very altars he had built. Then he told of a sign that would prove the truth of his words. The altar would burst apart and the ashes on it would fall to the ground. Jeroboam flew into a rage at that. He pointed to the man and told his soldiers to catch him. But as he did it, his hand withered and he could not draw it in again. And as he stood, the altar burst open, just as the prophet had said, and the ashes spilled out on the ground.

Then Jeroboam pleaded with the prophet to pray for him. When the prophet did so, the king's hand was made well again. Jeroboam was so pleased that he asked the prophet to come and feast with him in his palace. But the prophet refused. He had been commanded by God neither to eat nor drink until he was home again. Even if Jeroboam gave him half his riches, he could not stay. Neither must he travel home along the same road by which he came.

The Prophet is Killed by the Lion

In that time there lived in Beth-el an old prophet. His sons came to tell him what had happened at the altar after the young prophet spoke there. Immediately the old prophet rode after the young prophet, whom he found sitting under an oak tree by the wayside.

There he invited him to come home and eat with him, but the young man told him how God had commanded him to go straight home. Then the old prophet told a lie and said that an angel told him that he must bring the prophet back to eat with him.

So the young man went back with him to Beth-el, and ate in his home. But all the time he was unhappy, and at the table the Lord spoke to him again.

"Because you have disobeyed Me, you will die. But your body will not be buried in the grave with the bodies of your fathers," the Lord told him.

Immediately after eating, he saddled his donkey and turned

day his bones should be layed alongside those of the young prophet. At the same time he told the people that what the prophet had foretold would certainly happen. In the time God chose, His servant, Josiah, who was not born yet, would come and destroy the false place of worship Jeroboam had built in Beth-el, and all the other idols he had built.

Jeroboam reigned for twenty-two years altogether. Then his son Nadab became king in his place. But Nadab was just as evil as his father. He reigned for only two years, and then he was murdered by one of his own servants, Baasha. Baasha saw to it that every remaining member of Jeroboam's family was killed and not one of them remained.

Elijah, the Prophet of God

1 Kings 15 to 17

Baasha had learned too well the lessons taught by Jeroboam. He also worshiped idols, and was an evil man.

After Baasha came Elah, his son. Elah reigned for only two years. Zimri, one of his chariot commanders, slipped into the palace and stabbed him to death. Zimri took the throne in Elah's place, and killed all the family of Baasha and Elah.

back. On the way a lion attacked him and killed him. But then a strange thing happened. The lion did not tear up his body, nor did it attack the donkey, but the donkey and the lion both stood looking at the dead body of the young prophet. Passers-by were amazed at what they saw, and they went to the old prophet in Beth-el and told him. The old man went out with his donkey and brought back the body, and buried it in his own family grave. He felt so sad that his lies had caused this to happen, that he asked that one

After Zimri came Omri. He was an evil man, too, but he remained king for twelve years. When he died he was succeeded by his son, Ahab. Ahab was the worst king of them all. He married a horrible woman called Jezebel, a heathen from the kingdom of Sidon. She brought with her idols of Baal and Ashtaroth and taught the people of Israel to worship them. She hated those who loved the true God of Israel, the God of heaven and earth.

There lived in those days one brave and very great prophet. His name was Elijah. He went to King Ahab and prophesied to him the word of the Lord. "As the Lord God lives, there will be neither dew nor rain in this land until I give the word."

God told him to go and hide himself beside the brook Cherith, which flowed into the river Jordan. There he drank water from the brook. Every morning and every evening God sent ravens to bring him bread and meat to eat.

After a while, because of the drought in the land, even the brook Cherith dried up. A new place had to be found for Elijah. God sent him to a strange place, to Zarephath, in the land of Sidon, the very place from which the evil queen, Jezebel, had come. God told Elijah that He had already told a widow there that she must make ready a place for His servant!

Elijah went to Zarephath. At the gate of the city he came upon a widow gathering sticks for firewood. He spoke to her: "Please get me some water so that I may drink." As she was going to get the water, he called to her and said: "Please bring me a little piece of bread as well."

But she answered: "Truly, I haven't a single cake of bread, only a handful of meal in a barrel and a little oil in a jug."

Then Elijah said: "Go and bake me a little cake first, and after that bake for yourselves, because this is what God says to you, 'The meal will not become less in the barrel, and the jug of oil will not be emptied until I send rain again'."

Those were strange words, but the widow did exactly as Elijah had said, and God kept His promise. Elijah and the widow and her son had all the food they needed until the rains came again.

One day the widow's son suddenly became ill and died. Elijah took the boy's body from her and went up into his own room and laid the body on his bed. Then three times he stretched out over the body and prayed: "O Lord, Thou hast brought great sorrow to this widow by taking away the life of her son. Please give him life again!"

God heard the prophet's prayer, and the boy came to life again. Then Elijah took him to his

mother. When she saw him alive again, she knew that Elijah was a man who walked very closely with God. She said to him: "Now I know without any doubt that you are a man of God, and that the word of God in your mouth is truth."

Elijah's Prayer Brings Fire from Heaven

1 Kings 18

For three long years the drought continued in Israel before God sent Elijah to King Ahab again to tell him the rain was coming.

When Ahab saw Elijah, he cried out in anger: "Are you the one that troubles Israel?"

But Elijah answered him sternly: "I have not troubled Israel. It is you and your household who have turned away from the Lord God and are worshiping the false gods, the Baals of the Sidonians." Then Elijah told him to bring together on Mount Carmel all the four hundred and fifty priests of Baal which the evil Queen Jezebel had brought to the land.

When all these men were standing on the slopes of Mount Carmel, which overlooks the sea, Elijah cried out to them: "How long do you waver between two opinions? If the Lord be God, follow Him, but if it be Baal, then follow him." But the people were silent.

Then Elijah called for two bullocks to be brought, one for him to offer up to God, and one for the false prophets to offer up to Baal, so that rain might come. Elijah told them that they must place the wood in position, and then lay the meat of the bullock on top. He would do the same. The wood must not be set alight. They would pray, and the god that answered by fire would be the true God.

The men of Baal prayed from early morning until midday. They leaped up and down before the altar, but nothing happened.

Then Elijah called them to him. First he rebuilt the altar to God which the Baal priests had broken down. He made it of large stones, one for each of the tribes of Israel. Round about the altar he made a deep trench. On top of the altar he laid the firewood, and on top of that the pieces of the bullock's meat. Then he made them bring twelve barrels of water and pour it over everything on the altar.

At about three o'clock in the afternoon the work was done, and Elijah began to pray. "Lord God of Abraham, Isaac and Israel," he cried, "let it be known today that Thou art God in Israel, and that I am Thy servant, and that I have done all these things in obedience to Thee. Hear my prayer, O Lord God, hear, that these people may know that Thou art the Lord God, and may turn back to Thee."

As he finished, out of a clear sky fire came down from heaven and set alight the wood on the altar. The fire burned up the sacrifice and the water and even the stones of which the altar was made. When the people saw this, they threw themselves down on their faces and cried out: "The Lord, He is the God! The Lord, He is the God!"

Then Elijah called out to them to take the prophets of Baal, and not to let one of them escape. Down to the brook Kishon they were dragged, and every one of them was killed there.

To Ahab, Elijah said: "Go, eat and drink, because I hear the sound of great rains." And Ahab went. Then Elijah went right to the top of Mount Carmel and knelt down there and prayed. Suddenly he said to his servant: "Go and look out over the sea, and see if there is a cloud." The servant looked, and saw nothing. But Elijah told him to go seven

times and look. The last time he came back and said: "I see a cloud as big as a man's hand, rising from the sea."

Then Elijah cried out: "Hurry to Ahab and tell him to get his chariot, and go down from the mountain as fast as he can before the rain stops him." Even while he spoke the clouds gathered above, black and heavy, and the rain began to fall.

Ahab drove his chariot as fast as he could to Jezreel. But the Spirit of the Lord was upon Elijah so that he held up his cloak and ran, and reached the gates of Jezreel even before Ahab.

In one day the power of Baal was broken in Israel, and the great drought came to an end.

The Still, Small Voice

1 Kings 19

When King Ahab told Queen Jezebel all that had happened, she was very angry. The queen sent a message to Elijah, saying: "I shall see to it that you are as dead as those priests before another day is out." When Elijah heard that, he did not stop to think how God had protected him in the past, but ran. First he went to Beersheba and left his servant there. Then he went right on into the wilderness. He did not stop until he was a whole day's journey away.

There he sat down under a juniper tree, as miserable as a man could be. There in his sorrow and his weariness, he fell asleep.

While he lay there sleeping, a wonderful thing happened to Elijah. An angel touched him, and said: "Get up and eat." And when he looked, there was a cake baked on the coals, and a jug of water. Elijah ate and drank, and then lay down again. A second time the angel woke him up, and there was once more food and drink for him. This time the angel said: "Wake up and eat again, because there is a long journey ahead of you."

Elijah did as the angel said. And the food and drink he had then was enough to last him for a journey of forty days and forty nights to Horeb, the mountain of

175

God. This was where Moses saw the bramble bush that was on fire, but did not burn up. This was also where God gave to Moses the Ten Commandments. Sometimes this place is called Mount Sinai.

When he came to the mountain, Elijah found himself a cave to live in. There God spoke to him and asked him a question: "Elijah, why are you here?"

"O, Lord," he answered, "I have loved You, and worked as hard as I could for You. The children of Israel have broken their covenant with You, torn down Your altars and killed Your prophets. Now I am the only one left, but they want to take away my life, too."

Then God said: "Go and stand on the mountain slope, in the presence of the Lord your God."

While Elijah stood there, a sudden fierce wind rose up and tore down the rocks on the mountainside. But the Lord was not in that wind. Then came an earthquake, but the Lord was not in the earthquake. After that a fire swept across the face of the mountain, but the Lord was not in that either. Then all was silent, and Elijah heard a still, small voice. When he heard that voice, he hid his face in his cloak, and the Lord asked him: "What are you doing here, Elijah?"

Once more he answered: "Lord, I have been jealous for Your name's sake. The people of Israel have broken their covenant with You, torn down Your altars and killed Your prophets. I am the only one left, and now they want to kill me, as well."

God said to him: "Go back the way you came to the land of Syria from which you ran away. In the wilderness of Damascus you will find a man called Hazael. Anoint him to be king of Syria. Then look for Jehu, the son of Nimshi. Anoint him as king of Israel. After that, find Elisha, the son of Shaphat, in the town of Abel-meholah, in the land of the prophet in your place. Those who escape from the sword of Hazael will be put to death by Jehu, and those who escape from Jehu will be killed by Elisha. But I have preserved seven thousand in Israel who have never worshiped the false god, Baal. Those will not be hurt."

Then Elijah journeyed away from Horeb, until he came to Abel-meholah, in the land of the tribe of Manasseh. There he found Elisha, just as the Lord had said. Elisha was plowing with a team of twelve oxen before the plow. Elijah went up to him. Without saying a word, Elijah threw his own cloak over Elisha's shoulders. Elisha knew that meant that Elijah had chosen him to be his successor. Elisha knew that he must leave all his riches and his comfortable home and go with the old prophet.

Naboth's Vineyard

1 Kings 21

Apart from his palace in Samaria, Ahab, the king of Israel, had another palace in Jezreel on the plain of Esdraelon. Alongside the palace lived a man called Naboth, who owned a very fruitful vineyard. Ahab wanted Naboth's ground to make a vegetable garden for the palace. One day Ahab spoke to Naboth and made him an offer for the vineyard. But Naboth did not want to part with it.

When Ahab heard that, eventhough he was king, he sulked. He threw himself down on his bed and turned his face to the wall and refused to eat. While he lay there,

his wife came in, the evil Queen Jezebel. She asked him what was the matter. The sulky king answered that he wanted to buy Naboth's vineyard and Naboth would not let him have it. Then Jezebel said: "What, and you the king of Israel? Get up and eat and be happy. I'll see to it that you get Naboth's vineyard!"

Then Jezebel had Naboth falsely accused and he was murdered. Jezebel then went to Ahab and said: "Up, and take over the vine-

yard that Naboth would not give you, because now Naboth is dead."

In the meantime God had spoken to the great prophet Elijah and sent him to Ahab with a message.

Elijah went as God had said, and gave Ahab God's message, finishing with these terrible words: "As the family of Jeroboam was wiped out, and the family of Baasha, so the family of Ahab will be wiped out as well. And the body of Jezebel will be torn to pieces by wild dogs beside the wall of Jezreel, all because you have turned away from the Lord God."

When Ahab heard that, he was very sad, and mourned over his sin. Then God spoke to Elijah and said: "Do you see how Ahab has humbled himself before me? Because of that, I will not bring punishment on his family while he lives, but in his son's lifetime the punishment will come."

Elijah Goes Home in a Chariot of Fire

2 Kings 1 and 2

After the death of Ahab, his son Ahaziah became king of Israel. But Ahaziah reigned for only two years. One day he fell from a second-story window in his palace in Samaria and was very badly hurt. While he lay on his bed, he sent messengers to the temple of the idol, Baal-zebub, in the town of Ekron. The messengers were to ask if the king would recover from his injuries. But before the messengers could get to Ekron, the angel of the Lord went to Elijah and sent him to meet those messengers. He asked them: "Is there not a God of Israel, that you go to this heathen idol? Go back to Ahaziah and tell him that he will never get up from his bed, but will die."

When the messengers returned

to the king, he asked them why they had come back so soon. They told him of their meeting with a strange prophet. They did not know who he was, but told the king that he was a hairy man with a girdle of leather around his hips. And Ahaziah said: "That was Elijah, the Tishbite."

Ahaziah was angry. He sent an officer with fifty soldiers to catch Elijah and throw him into prison. But when those men found Elijah he called down fire from heaven and they were all burned up. A second time the king sent fifty men to get Elijah, and the

same thing happened. The third time the captain in charge went down on his knees in front of Elijah, and begged the prophet to spare his life and the lives of his men. This time Elijah went with them to see the king. To the king the prophet gave the same message as he had first given to Ahaziah's messengers. Soon afterward Ahaziah died.

Now the work of Elijah was done. The time was near for God to take His servant into Heaven. Elijah knew this. One day when he was walking to Gilgal with his servant and disciple Elisha, he asked Elisha to wait for him at Gilgal while he went on to Beth-el, where the Lord had sent him. However, Elisha felt that something unusual was going to happen, so he refused to stay at Gilgal. The two of them went on together to Beth-el. There they met a group of young men, who were called the sons of the prophets. They were being taught by the prophets. When they were older some of them would become prophets, too. These young men ran to Elisha and said: "Don't you know that God is going to take away your master from you today?" And Elisha answered: "Yes, I know. Be quiet now."

Then Elijah asked Elisha to stay at Beth-el, while he went on to Jericho. But again Elisha would not, and they went on together until they came to Jericho.

There another group of the sons of the prophets came to Elisha and asked him the same question as the others had done at Beth-el. Elisha gave the same answer.

At Jericho, Elijah told Elisha that the Lord wanted him to go to the river Jordan. Elijah asked Elisha to stay behind at Jericho. Once more Elisha refused to stay. The two of them went down to the river, followed by fifty of the sons of the prophets. There Elijah took off his cloak, wrapped it in a long bundle, and hit the waters of the river with it. The waters parted so that Elijah and Elisha could walk through to the other side.

Once through the Jordan, Elijah said to Elisha: "Tell me what I must do for you, before I am taken away." And Elisha answered: "I beg you, let a double portion of your spirit rest on me."

Then Elijah said: "You have asked a hard thing. However, if you see me when I am taken away, you will be given what you have asked for. Otherwise you will not receive it."

The two of them walked on together. Suddenly there appeared from heaven a chariot of fire and horsemen of fire, and Elijah went up in a whirlwind into Heaven. Elisha saw what was happening and cried out: "My father, my father, the chariot of Israel, and the horsemen of Israel." And then Elijah vanished from his sight.

Elisha picked up Elijah's cloak that had fallen from his shoulders, and turned back to the river Jordan. There he did what Elijah had done before. He rolled up the cloak, and with it he hit the waters of the river. Once again the waters parted and he was able to walk through to the other side.

When the sons of the prophets saw Elisha come through the river like that, they cried out that the spirit of Elijah now rested on him. They ran to meet him, and bowed down in front of him.

The Jug of Oil That Overflowed

2 Kings 4 and 6

God gave to Elisha power to do many wonderful things.

Once one of the sons of the prophets died. His widow was left with two little sons, and no money and no food to give them. She came to Elisha and asked him to help her. She owed money, and the man to whom she owed it was coming to take her two sons away to be his slaves. Elisha asked her what she had in her house, and she told him there was nothing except a pot of olive oil. Then Elisha said she must go and borrow as many empty jugs and pots as she could get from her neighbors. Then she and her two sons must go into the house and close the door behind them. There they must pour oil from the pot into all the others, and put all the full ones on one side.

When all the pots were full, the oil stopped coming out of the pot.

The Boy Who Died and Lived Again

2 Kings 4

One day Elisha the prophet passed the home of a great lady who lived in the town of Shunem. When she heard he was going by, she sent out and asked him to come and eat with her. After that, whenever Elisha went along the road, he would stop awhile and have a meal in the great lady's home. This happened so often that she and her husband built a little room against the wall of the house where Elisha could stay whenever he wanted to.

It happened that one day Elisha asked her what she would like as a reward for her kindness to him. But she said to him: "I live amongst my own people. I need nothing, thank you." Then Gehazi, Elisha's servant, remembered that she had no son, although she longed for one.

Elisha said to her: "About this time next year you shall have a baby boy." But the lady would not believe him.

Still, the next year, there was the baby boy, just as Elisha had said.

One day, when the child had grown, he went out to help his father reap the crop. Suddenly he felt very ill. His father told a servant to take him back home at once. There his mother nursed him on her lap, till at noonday he died. His mother was sad. She took his body and laid it quietly on the bed in Elisha's room. Then she sent to her husband and asked for one of the servants and a donkey, so that she could go to look for Elisha.

Off she went, as fast as she could, until at Mount Carmel she found the prophet. He saw her coming a long way off, and said to Gehazi: "Look, there is the Shunammite woman. Run to meet her and ask her if her husband and the child are well." All she said to Gehazi was: "It is well." But when she reached Elisha, she threw herself down and took hold of his feet. Gehazi wanted to push her away, but Elisha stopped him and said: "Leave her alone."

Then the Shunammite lady told Elisha why she was so sad. Elisha sent Gehazi ahead and said: "Go as quickly as you can, and lay my staff on the face of the child."

The Shunammite lady would not go back without Elisha, so he went with her. When they came near to her house, Gehazi came out and told them that the child was still dead. Elisha then went into the room and closed the door. First he prayed to God. Then he went and lay over the child with his eyes on the child's eyes, his mouth on the child's mouth and his hands over the child's hands. Slowly the cold body became warm again. Then Elisha went out of the room and walked back and forth in the house. He went back and stretched himself over the little boy again. This time the boy sneezed seven times and then opened his eyes.

Elisha called Gehazi then, and sent for the Shunammite lady. When she came, he said to her: "Pick up your son."

She was so happy that she threw herself on the ground in honor of Elisha. She then picked up her little boy. He was well again.

Only a Little Girl, But She Helped to Heal a Great Warrior

2 Kings 5

When Elisha was God's prophet in Israel, the king of Syria had as the commander of his army a great man whose name was Naaman. Naaman was a mighty warrior, but he was a leper. The Syrians were still the enemies of Israel, and some of their soldiers had raided Israel and brought away a number of prisoners to be slaves in Syria. One of them was a little girl.

One day that little girl said to her mistress: "O, I wish my lord Naaman could see the prophet that lives in Samaria. I am sure he would be able to make him well again." Someone heard her say this and went in and told Naaman about it. The king heard, too, and decided to send Naaman to the king of Israel with a letter.

When the king of Israel opened the letter, this is what he read: "With this letter, I am sending to you my general, Naaman, so that you can have him cured of his leprosy." The king was shocked to read that. He thought the Syrian king was asking him to do something impossible, just to be able to pick a fight with Israel if Naaman was not cured.

News of this was taken to Elisha. Elisha sent back a message to the king, saying: "Why is the king upset about this? Send the Syrian to me, and he will learn that there is a prophet of God in Israel."

Naaman came with his horses and chariot to the door of Elisha's house, but the prophet did not come out to speak to him. He sent out his servant Gehazi instead, to tell Naaman to go and dip himself seven times in the river Jordan.

Naaman was a very proud man, and this made him very angry. "Surely the prophet could have come out and prayed over me, touched the leprous place and

that there is no other God on earth except the God of Israel. Please, will you now accept a reward from me?"

But Elisha would not take anything. Then Naaman asked a strange thing: "Let me take away two mule-loads of earth, so that I can build in my own land an altar to the God of Israel. I shall not worship Rimmon any more, but the true God only." Then Elisha blessed him, and said: "Go in peace."

Gehazi was very different from Elisha, though. When Naaman's party was a little way off Gehazi ran after the Syrians. When Naaman saw him running after them, he waited to hear what message he brought.

Then Gehazi told an untruth, and said: "My master has sent me to tell you that two of the sons of the prophets have just arrived from the land of Ephraim. Will you please leave for them a talent of silver and two changes of clothes?" Naaman was so pleased over what Elisha had done for him that he sent back instead two talents of silver with the two changes of clothes.

Gehazi took the gifts and hid them. Then he went into the house of Elisha. But there the prophet just looked at him, and said: "Where have you been, Gehazi?"

The servant lied again: "Nowhere, my master!"

made me well," he said. He turned away in a rage, ready to go back home.

But there was one of Naaman's servants who was more sensible. He pleaded with the great man. "Why do you not go down to Jordan and wash yourself, as he said?" So Naaman went to the river Jordan, and dipped himself seven times in its water. His flesh was made clean and all the leprosy left his body.

Then Naaman went back to Elisha with all his party of men and said to him: "Now I know

Then Elisha said: "You cannot deceive me. Because you have sinned like this, you will become a leper just as Naaman was." And Gehazi's skin was turned as white as snow by the leprosy.

The Army That Fled and Left Its Tents Behind

2 Kings 6 and 7

There was peace between Syria and Israel for a number of years. But then the old hatred flared up again. A great Syrian army moved into Israel and besieged Samaria, the capital.

Elisha, the prophet was in Samaria with the king of Israel at the time. He would not let the Israelites give in to the Syrian army. The king, Joram, was so worried about the terrible conditions in Samaria that he wanted to have Elisha killed for telling him to hold on. But Elisha gave a strange message to the elders. When conditions in Samaria were at their very worst, and there was hardly a morsel of food of any kind to be found anywhere, he told them that by the same time the next day food would be so plentiful that it would be almost given away.

While Elisha was talking to the elders, four lepers were standing at the gate of the city. These men were most unhappy. It would not help them to try to get into the city. They would try instead to link themselves with the Syrian army and see if they could get help there. At the worst the Syrians would kill them swiftly.

That evening at dusk the four lepers went into the Syrian camp. How surprised they were to find it deserted. They did not know it, but the Lord had made the Syrian army hear a noise like the noise of a great army of chariots and horsemen approaching. The army was so terrified that, without waiting a moment, they ran away,

look around the Syrian camp, and to scour the hills for the enemy army. The rest of the Israelites would watch from the city walls. So early in the morning two chariots were sent out to look. They went through the camp, then into the hills, and right on until they reached the river Jordan. All they found was clothing and articles of equipment scattered by the wayside. Every Syrian had fled right across the river. The charioteers hurried back to tell the king what they had seen. The wonderful news was soon known right through the city. The people thronged together at the gates to see what was brought in from the camp. There was food, more than enough for all the people of the city, and it was just as cheap as Elisha had said it would be.

leaving all their goods and riches.

The four lepers moved from tent to tent taking all the food they needed.

Suddenly the lepers remembered the poor, starving people inside the city. They said to one another: "Let us go quickly and tell the king."

When the king was told, he was very suspicious about the news. He felt that the Syrians were setting a trap for them.

Then one of King Joram's servants had an idea. They must send out a little party of men to

Jehu, the King Who Drove Wildly

2 Kings 8 to 10

In the days of Elisha, Ben-hadad, the king of Syria, became ill. Elisha went to Damascus, where the king lived. When he heard about this, Ben-hadad sent one of his princes, Hazael, to ask Elisha whether he would recover. When Hazael came to Elisha, he said to him: "Your son, Ben-hadad, king of Syria, has sent me to you, to ask you if he will recover from his illness."

Elisha's answer was not comforting. He said: "Go and tell him that he will recover, but the Lord has shown me that he will certainly die." Then Elisha looked Hazael straight in the eyes, until Hazael blushed and was ashamed, and the prophet wept. When Hazael asked him why he was crying, Elisha said: "It is because I see what terrible harm you will do to the children of Israel." Hazael was amazed. "Who am I," he asked, "to be able to do things like that?" Then Elisha answered: "The Lord has shown me that you will be king of Syria."

When Hazael went back, the king asked him what Elisha had said, and he replied: "The man of God said that you will get well again." But the next morning Hazael went to the king's bedroom and took a wet cloth, and held it over the king's face until he suffocated and died. Then Hazael became king of Syria.

It was not long before Hazael launched an attack against Israel. A great battle was fought at Ramoth-gilead. Joram, the king of Israel, was wounded. After the battle he was taken down to Jezreel to recover from his wounds. While he was there Ahaziah, the king of Judah, went to see him.

By now Elisha was back in Israel. He sent one of the sons of the prophets to Ramoth-gilead, to call out Jehu, the son of Nimshi, to be king of Israel, even though Joram was still alive. The young man went to Ramoth-gilead and found the captains of the Israelite army sitting together. Jehu was with them. To Jehu he said: "I have come on an errand to you, Captain." So Jehu led him into the house, where the young man poured oil on Jehu's head and said: "The Lord has sent me to anoint you king of Israel. You will destroy all who belong to the family of Ahab, so that the Lord may avenge the blood of all the prophets and all His servants who were killed by Ahab and his evil wife, Jezebel."

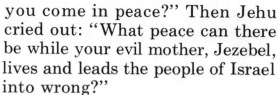

Joram was in Jezreel. Jehu decided to tell Joram the news himself.

On the tower of Jezreel a watchman saw the cloud of dust approaching. When he told Joram, a horseman was sent out to meet the soldiers and ask them if they came in peace. But Jehu said: "What have you to do with peace? Fall in behind me." So the messenger did not return to Joram. A second was sent out, and the same thing happened. Then the watchman cried out to Joram: "I think it is Jehu who is coming, because he drives his chariot furiously." When he heard that, Joram was afraid. He took his chariot, and with his visitor, Ahaziah, the king of Judah, he went out to meet Jehu. That meeting took place exactly where Ahab, the father of Joram, had stolen Naboth's vineyard. When Joram saw Jehu, he asked: "Do you come in peace?" Then Jehu cried out: "What peace can there be while your evil mother, Jezebel, lives and leads the people of Israel into wrong?"

At that Joram shouted to the king of Judah: "There is treachery, Ahaziah. We must flee." So they swung their chariots around to race back to Jezreel. But Jehu took his bow and shot an arrow after Joram. It struck him in the heart. Then Jehu told his captain, Bidkar, to take Joram's body and throw it down in the field of Naboth, so that the word of God, which Elijah had spoken to Ahab, could be fulfilled. Elijah had said: "I have seen the blood of Naboth in this place, and in this place the punishment of Ahab and his sons will also be carried out."

When Ahaziah, the king of Judah, saw this he ran away as fast as he could. But Jehu sent men after him, and killed him. Ahaziah was a grandson of Ahab and Jezebel, and a bad man, too.

When Jehu came riding in through the gates of Jezreel, Jezebel knew that her days were numbered. Dressed like a queen, she sat on a balcony and waited for Jehu. When she saw him, she said: "Greetings, Jehu—you who, like Zimri, have murdered your master. Do you expect to have peace?" But Jehu did not answer her. He simply called out to her servants, standing behind her on the balcony: "Who is on my

side?" Two or three of the men showed that they would follow him. Jehu told them to throw Jezebel down from the balcony. When they did, he drove his chariot over her body. Then Jehu told his men to bury her because, after all, she was the daughter of a king. When they came to the place where she had died there was hardly any of her body left. Wild dogs had torn it to pieces, just as Elijah had said would happen. After this, Jehu had every member of Ahab's family put to death. There was terrible bloodshed. Jehu told everyone that he was doing this because Ahab's people had served the false god, Baal, and he wanted to honor the Lord. But when he was strong and the people were all following him, he did something that must have seemed strange. He sent out a messenger, saying: "Ahab served Baal a little, but Jehu will serve him much." Then he arranged a great feast, and a great sacrifice to Baal. He sent for all the worshipers of Baal to come, and all the priests of Baal to get ready to sacrifice to the idol in its temple. When they were all gathered, he sent his soldiers to surround the temple and to kill every Baal priest in the place. After that they went out and destroyed every idol throughout the land. Only the worship of God was allowed.

But Jehu did not destroy the golden calves that Jereboam had put in Beth-el and Dan. Because of that he was not always careful to keep God's commandments. He did not see to it that the people of Israel were obedient. Although God promised him that he and his sons would rule over Israel up to the fourth generation, he and the people of Israel still had to be punished for the wrong they did. The Syrians, under Hazael, attacked them, and took away much of their land. In all the twenty-eight years of Jehu's reign, there was no peace in Israel.

Elisha and the Bow

2 Kings 13

After the reign of Jehu, his son, Jehoahaz, became the king of Israel. Jehoahaz was a bad king, like so many of the others who had ruled before him. He was weak, too, and a poor soldier. Soon much of the land was in the hands of the Syrian kings, Hazael and his son Ben-hadad. Many of the people of Israel fled from the towns and villages and lived in tents out in the fields to get away from the Syrians. The army of Israel was so badly defeated that in the end Jehoahaz had only fifty horsemen, ten chariots and ten thousand foot soldiers. But God saw to it that the Syrians did not defeat the Israelites altogether.

When Jehoahaz died, his son, Jehoash, became king. Jehoash reigned for sixteen years, just one year less than his father. He followed in his father's footsteps. The people still worshiped idols, and the Syrians still overran the country.

By this time the prophet Elisha was an old and sick man. He could no longer travel about the country. One day the young king of Israel went to see Elisha because he felt angry at the way the Syrians were sending their bands of raiders into all parts of the land. When he saw how weak the old man was, he wept and said: "O, my father, you mean more to Israel than horsemen and chariots." Elisha replied: "Take your bow and arrows." When he did, Elisha commanded him to open one of the windows toward the east. Then he told him to take hold of the bow, ready to shoot, and he placed his own hands on the king's hands. As the king shot, he said: "The arrow of the Lord's deliverance, and the arrow of deliverance from Syria, because you will defeat the Syrians at Aphek until you have destroyed them." Elisha then told Jehoash to take the arrows and strike the ground with them. The king did so and hit the ground three times. But Elisha was annoyed with him and said: "Why did you hit three times only? You should have beaten the ground five or six times. Then you would have conquered the Syrians altogether, but now you will defeat them three times only."

Not long after this Elisha died, and they buried his body in a cave in the hills. About a year later the Moabites invaded the land from the southeast. One day a party of Israelites were burying a man in the same place where Elisha was buried. Suddenly they saw a band of Moabites rushing up. They were frightened. They quickly let down the body into Elisha's grave. When the body touched Elisha's bones, the man came to life again and stood up. Even after his death, Elisha still had miraculous power.

Jehoash did not forget what Elisha had told him. He went to war against the Syrians. Three times he defeated the armies of Ben-hadad, king of Syria. Jehoash took back all the cities which the Syrians had taken away from Israel during the reign of Jehoahaz. After all Elisha, the servant of God, had done to help him, King Jehoash still led the people in the worship of Idols and did not turn back to God.

After Jehoash came Jeroboam, the second king of that name. Jeroboam turned out to be the strongest of all the kings of Israel. In his reign the country became rich and strong once more. Samaria became a great city.

Although the Syrians had been

defeated, there was another enemy becoming stronger and stronger. This was the Assyrian Empire. Their great city, Nineveh, stood beyond the river Tigris. One by one they were conquering all the countries round about. The Israelites began to be afraid of what might happen to them.

Jonah and Nineveh

Jonah 1 to 4

In those days there was a prophet in Israel named Jonah. God spoke to him and said: "Go to Nineveh, that great city, and speak to them for Me about their great wickedness."

But Jonah was afraid, because the people of Nineveh, the Assyrians, were the enemies of the Israelites. They would rather kill him than listen to him. So he ran away to the seaport town of Joppa to find a ship that would take him to Tarshish, away across the Mediterranean Sea. He boarded the ship and set sail. But Jonah should have remembered that you cannot run away from God.

God knew what Jonah was doing. Once the ship was well out from the coast, God sent a great storm which raged so fiercely that it seemed as if the ship would go down. The sailors threw overboard everything they could, to try to lighten the ship. But nothing helped. Then each one cried out to his god for help, but the waves still tossed the ship about. All this time Jonah was asleep below deck. The captain went down to him, woke him up and said: "How can you sleep at a time like this? Wake up and call upon your God. Perhaps He may be able to save us."

But the storm grew worse and worse until the sailors said, one to another: "There is someone on board who has caused this trouble

to come to us. Let's draw lots to find out who it is." And when they did, they found out that it was Jonah. Then he told them he was trying to escape from God. "What must we do with you?" they cried out. "While you are on this ship we are all in danger of losing our lives."

So Jonah told them to throw him into the sea. Then the sea would become calm and they would be safe. At first they would not, because they did not want to let Jonah drown. But the sea did not become calm, and, try as they would, they could not get the ship any closer to land. They cast Jonah into the sea, and at once the waves calmed and the wind lessened.

What happened to Jonah? God sent a great fish to swallow him up. For three days and three nights Jonah was in the stomach of that fish. There he prayed to God. In his terror, Jonah begged God to save him, and forgive him for his great sin in trying to run away. On the third day the fish vomited him up on a beach nearby.

After this, God spoke to Jonah a second time. God told Jonah once again to go to Nineveh and preach there the words God would give him. This time Jonah went.

Nineveh was a very large city. It took three days to walk around its walls. Many people lived there.

As Jonah walked in he cried: "Another forty days, and Nineveh will be destroyed." Soon the people began to gather around. Then he spoke to them about God's anger over the wickedness of their city. When they heard, the people began to be sorry for what they had done. Soon even the king believed, and with all the people prayed that God would forgive them. They all fasted, and wept over their sins. Even the cattle were not allowed to eat during the days of fasting. When God saw this, He forgave them.

When the forty days Jonah had spoken about were past, the city was not destroyed.

Jonah was very angry about this. He prayed to God and said something he should not have said at all: "O Lord, isn't this what I said would happen when I was still in my own country? This is why I tried to go away to Tarshish, because I knew that my work would be for nothing, and that in Your kindness and Your mercy You would forgive these people and spare their lives. Now

take away my life. It would be better for me to die than to go on living."

But God was not angry. All he said to Jonah was: "Is it sensible of you to get cross about this?"

Then Jonah went out of the city gate. A little way east of the wall he made himself a shelter and sat in its shade to see what would happen to the city. While he sat there, God made a wild plant to grow up over the shelter to make it cool. Jonah was very pleased. The next day, however, God made a worm to eat at the stem of the plant until it withered and died. Then a hot east wind began to blow. The sun beat on Jonah's head until he was very cross and wished he were dead.

Now God spoke to him again: "Is it right for you to be angry about the plant?" Jonah said: "It is right for me to be angry!" But God said: "You are upset about the death of the plant, which really was nothing. You had nothing to do with its growth, it came up in a night and died in a night. Yet you do not want me to spare the great city of Nineveh. There are more than a hundred and twenty thousand children in it, and many cattle. Jonah, Jonah, think this over again, will you?"

God's specially chosen people were the nations of Israel and Judah, but in this story we learn that God showed His love for other nations and people.

How the Ten Tribes Were Lost

2 Kings 15 and 17

The reign of Jeroboam II was a time of great prosperity for Israel. But after his reign the whole kingdom fell to pieces. After Jeroboam, the next king was his son, Zachariah. He reigned for only six months and then he was murdered by one of his own people, Shallum, who became king in his place. But Shallum lasted for one month only. Then Menahem murdered him and took the throne. Menahem was a cruel and evil king, but he reigned for ten years. By this time armed bands of Assyrians were already raiding the land, but Menahem made all the rich people of Israel pay a special tax of silver. He gave the tax to Pul, the king of the Assyrians, so that he would stop his people from attacking the Israelites.

After Menahem, came his son, Pekahiah, but two years later one of his captains, Pekah, rose in revolt against him, and murdered him. Pekah reigned for twenty years, but like the kings before him, he did not serve God nor teach his people to do so. In his time Tiglath-pileser, the king of Assyria, attacked the land of the tribe of Naphtali and took all its cities and carried away the people into Assyria. After this terrible defeat, Hoshea rebelled against Pekah and murdered him. Another reign came to its end in bloodshed. Hoshea remained in power for nine years, but it was nine years of wickedness and shame and defeat. At the end there was no longer a kingdom of Israel, for God let their enemies overpower them.

Shalmaneser, the king of Assyria, brought his armies up to attack Israel, but Hoshea gave him presents, and promised to be his servant, so there was no war. But Shalmaneser found out that Hoshea was trying to buy the help of So, king of Egypt. To punish Hoshea, he threw him into prison. Shalmaneser then sent up his armies to surround Samaria, and

for three years the city was besieged. Before the end of the siege, Shalmaneser himself had died, but his general, Sargon, completed the task. The capital of Israel was captured. The people of Israel were dragged away into Assyria, to lands far away, around the Caspian Sea, and to Mesopotamia and Media. This was the end of the Ten Tribes. They never went back to their own land again. They married into the heathen nations, so that we cannot tell today what happened to them.

The king of Assyria brought people from many other countries to live in the land of Israel. They lived in the great cities of Israel like Samaria. The land became a heathen land. Soon, however, lions and other wild animals became a nuisance to these new settlers and killed many of them. The king of Assyria thought that this was because they did not serve the god of the country they lived in, but still served the gods of the countries they had come from. He thought that each nation had its own god. He knew nothing at all about the one true God. So, to protect the people in Israel from the wild animals, he sent one of the priests they had taken prisoner to teach them how to worship God. This man went to live at Beth-el. He tried hard to teach the people the true faith, but they still clung to their old idols which they had brought with them, while claiming also to serve God.

A nation with mixed beliefs came into existence. In time they were given the name of Samaritans. Many centuries later they dropped their worship of idols, but they never became friendly with the people of Judah.

The First Four Kings of Judah

2 Chronicles 12 to 20

The last stories have been about the northern kingdom of Israel; but in the meantime interesting things were happening in the southern kingdom of Judah, and in Jerusalem, its capital.

The first king of Judah was Rehoboam. He was like the Israelites in the north who forgot the laws of God. Because of this, very soon the people of Judah were worshiping idols. God became very angry with them. In the fifth year of Rehoboam's reign God allowed King Shishak of Egypt to bring a great army against Judah, even taking Jerusalem and carrying away the treasures from the Temple.

Rehoboam reigned for seventeen years. After his death his son, Abijah, became king. Not long after the beginning of his reign, Jeroboam of Israel brought a great

army to make war against Judah. Abijah bravely led out his men to defend their land, but they were heavily outnumbered. Soon Jeroboam's army had surrounded them. Abijah called out to his men to stand firm and to trust in God. Abijah knew God would help them. The army of Judah shouted loudly as they attacked Jeroboam's men, and God was with them. That day they won such a great victory over Israel that Jeroboam never attacked them again.

Abijah was king for only three years. He was followed by his son, Asa, who was a brave and clever

man. But, most important of all, Asa was a man who loved God. For ten years there was peace in the land. The king saw to it that as many of the altars and idols of the false gods as could be found were destroyed. At the end of the ten years of peace, great armies came up from Ethiopia, far south of Egypt, to attack the little kingdom of Judah. Asa drew up his tiny army at a place called Mareshah: but what hope had they against all the Ethiopians? Still, Asa was not afraid. He stood before his men and cried out to God, saying: "O God, it makes no difference to Thee whether we be many or few. Help us, we beg Thee." God helped them. The Ethiopians were badly beaten.

Not long afterward God sent a prophet called Azariah to Asa to give him some very good advice. He said to the king: "As long as you remain with the Lord, He will stay with you. If you seek Him, you will find Him, but if you turn from Him, He will turn from you." When Asa heard this, he took courage and called a great feast day in Jerusalem. On that day the whole nation brought sacrifices to God. Many of the people of Israel who had come to live in Judah because Israel was so ungodly sacrificed with them.

When Asa was a very old and sick man, he made a bad mistake. Instead of looking to the Lord for help, he asked for the help of men.

These men called themselves doctors, but they tried to heal people by praying to false gods. This taught the people of Judah wrong ways again. When Asa died, they put up idols again all around the country.

After Asa, his son Jehoshaphat became king. Jehoshaphat was the strongest and wisest of all the kings the country had. He loved and served God. He watched carefully over the ways of his people. Into all the cities and towns he sent princes and Levites and priests to teach the people the law.

In all the cities of Judah, Jehoshaphat appointed judges, to see that the laws were properly kept. He warned those judges that they were not there to serve man, but first of all to serve God. They must never take bribes or give wrong judgments. God would punish them for these things.

Some time afterward news reached Jehoshaphat that some of the nations round about were drawing their armies together to attack Judah. It was a rich country now, and they felt there was great spoil to be taken. The Moabites, the Ammonites and other smaller nations had made an agreement with the Syrians. They planned to attack Jehoshaphat and his people. Jehoshaphat knew that the men of Judah were far too few to fight against these great numbers, but he knew where to turn for help. He proclaimed a day of fasting throughout the land. He called all his soldiers together in front of the Temple in Jerusalem. There he prayed that God would help them in the great battles that must take place soon.

Then God spoke to Jehoshaphat and the people of Judah through a prophet called Jahaziel, one of the Levites: "Do not be afraid or dismayed because of these great armies. The battle is not yours, but God's. Go out to meet them tomorrow. Do not be afraid. You will not have to fight at all in this battle. The Lord will see to the victory."

When they heard that, all the people bowed their heads to the ground and worshiped God. Early the next morning the army moved out to meet the enemy. At the head of the column marched singers and musicians from among the Levites to praise God as the army moved along. But when they reached the enemy camp, what a surprise they had. There was a terrible battle raging in the camp. The Ammonites and the Moabites were fighting against the rest and there were bodies lying all around. Some of the enemy soldiers were already fleeing into the desert. There was no army for the men of Judah to fight. Without a single moment of fighting, they were able to take back to Jerusalem great quantities of gold and silver and jewelry, so

much that it took them three whole days to collect it all together.

On the fourth day they gathered in a valley nearby to praise God for what He had done. Ever since then the place has been called the valley of Berachah, which means "blessing," because there they blessed the Lord's name.

After that wonderful victory, none of the nations around Judah dared to trouble Jehoshaphat. Till the end of his reign there was

peace in the land, and the people praised and served God.

How different were the first kings of Judah from the first kings of Israel!

A Little Boy Becomes King

2 Chronicles 21 to 24

When the great king of Judah, Jehoshaphat, died, his son, Jehoram, became the next king. Jehoram was married to the daughter of Ahab and Jezebel. She taught him to be a wicked man, too. As soon as he came to the throne, he murdered all his brothers and

many of the other princes of Judah. He reigned for eight years, and they were very bad years. Elijah, the prophet who lived in Israel at that time, sent him a letter warning him of what would happen if he did not turn back to God. God would send an awful disease which would strike all his family. Jehoram would die of it in terrible pain.

Then the Philistines and the Arabians in the south began to raid deep into the land of Judah. They reached even to Jerusalem, broke into the palace, carried away all his treasures, and killed all the king's sons except Ahaziah.

The king was away at the time, but before long he fell ill with the disease Elijah had warned him about. He died in terrible pain.

The next king, Ahaziah, was the only son of Jehoram left after the Philistines and Arabians raided Jerusalem. Ahaziah reigned for one year only. He went to visit his uncle, Jehoram, the king of Israel, who had been wounded in a battle against the Syrians, and at Jezreel they were both murdered by Jehu.

When his mother, Athaliah, heard the news of this, she had all the other men in the royal family killed, but the youngest son of Ahaziah, Joash, was saved by his aunt, who hid him in his nurse's bedroom. Later she took him secretly to the Temple and

205

asked the High Priest, Jehoiada, to hide him there and look after him.

Athaliah made herself queen of Judah and ruled for all the six years that Joash was hidden away. She stopped all the services in the Temple and built a temple for the idol, Baal. She made the people of Judah worship there. But while this was happening, Jehoiada, the High Priest, was planning how to make Joash king of Judah. He arranged a special gathering of leaders of the people in the Temple. He brought out the little boy, Joash, who was only seven years old, and anointed him and crowned him king. Around the Temple stood soldiers to protect the young king. When he stood there in front of them, the people shouted out: "God save the king!"

When Athaliah the queen heard all this shouting, she came out of her palace to see what was happening. When she saw the young king standing there, she cried out: "Treason, treason!" Then Jehoiada called to the captains of the soldiers to take her and kill her because of her evil deeds. They took her away from the Temple so that her blood would not be shed in the house of the Lord. At the horse gate to the palace they killed her. When they heard what had happened, the people of Jerusalem rejoiced, but they still needed a warning from Jehoiada. He warned Joash and all the people to be the Lord's people, and to serve Him. They were not to follow the false gods that Athaliah had served.

Three Kings and the Great Prophet Isaiah

2 Chronicles 25 to 28; Isaiah 6
Amaziah was the next king of Judah after Joash. He began by serving God well, but in his heart there was always a longing for what was wrong. In the reign of

King Jehoram the Edomites had rebelled against Judah. Now Amaziah decided that they must be conquered again.

Amaziah led his men out against the Edomites. With God's help Judah won a great victory against the Edomites in the valley of Salt. But Amaziah was very cruel and murdered thousands of the people that were captured. He also showed what a faithless person he was by taking back the idols of wood and stone which the Edomites had worshiped. He made them his own gods, and the gods of his people. God was angry and sent a prophet to speak to Amaziah. "Why are you worshiping these gods which were not able to save the Edomites from defeat?" The king flew into a rage and said: "Who asked you to give the king advice? Be silent, or you will be put to death." The prophet answered: "I know that God will destroy you, because you have done this and will not listen to my advice."

Amaziah did not have to wait long for his punishment. The departing army of men from Israel had already attacked some of the towns of Judah and done a great deal of damage. But now Amaziah listened to bad advisers and sent a challenge of war to Joash, king of Israel. Joash laughed at him, and tried to make peace with him, but Amaziah kept on until the two armies met at Beth-shemesh. The

Israelites inflicted a very great defeat on the army of Judah, and captured Amaziah himself. They broke down the walls of Jerusalem and took away all the treasures of the Temple and from the king's palace. After this terrible defeat, Amaziah reigned for another fifteen years. He was such a hated man that in the end his own people drove him out of Jerusalem and killed him.

After Amaziah came his son, Uzziah, who was only sixteen years old when he began to reign. Uzziah ruled for fifty-two years.

For most of his reign he served God faithfully and did what was right in God's sight.

When Uzziah became king, the land was very poor. He began to build it up again. First of all he took the seaport town of Eloth on the Red Sea, and built it up to be a trading place. He attacked the Philistines and broke down the walls of several of their fortress towns, like Gath and Ashdod and Jabneh, to make the south of Judah safe from their attacks. Then he defeated the Arabians as well. When they saw how many victories he was winning, the Ammonites brought gifts to him and asked for peace. In Jerusalem, he repaired the walls which the Israelites had broken down during the reign of his father. He built new watchtowers on the walls and fortified them so that it would not be easy for the enemies of Judah to break into the city. Throughout the land other watchtowers were built, too, so that the watchmen could see from a long way off the approach of any enemy bands.

Under the control of King Uzziah, Judah became so rich and so strong that in all the lands round about they spoke of his greatness. But then Uzziah began to think too much of himself and to ignore God's commandments. He wanted to be not only king, but priest as well, and that was against God's Law. One day he forced his way into the Temple to burn incense on the special altar of incense. Azariah, the High Priest, went in after him with eighty of the other priests to try to stop him from breaking God's Law. Azariah said to him: "Uzziah, you cannot do this. It is only the priests whom God has chosen from the sons of Aaron who are allowed to burn incense here or to go into the holy place." When Uzziah heard that, he was very angry and lifted up the censer to burn incense. But as he did it, a great white blotch came on the skin of his forehead. It was leprosy! From then on, Uzziah was not allowed to have anything to do with other people because they might catch

the disease. His son Jotham became king in his place.

Jotham reigned for sixteen years. He obeyed and served God faithfully all the time.

After Jotham came Ahaz. Ahaz was the worst of all the kings of Judah. He was an idol worshiper from the beginning, just like the kings of Israel. He even sacrificed his own children to the idols. What a terrible time this was for the people of Judah! First the Syrians attacked them, took many of them prisoner, and carried away their possessions. Then Pekah, king of Israel, made war against them. After killing a hundred and twenty thousand men in one day's fighting, he took away two hundred thousand women and children as prisoners to Samaria. There, one of God's prophets reasoned with the Israelites: "Judah was defeated in battle because God is angry with them for their sins. But you cannot make slaves of your own brethren, the people of Judah. You have also sinned against God.

Listen to God's word, and let your brethren go back to their own land."

The state of the country was worse than ever before. The Edomites had attacked them again. The Philistines had taken many towns in the south, near the Mediterranean Sea. It looked as if the whole country would be destroyed. Then Ahaz sent to the king of Assyria for help. When the Assyrians came they did not help, but took over the whole country. They carried away all the treasures that were left, and made Ahaz promise to pay great taxes every year to the king of Assyria.

A Great Prophet

In the time of the three kings, Uzziah, Jotham and Ahaz, there lived in Jerusalem a young man called Isaiah. God used that young man to bring His message to the people of Judah.

In the year that King Uzziah died, Isaiah was still a young man. One day when Isaiah was in the Temple praying, he had a wonderful vision. It was as if he saw God sitting upon a great throne, and around Him were angels. Before the throne stood angels called seraphs, each with six wings, two to cover their faces, and two to cover their feet, and two for flying. One to another they cried out, saying: "Holy, holy, holy, is the Lord of hosts: the whole earth is full of His glory." As they cried out, it seemed as if the whole Temple building shook. It was filled with smoke. Isaiah was terrified, and he cried out: "Woe is me, I am lost; because I am a man of unclean lips, and I live among a people of unclean lips; for my eyes have seen the King, the Lord of hosts." Then one of the seraphs flew toward Isaiah carrying the tongs which were used at the altar in the Temple. In the tongs the seraphim carried a glowing coal which he had taken from the altar. With it he touched Isaiah's lips, saying: "This coal from God's altar has touched your lips, and now your sin is taken away and you are pure." Then Isaiah heard the Lord Himself say: "Whom shall I send, and who will go for Us?" And Isaiah answered: "Here am I; send me."

Then God said: "Go and tell this people My message. But they will not listen to you, and they will not understand your words. It will seem as if their ears are blocked and their eyes shut. They will not see, nor hear, nor understand, and they will not be converted to Me nor healed from their wrongs." Isaiah asked: "For how long will this be, O Lord?" The Lord said: "Until all the cities are destroyed and there are no people living in them any more, and until the whole land is ruined. The people will have been taken far away, but a tenth part will be kept and brought back. Then the land will grow up again, just as the stump of a tree does after it has been cut down."

Hezekiah the Godly

2 Kings 18 to 21; 2 Chronicles 29 to 32; Isaiah 36 to 39

When Ahaz died, his son Hezekiah became king of Judah. He was

very different from his father. He
tried to keep all commandments,
and to live as his great forefather
David had done. At once he began
to put right the wrong Ahaz had
done. He had all the heathen
places of worship broken down
and all the idols destroyed. In the
very first month of his reign he
had the Temple doors opened. He
had the whole building repaired.
Then he sent in the Levites to
clean every part of the Temple. It
took them sixteen days to finish
the work. When this was done, the
sacrifices and services began again
just as the Law of the Lord said
they should be carried out.

For many years the Passover
Feast had not been kept as the
Lord commanded. Hezekiah felt

that now was the time to begin once again to keep the feast. He felt that Israel and Judah should keep it together, so he sent messengers to the northern kingdom to invite the people to Jerusalem. But many of the Israelites were serving the idols of the Assyrians, and they only laughed at the messengers from Judah. In the tribes of Ephraim and Manasseh not a single person would come at first, but later some did come from Asher, Manasseh and Zebulun to join in the feast in Jerusalem.

When Hezekiah became king, Judah, Israel and Syria were all in the hands of the Assyrians.. Each of these nations had its own king, but all three kings were servants of the Assyrian king, and had to pay very heavy taxes to him every year. In the fourteenth year of his reign, Hezekiah felt that it was time Judah was free again. He did not pay taxes to the Assyrian king, but instead strengthened the walls of Jerusalem and prepared his soldiers to defend their country against any Assyrian attack. When this happened, Sennacherib, king of Assyria, brought up great armies. Before very long many of the cities of Judah on the west side of the country had been captured. The Assyrians moved on toward Jerusalem itself. Hezekiah saw that he had made a mistake. His country was not strong enough yet to fight against the Assyrians. Hezekiah sent messengers to the headquarters of the king of Assyria in the town of Lachish to ask for peace. He promised to pay whatever tax the Assyrians asked for. The tax was so heavy that Hezekiah had to have the gold cut off the doors and the pillars of the Temple. This was the gold which Hezekiah had put on the Temple when he first became king.

Sennacherib, the Assyrian king, was not even satisfied then. He sent three of his princes with a mighty army of men to attack Jerusalem. When they came near to the city, the princes went ahead with a letter to Hezekiah. They also shouted out a message of

mockery to the defenders of the walls of Jerusalem.

When Hezekiah received Sennacherib's letter, he was very worried and upset, but he did the right thing. He took the letter to the Temple and laid it before the altar of the Lord. Hezekiah asked God to come to the help of His people in their great need. Then he sent his own princes, Eliakim and Shebna, to the prophet Isaiah to ask if there was any message from God. This was the word they brought back: "The Lord says, 'Do not be afraid of what the Assyrians have said. The king of Assyria will not come into this city nor even shoot an arrow into it nor attack it in any way. He will go back to his own land by the same way along which he came. In his own land he will be killed with the sword. For the sake of the memory of My servant David, I shall protect this city.'"

While this was happening, Sennacherib received news that a mighty army was coming from Ethiopia to attack him. To prepare for war against them, he called back his men from Jerusalem to Lachish. There a terrible thing happened to them. In the night an angel came from God and spread disease in the Assyrian camp. Before morning one hundred and eighty-five thousand of the soldiers were dead. When this happened, Sennacherib gathered together all the men that were

left. He went back to Nineveh in his own country. There some time afterward his own sons killed him with the sword while he was worshiping before an idol. God had saved the city of Jerusalem and the people of Judah from the Assyrian enemy.

Hezekiah Falls Ill

While the Assyrians were still in the land, Hezekiah fell seriously ill. The prophet, Isaiah, came to him and said: "You must settle your affairs, because God says that this sickness will take away your life." When Hezekiah heard that, he turned his face to the wall and wept bitterly, and prayed: "O God, remember that I have always served You with my whole heart, and done what is good in Your sight, I beg You."

God heard that prayer. He called back His prophet, Isaiah, and gave him a new message to take to Hezekiah. He must go back and tell the king that God had heard his prayer and seen his tears. God would make him well again. In three days' time he would be able to go to the Temple to worship. He would live for fifteen more years. In all that time the Assyrians would be kept from attacking Jerusalem. Hezekiah was very pleased to receive this message, but he wanted a sign to prove that God would really heal him. Isaiah asked him which he wanted. Isaiah asked, "Must the shadow on the sundial move back ten degrees or forward ten degrees?" Hezekiah answered that it was an easy thing for the shadow to go forward. He said "Let it go ten degrees backward."

So Isaiah prayed to God. God brought back the shadow on the sundial by ten degrees so that Hezekiah could be sure of the truth of the promise.

For fifteen years after that Hezekiah continued to reign. There was peace in the land in all that time.

The Book of Law is Found

2 Kings 21 to 23; 2 Chronicles 33 to 35

After the death of Hezekiah, Manasseh became the king of Judah. He was a boy of twelve when he came to the throne. He reigned for fifty-five years. But he was not at all like his father, Hezekiah. From an early age he encouraged the people of Judah to turn back to the worship of idols, and of the sun, the moon, and the stars. Even in the Temple of God he had altars built for all these false gods. When he was older and had children of his own,

he made them go through fire in honor of the gods.

Because of this, the Assyrians turned their attention again to Judah. In the war, Manasseh was captured and taken away in chains to Babylon. While he was in prison there, King Manasseh began to think over his ways. He began to realize that he had done wrong in turning away from God. He prayed for forgiveness. God made the Assyrians free him again and take him back to Jerusalem. Then Manasseh knew that the Lord was the true God. From that time on he served God only.

When Manasseh died, his son, Amon, came to the throne. Amon reigned for only two years in a very evil way. Then he was murdered by his own servants.

Josiah Becomes King

The next king was Josiah, a little boy who was only eight years old when he became king. At first one of the princes ruled for him, because he was so young, but all the time he was doing his best to serve God in the right way. As soon as he was old enough, he commanded that all the idols and altars to false gods in the land should be broken down and burned. With his servants he even crossed into Israel, which now had very few people left after the Assyrians had taken the rest away. Josiah broke down the altars there. When he came to Beth-el where Jeroboam had built a temple two hundred years before and made the golden calves for the people of Israel to worship, he broke the temple and the altar. He burned everything that would burn. When all this work of cleansing was done, Josiah went back to Jerusalem. There he saw that all that had anything at all to do with idol worship was taken away and destroyed. While his workmen were busy around the Temple, Hilkiah, the High Priest,

217

found there the book of the Law. Hilkiah took it at once to the king. Shaphan, the king's scribe, read the book to him. When the king heard the Law, and understood how much wrong had been done in the land, he was so upset that he tore his clothes. Then he told the Temple leaders to ask God what he and the people of Judah must do to be forgiven because they and their forefathers had broken His laws. He knew they were all in great danger. He was sure that God would punish them for what they had done. The Temple rulers went to a prophetess called Huldah, and told her the king's request.

This was Huldah's answer: "This is what the Lord God of Israel says: 'Go and tell the man that sent you that I will cause great disaster to come upon this place and its people, because they turned away from Me and served idols. This land and this people must be punished for the evil they have done. But because King Josiah has served Me faithfully and is sorrowful over all the sins of the nation, I will not punish Judah in his time. These terrible things will happen to Judah only after his death.'"

After receiving this message, the king called together the elders from all parts of the land and all the people of Jerusalem to a great meeting at the Temple gates. He stood beside one of the great pillars at the door and read to them the laws from the book that had been found. Then together they made a solemn promise to keep all those laws faithfully. To the end of Josiah's life they were careful to live according to the laws and commandments of God. But the king did not live for many years after that.

Up to this time, Judah, like all the nations around about, was part of the Assyrian Empire. But the Empire had become weak and was falling apart. Egypt was getting stronger, and decided to make war against the Assyrians. To attack them,

Pharaoh-Nechoh led his army up through Judah. Josiah felt that because his country was still part of the Assyrian Empire, he must try to stop the Egyptian advance. Then Pharaoh sent messengers to tell him that he had no fight with Judah, but only with the king of Assyria.

Josiah would not listen. His army fought against the Egyptians in the valley of Megiddo. That day the men of Judah were very badly beaten. An arrow hit King Josiah himself and he died in his chariot. His body was taken back to Jerusalem to be buried there.

The Last Four Kings of Judah and the Prophet Who Wept

2 Kings 23 to 25; 2 Chronicles 36; Jeremiah 22, 24, 29 and 36 to 43

When Josiah died, the people of Judah made his son, Jehoahaz, their king. Josiah had been a very good king, but his son was a wicked man.

At that time the whole Assyrian Empire was crumbling to ruins. The capital, Nineveh, that great city, had been destroyed. War was raging on all sides. For a time the Egyptian king, Pharaoh-Nechoh became the ruler of all the land from Egypt right up to the River Euphrates. Jehoahaz and the peo-

ple of Judah had to pay tribute to him, but Pharaoh-Nechoh did not trust Jehoahaz and took him away into Egypt as a prisoner. In his place Jehoahaz made one of his brothers, Eliakim, king of Judah, but changed his name to Jehoiakim. Jehoahaz had been king for only three months. He died in prison in Egypt. The prophet Jeremiah had foretold this near the end of Josiah's reign.

Jehoiakim reigned for eleven years. He was like his brother, an ungodly man who led the people

in worshiping idols. In his reign the armies of Babylon began to conquer the Egyptians. For three years Judah was under the control of the Babylonians. Then Jehoiakim rebelled. But the Lord was no longer on his side. He had sinned too much, and had even tried to kill God's messenger, Jeremiah.

The king would not allow Jeremiah to go about among the people bringing God's messages to them. Jeremiah was not allowed even to speak in the Temple any more. But that did not silence him. He was God's servant. He could not be quiet. His scribe, Baruch, wrote down on a parchment all that he said, then Baruch would go read the message to the people. One winter day the king's officers came and snatched the parchment roll away from Baruch. They took it to the king, who was sitting warming himself by the fireside. Section by section the officers read the document to him. Section by section he took it and cut it to pieces with his knife, throwing the pieces into the fire. Even some of the princes were horrified and asked the king not to do this. He would not listen to them. Instead he sent some of his officers to throw Jeremiah and Baruch into prison, but the Lord hid them. While they were hidden away, Baruch wrote down again what the Lord had said through Jeremiah. We still have those words in our Bibles today.

Not long afterward the Babylonian armies returned to Judah. Nebuchadnezzar, the king of Babylon, took Jehoiakim prisoner. Three years later the Babylonians let Jehoiakim free, but he died in disgrace a short while afterward.

Jeremiah's Vision

After Jehoiakim, his son Jehoiachin became king, but he was only eight years old. In three months his reign was over because the Babylonians under Nebuchadnezzar came back. They took Jehoiachin and his princes away as prisoners. They also carried away all the treasures still left in the Temple. They made Jehoiachin's uncle, Zedekiah, king in his place. The king and the princes who were taken prisoner loved God. They worshiped and served Him even when they were in Babylon. The new king was a bad man who mocked God's prophet, Jeremiah.

Soon after Zedekiah became king, Jeremiah was sitting in the Temple one day. There he saw a vision. In that vision God told him all that would happen to the people of Judah. He saw two baskets of figs. One was full of beautiful fruit, but the other had only rotten fruit not fit to be eaten. Then the Lord asked him: "What do

you see, Jeremiah?" Jeremiah answered: "I see figs. The good figs are very good, but the bad figs are so bad that they cannot be eaten." Then the Lord said: "The good figs are the people I have already made to be carried away to Babylon. I shall bless them and bring them back again to their own land. I shall make them love Me more and more. They will return to Me with all their hearts. The bad figs are Zedekiah and the people of Jerusalem and all Judah who have remained behind. They will suffer

very much, by famine and disease and armed attack. Those that are left will be scattered throughout the kingdoms of the world. None will be left in this land."

Afterward Jeremiah sent a letter to the prisoners in Babylon to encourage them. He was giving them a message from God. He wrote: "Build houses for yourselves and live in them. Make gardens and eat the fruit from them. Marry, and have children, and let your children marry, too. Pray for the peace of the city and the land in which you are living, because you and your children will live there for seventy years. After seventy years you will return again to your own land. It is My plan to bless you with peace and prosperity. Pray to Me and I will hear you. If you search for Me with your whole hearts, you will certainly find Me."

Zedekiah was made king of Judah by the Babylonians. He promised to be faithful to Nebuchadnezzar, the king of Babylon, but it was not long before he had persuaded his princes that they should rebel. At the same time, he taught them to turn away from God and worship idols.

Zedekiah had heard that Pharaoh's army was moving out of Egypt to make war against the Babylonians. He planned to break his promise to Nebuchadnezzar and fight on the Egyptian side in the war. But Jeremiah warned him not to break his promise. God had told him that the Egyptians would turn back to their own land, and that the Babylonians would come and de-

stroy Jerusalem. Jeremiah warned Zedekiah that the Babylonians would not leave the land of Judah.

When they heard this, Zedekiah and his princes were very angry. They said that Jeremiah was a traitor and must be killed. Zedekiah told the princes to do what they liked with Jeremiah. So they took him and let him down with ropes into a muddy dungeon under the floor of the palace prison. There was a kindhearted man in the palace, a man called Ebed-melech. He was upset over the thought of Jeremiah lying there in the mud, starving. He went to the king and asked permission to move the prophet to another part of the prison. The king allowed him to move Jeremiah to a warm and dry place.

By this time Nebuchadnezzar and his armies were hammering at the walls of Jerusalem. Soon the walls came tumbling down, and the fierce soldiers swarmed into the city. The king and his family tried to flee out of the city, but the Babylonians soon overtook them and made them prisoners. Zedekiah was dragged in front of Nebuchadnezzar and had to watch the Babylonians kill his own sons. Then they blinded him, fastened him with chains and took him away to Babylon. In the meantime, all the buildings in Jerusalem were burned down. All the people, except the very poorest, were driven like a flock of

223

sheep toward Babylon, far away in the east. That was the end of the kingdom of Judah. Zedekiah was the last king, and there was none to follow him.

Nebuchadnezzar was friendly toward Jeremiah because he had warned Zedekiah not to side with the Egyptians. Jeremiah chose to stay in Jerusalem, even though the city was destroyed. A short while afterward, enemies of the king of Babylon captured Jeremiah and carried him away to Egypt. That is where he died.

Jeremiah was the "Weeping Prophet." He had to warn his people all the time of the terrible fate that lay ahead of them. Jeremiah could not help sorrowing about it. But he was faithful to God Who had called him to be a prophet. However hard it was, he gave God's messages to the people of Judah until, four hundred years after Rehoboam had become its first king, the kingdom of Judah came to an end.

The Dry Bones that Became Living People

Ezekiel 37

All that was left of the tribe of Judah, once so great, was now a weary band of prisoners in the land of Babylon, or Chaldea, as it was also called. They had had a long journey from the ruins of Jerusalem, through hot and thirsty deserts. Many had died by the wayside, but when they reached the land of the Babylonians they were not treated cruelly. It was a fertile land, and they were even given plots of land on which they could grow food for themselves. Some of them went to work in the cities. A few even became important officials in the king's palace.

The best of all was that they were not made to worship the idols of the Babylonians, but were allowed to serve the one true God of Heaven and Earth. They started schools for their young people, to teach them God's laws. They built special places where they could worship every sabbath. But this was not their own land. It was not home. Sometimes they were very homesick and sad. They would even sing of their longing to return to Jerusalem. One of those songs is in the Bible, in the Book of Psalms. Psalm 137 tells us how they mourned.

The Lord was good to these people. He did not turn away from them. There were still prophets, whom God used as His messengers to the people. One was Daniel. Another was Ezekiel, who saw strange visions of angels and the throne of God.

Once in a vision, Ezekiel was carried away into a wide valley.

When he looked around, he found there were men's bones scattered all around, as if there had once been a great battle there. Then the Lord spoke to him: "Son of man, can these bones come to life?" Ezekiel answered: "O Lord, Thou knowest if they can come to life again." Then God said to him: "Preach to the bones, and say to them, 'O dry bones, listen to the word of the Lord. This is what the Lord says to you: I will make the breath of life come into you again, and make sinews and flesh come on you. You will live. You will know that I am the Lord.' "

Ezekiel obeyed, and as he spoke, there was a great noise. The scattered bones came together, and sinews and flesh and skin formed on them. But there was no breath in them. Then God spoke to him again and said: "Preach to the breath now. Tell it to come from the four winds, and make these bodies live." So Ezekiel did. And those bodies stood on their feet, like a great army, filling the whole valley. Then God said to Ezekiel: "Son of man, these bones represent the whole house of Israel. They feel that there is no hope for them any longer. But, as life has come into these dead bones, I will bring life into the house of Israel again. I will gather them from among the heathen. I will take them back to their own land. They shall be a nation once more. I will be their God, and they shall be My people. Israel and Judah will not be separate any more, but will live as one people in their own land."

When Ezekiel told his people that wonderful message from God, they took courage and looked forward with joy to the day God would lead them home once more.

Jewish Prisoners in the Palace of Babylon

Daniel 1 and 2

When Jehoiakim was king of Judah, Nebuchadnezzar of Babylon came and besieged Jerusalem. When the city surrendered, Nebuchadnezzar took away the king and a number of the princes as prisoners to Babylon.

When they arrived, Nebuchadnezzar told the ruler of the servants in his palace to select from among the prisoners a group of young men who could be trained to work in the palace.

Among these young men were Daniel, Hananiah, Mishael and Azariah. Those were their Jewish names. The ruler of the palace had them changed to Chaldean names. Daniel became Belteshazzar. Hananiah became Shadrach. Mishael became Meshach. Azariah became Abednego. The king wanted these men to have the very best food. He had some of the dishes from the royal table sent to them. Since this food had first been offered to the Babylonian idols, the young men would not eat it.

When they told the palace ruler they would not eat the food, he was very worried. He loved these young men. He was afraid that if they did not eat the rich food the

king sent, they would become thinner. He knew the king would be angry with him. But Daniel said to him: "Put us to the test for ten days. Give us only vegetables and water. Then examine us, and see if we are thinner than the men who eat the meat that comes from the king's table. If we are, then you can change the food we eat." After ten days that ruler was amazed. The four young men looked fatter and healthier than all the others! He took them in to King Nebuchadnezzar's throne-room, to be tested by the king. The king asked them all kinds of questions. He found them to be ten times more clever than all the magicians and astrologers in his kingdom. The king gave them the highest posts in the land.

One day the king called in all his wise men. He had dreamed a dream. Now he wanted very much to know what it meant. But even though he was very worried about it, he could not remember the dream. All the same, he told his wise men that if they could not tell him the dream, and explain its meaning to him, he would have them all cut to pieces.

As you can imagine, the men were very worried. How could they possibly explain a dream that the king could not even remember? Then Daniel stepped in. He went to Arioch, the chief of the royal guard. Daniel told him not to kill the wise men yet. After that he went to the king and asked to be given a little time. If given more time, David told the king, he would tell him the dream and explain it.

When the king agreed, Daniel went back to his friends, Hananiah, Mishael and Azariah. He asked them to pray with him that God would show mercy to them and reveal to them the secret. God answered their prayer. That night in a vision God told the whole matter to Daniel.

In the morning Daniel went to Arioch and asked to be taken to the king. The captain took Daniel immediately to Nebuchadnezzar. The king asked him: "Are you able to tell me what I dreamed, and what my dream means?" Then Daniel answered: "The wise men of Babylon, the astrologers and magicians, cannot tell the king the secret of his dream. But there is a God in heaven that reveals secrets. He knows everything, and has told me, His servant, the meaning of the dream. This is your dream. O king, You saw a great statue, which was beautifully made, but terrible to look at. Its head was made of gold, its chest and arms of silver, its stomach and sides of brass, its legs of iron, its feet partly of iron and partly of clay. While you watched, a rock not cut out by human hand smashed against the feet of the statue and broke them to pieces. The whole statue fell to the

ground. The gold, silver, brass, iron and clay lay in pieces on the ground, and became like chaff on a threshing-floor. The pieces were so fine that the wind blew them away. But the rock became a great mountain, and filled the whole world. This was the dream. Now I will tell you the meaning of it. God has given you this dream so that you may know what is going to happen in the future. You are the golden head of the image, for

God has given you a great kingdom. The chest and arms of silver are a kingdom that will come after yours, but will not be so great. The third kingdom, of brass, will rule over all the world. It will be followed by a fourth kingdom, as strong as iron, that will conquer all its enemies. But the feet of the image were partly clay and partly iron. They tell of a kingdom that will be partly strong and partly weak and easily broken. Each kingdom will be weaker than the one before it, until this last kingdom comes, that will break to pieces, when the rock not cut out

by human hand smashed against it. That rock will be God's own kingdom that will not pass away. Like the rock in the image it will break to pieces all the other kingdoms, and will grow and grow and take the place of all others. It will stand for ever, a kingdom over the whole earth."

When Nebuchadnezzar heard this, he was so amazed that he threw himself down and worshiped Daniel as if he were a god. At the same time, he did not forget what Daniel had said. "Truly," he said, "your God is a God of gods and a Lord of kings and a revealer of secrets."

Then he made Daniel a great man in the land and ruler of the province of Babylon and gave him many gifts. Shadrach and Meshach and Abednego were not forgotten either. They were also made important officials in the province of Babylon.

The Golden Image and the Fiery Furnace

Daniel 3

Nebuchadnezzar knew the greatness of God, but he did not understand that he must not worship idols. Not long after Daniel had told him his dream and explained it to him, Nebuchadnezzar had his workmen make a great statue of a man. The statue was covered with gold from head to toes. It was ninety feet high and nine feet wide. Nebuchadnezzar had it set up on the plain of Dura near to Babylon.

Then he sent heralds out into all the country round about. They told the princes and governors and judges and treasurers and all the other important people that they must come to a great service where they would worship the idol Nebuchadnezzar had set up. When they came to the idol, they would find a number of musicians there. When the musicians played on their instruments, all the people must fall down and worship. If they did not they would be thrown into a great furnace and be burned to death.

When the music sounded, there were three men who stood there and would not bow down and worship. These men were Shadrach, Meshach, and Abednego. Daniel was away that day. Some of the Babylonians went straight to tell the king, and he had the men brought before him. Nebuchadnezzar was furious with them for not listening. He told them that he would have the trumpets sounded again and the music played once more. If they did not do as he commanded, he would certainly have them thrown into the furnace and no god would be able to save them. But those three

were very brave men. Without a moment's doubt they answered: "O king, we are ready to give you our answer right now. If you have us thrown into the furnace, the God Whom we worship is able to save us if it is His will. But even if it is not His will, we tell you now, O king, that we will not bow down and worship before your golden idol, nor any other of the gods of Babylon."

Nebuchadnezzar was very angry when he heard that. He gave orders that the furnace should be stoked until it was seven times as hot as usual. Then the three men were to be bound with ropes and thrown into the fire. When they were thrown in, the fire was so

hot that the soldiers who threw them in, were burned up by the flames. Shadrach, Meshach and Abednego fell right into the middle of the furnace.

The king was watching what happened. Suddenly he said in amazement, "Didn't we throw three bound men into the fire? But how is it that I see four men walking around in the fire, and not one of them is tied up? And the fourth man looks like the Son of God?" As soon as the heat of the fire had died, he went closer, and called out to the men: "Shadrach, Meshach, and Abednego, you servants of the most high God, come out of the furnace, and come to me." But when they came, it was only three men who came out of the fire, and those three men were still in their clothes. Not one piece of clothing had even been singed. When the king saw this, he said to all the princes and other high officials gathered there: "Blessed is the God of these three men, Who has sent His angel to save them from the fire because they would not serve any other god. I give commandment now that any person in my empire, whatever his nation or language, who says anything against the God of Shadrach, Meshach and Abednego, will be cut to pieces, and his house will be torn down."

Then the king gave to the three men higher positions than they had before. They became some of the most important men in the land of Chaldea.

The Tree That Was Cut Down But Grew Again

Daniel 4

King Nebuchadnezzar told a story of things that happened to him to all the people in his empire. The story was of a dream, of how Daniel told him the meaning of the dream, and of how the dream became true. This is what Nebuchadnezzar told the people.

One night I had a dream which made me very frightened. I could not understand what I had dreamed. I sent for all the magicians and the other wise men to tell me what it meant, but they could not. Daniel, in whose heart live the spirits of the gods, came to me and I told him my dream. This is what I had seen. I saw a great tree that reached right up to heaven. It had beautiful leaves, and so much fruit that there was enough for all to eat. The beasts of the field sheltered in its shade. The birds of the air lived in its branches. Then I saw a heavenly messenger come down, and cry out these words: "Chop down the tree, and cut off its branches. Shake off its leaves and scatter its fruit. Let the animals go away from under it, and the birds leave its branches. But leave its stump in the ground. Fasten it with a band of iron and brass. Let the grass of the field grow around it. Let it be wet by the dew of

233

heaven, and let it remain between the animals that graze round about. Let seven years go past, and let all that live know that God rules in the kingdoms of men and gives them to whoever He wishes." This is the vision I saw, O Daniel. Tell me what it means.

Then Daniel said: "O king, I wish that the dream belonged to your enemies and not to you. The tree you saw is yourself. Your kingdom is great, and reaches to the ends of the inhabited world. But the heavenly messenger who came down, told of God's verdict over you. They shall drive you away from other human beings, and you will live with the animals of the fields. You will have to eat grass like oxen. You will be wet by the dew, because you will have no roof over your head. And this will go on for seven years. But because the messenger said that the stump of the tree was to be left in the ground, the kingdom will not be taken away from you altogether. When you have learned that God is the ruler of all, then the kingdom will be given back to you again. O king, be warned. Turn away from your sins, and be merciful to the poor, and perhaps God will turn these things away from you."

This is exactly what happened to me, my people. At the end of the year I was walking in my palace, and boasting of the great city which I had built by my own power and greatness. Suddenly I heard a voice from heaven, saying: "O king Nebuchadnezzar, the word is spoken against you. The kingdom is taken away from you!" From that moment all my understanding went from me. I became like a beast of the field. I was driven away from other people. I had to live among the animals. My hair grew long like the feathers of an eagle. My nails became like birds' claws. After seven years like that, my mind became well again. I came back

to my palace. But I had learned the greatness of God. I blessed and praised Him and honored Him, Who is the everlasting King. Then my kingdom was given back to me, and I reign once more over all the lands in the empire.

"Now I, Nebuchadnezzar, praise and glorify God, Whose ways are righteous, and His works all truth, and Who is able to humble the proud."

That is the story Nebuchadnezzar, the great king of Babylon, told his people so that they would understand that there is only one King of kings.

The Writing on the Wall

Daniel 5

After Nebuchadnezzar's death, the great Babylonian empire began to break up. Nebuchadnezzar's son was murdered, and so were several of the men who followed him. The last king was Nabonidus who ruled together with his son, Belshazzar. Belshazzar was king of Babylon, while his father took care of other parts of the kingdom.

Those were dangerous times. While the Babylonian empire became weaker, there was another empire, further to the east, that was becoming stronger and stronger—the empire of the Medes and the Persians. While Belshazzar was king of Babylon, the fierce soldiers of this empire were encamped not far away, waiting for a chance to break into the city.

One night Belshazzar held a great feast for his lords. A thousand people were present. Belshazzar sent for the gold and silver vessels which Nebuchadnezzar had brought out of Jerusalem so that his guests could drink wine out of them.

While the king and all his guests were drinking and eating, Belshazzar suddenly saw something that frightened him very much. On the wall he saw the fingers of a man's hand, writing. There was no hand or body attached, that he could see. Just fingers writing! The king became pale with fright. He trembled all over. He called for the magicians and the wise men to be brought in at once to read the words on the wall to him, and tell him what they meant. He said to them: "If any man can explain this writing to me, I will clothe him in the richest robes and give him a golden chain, and make him third ruler in the kingdom."

Then the queen suddenly remembered Daniel. He was an old man now. Most of the people had forgotten the great work he had done when Nebuchadnezzar was still king. But the queen still remembered. She suggested that Daniel be called.

When he was brought, Belshazzar promised him the same reward he had offered to the other wise men. Daniel would not hear of taking the gifts, but he promised to explain the words. This is what he said: "O king, the most high God gave your forefather, Nebuchadnezzar, a great kingdom. He had much power and his wealth could not be counted. But he became proud, and thought he had won all this by his own efforts. Then God had his kingdom taken away from him, and even his understanding. He was driven out amongst the animals. Only when he had learned that

God is the Ruler of all, and gives the kingdoms of the world to those He wishes, was he allowed to rule once again. But you, O Belshazzar, have not humbled your heart, although you knew all about Nebuchadnezzar. You have become boastful, and now you have even allowed the vessels from God's Temple to be used for wine drinking. The words on the wall are God's message to you. These are the words: MENE, MENE, TEKEL, UPHARSIN. And this is what they mean. God has numbered your kingdom, and brought it to an end; you are weighed in the balance and found wanting. Your kingdom is divided and given to the Medes and the Persians."

Belshazzar gave Daniel the rewards he had promised, although Daniel had said he did not want them. During the same night the Persians captured the palace and killed Belshazzar himself. While the feast was going on, the Persian soldiers were already creeping into the city and surrounding the palace.

The Lions that Could Not Bite

Daniel 6

Darius was the king of the Persian empire. He was a Mede by birth. Darius chose one hundred and twenty princes to control the different parts of his empire. Over the princes were three presidents. Daniel was the first among the presidents. He did his work faithfully and well, but the other presidents and many of the princes were jealous of him.

They had an idea. They thought they might be able to trap him because he was so faithful to God and would not have anything to do with the worship

of idols. They worked out a very clever plan. A number of them went to the king and told him that they wanted him to make a special law that for thirty days no one was allowed to pray to any god or man except the king. Anyone who broke the law would be thrown to the lions in the king's private lion cage. Now this flattered the king. He was glad they thought so much of him, so he signed the law without argument.

When Daniel heard of the new law, he was not worried. He had always been faithful to God, and he would not change now. He went into his room. At the open window facing toward Jerusalem, he prayed to God three times a day just as he had always done.

That was the chance his enemies were waiting for. They watched him at prayer. Then they went to tell the king and to demand that Daniel be thrown to the lions. Darius was very unhappy. He tried his best to save Daniel, but there was nothing he could do. That evening at sunset, the old prophet was brought to be thrown to the lions. But before that happened, the king spoke to him to encourage him. These were the wonderful words he said: "Your God Whom you always serve, will save you." Then Daniel was put into the lion cage, which was a big cave. A stone was put over the mouth of the cave so that Daniel could not get out. The king and his lords sealed the stone with their special signets so that no one could tamper with it. Then they went away to their beds.

Darius was very sad. He would not eat, nor listen to any music from the royal musicians and that night he did not sleep at all. Early in the morning, before anyone else was awake, he went quickly to the lions' den. He called out in a sad voice: "O

Daniel, servant of the living God, is your God Whom you serve so faithfully, able to save you from the lions?" How thrilled he must have been to hear Daniel answer! "O king, may you live for ever," Daniel said. "My God sent His angel to close the lions' mouths. They have not hurt me. My God knew that I had done no wrong against Him, nor against you, either, O king!"

Then Darius told his servants to get Daniel out of the lions' den. The men who had tried to cause Daniel's death together with their wives and children were thrown in. The lions tore them to pieces as they fell in.

Darius had always loved Daniel, but now he knew the greatness of Daniel's God, too. He was never cruel again to those who served God.

The Jews Return Home

Ezra 1 to 3

King Cyrus of Persia was very fond of Daniel the prophet. He was fond of the Jewish people as well. It had been seventy years since the first of those people were carried away as prisoners by Nebuchadnezzar, the king of Babylon. The Jewish people were not thought of as prisoners any more. They lived in their own homes. They tilled their own land, but they were still not allowed to go back to Jerusalem. In the first year of the reign of Cyrus, the Lord put it into his heart to give the Jews permission to return to their own land.

He did even more than that. He issued a proclamation in which he said that God had commanded him to see that the Temple was built again in Jerusalem!

Jeremiah had prophesied many years before that the people would be taken away from Jerusalem and remain in captivity for seventy years. Isaiah had even said, two hundred years before, that the man who would send them home would be called Cyrus. There wasn't even a Persian army when Isaiah told the people. Now it was all happening. The seventy years were past. Most of the people who were brought away prisoners from Jerusalem had already died, but their children still longed to go back to their own country. How glad they were to hear Cyrus's proclamation! This is what he said: "The Lord God of heaven has given me power over all the kingdoms on earth. He has told me to build Him a house at Jerusalem. Which of you among all His people wish to go back to your own land? May the Lord bless you, and bring you safely to Jerusalem to build His house there again. I give command that wherever you stop on the way, the people of that place must help you with gifts of silver and gold and other goods, together with animals to carry these treasures. They must also bring to you their free will offerings of money for the building of the Lord's House!"

The Jews in Babylon were so thrilled at the news, that one of them composed a special Psalm, which we still read and sing. It is Psalm 126.

Many of the Jews began to get ready to go back to the land of Judah and the ruins of the city of

Jerusalem, but most of the rich men and the nobles decided to stay in Babylon. Still, they did give rich gifts to those who were returning. The king himself, although he was not a Jew, but a Persian, gave to them all the treasures which Nebuchadnezzar had brought back from the Temple when he destroyed Jerusalem. There were five thousand four hundred pieces altogether.

When the first party came together to start the long journey to Jerusalem, there were forty-two thousand three hundred and sixty of them. And what a joyful company they were. They even had two hundred singers to pro-

vide them with music on the way. On horses and mules and donkeys and camels, and some on foot, they moved along slowly. In all the villages and towns by the wayside they gathered more and more riches. By the seventh month they were all settled in Judah.

In that month all the men came together in the ruins of Jerusalem, to bring sacrifices once again to God as they had done before the exile. On the rock, which had long ago in the days of king David been the threshing floor of Ornan, they built the altar. There Joshua the high priest made the first offerings to God. Every day the

morning and evening sacrifices were offered there, but the altar stood out in the open. There was no temple as there had been long ago. Not even the foundations were left. But the work of building was soon begun. Money was paid to stonemasons and carpenters to begin setting up the new temple. The leaders sent to Tyre and Sidon for more cedar wood, just as had been done long before in the time of king Solomon.

In the second year after the Jews returned, the work was begun. Zerubbabel the prince was their leader. He saw to it that all

was done properly. One day they would be able to worship God again as their fathers had done long ago.

A New Temple Is Built on Mount Moriah

Ezra 3 to 6; Haggai 1 and 2;
Zechariah 4

When the work of Temple-building began in Jerusalem, it began with a special ceremony of the laying of the foundation. All the men of Jerusalem came together at the Temple site. All the priests and Levites were there dressed in their ceremonial robes. When the stones were laid by the builders the Levites made music with their cymbals. The priests sounded their trumpets. Then a song of praise was sung to the glory of God. This is what they sang:

"Praise the Lord, for He is good;
For His mercy endureth for
ever toward Israel."

The whole company of men shouted with joy as the stones were cemented into place. But there were a few that wept—the old men who could still remember faintly the beautiful Temple of Solomon which Nebuchadnezzar had broken down.

This is how the work of building began, with great joy and enthusiasm. But there were some who did not approve of what was being done. They were the Samaritans who lived in the north. These were the people who had married into the heathen families brought into the land when the Babylonians took away the people of Judah. They said that they served God, but they also served heathen idols. They came to Zerubbabel and asked to be allowed to help with the building of the Temple.

But Zerubbabel said to them: "You have nothing to do with us in this work. This is our work, and we have been commanded to do it by Cyrus, king of Persia." That made them very angry. From then on they did their utmost to hinder the work of the builders. They tried to frighten the people of Jerusalem by threatening to attack them. They even went so far as to send messengers to Cyrus to tell him he should stop the work that was being done in Jerusalem. They went on doing this after the death of Cyrus, even right through to the reign of Darius about twenty years later.

When Artaxerxes was king, the enemies of the Jews sent a special letter to him, complaining about the building that was going on in Jerusalem. These are some of the things they wrote: "O king Artaxerxes, this letter comes from your loyal people on the other side of the river Jordan. We are worried about what is happening at Jerusalem. If that city

is built again and the walls raised once more, the people of Judah will refuse to pay taxes. The king's revenues will be damaged. We advise the king to study the records of the empire. He will find that Jerusalem has been a rebellious city before. We are sure that once it is built up again, the people of Judah will rebel once more. The king will have no dominions on this side of the river."

Artaxerxes did not understand their hatred for the Jews. The answer he sent back to the Samaritans was this: "Your letter has been read to me. I have made my scribes search through the history of Judah. It is true. Jeru-

salem has rebelled against her rulers before. Go now, and command these men in my name to stop the work of building, until I send instructions for the builders to begin again."

The leaders of the Samaritans, Rehum and Shimshai, were very pleased to receive the letter and they rushed off at once to Jerusalem to show it to the Jews and stop the work. Everything came to a standstill. Not another stroke of work was done until the second year of the reign of king Darius.

When the Jews came back from Babylon, there was no prophet with them to bring them God's message. Now there were two men whom God used to pass on His Word. Their names were Haggai and Zechariah. Their message to the people of Jerusalem was that they should begin again with the building of the Temple and the walls of the city. These were Haggai's words: "Is it a time for you to live in your fine houses, while the house of the Lord lies in ruins? Consider your ways. Go up to the mountain, and bring wood, and build the house; and I will take pleasure in it, and I will be glorified, says the Lord. The first Temple was glorious, but this Temple will be greater still."

Zechariah, the other prophet, encouraged the people in the same way: "This is the word of the Lord to Zerubbabel, saying, Not by might, nor by power, but by

My Spirit, says the Lord of hosts. The hands of Zerubbabel have laid the foundation of this house; his hands also shall finish it."

Then Zerubbabel the prince, and Joshua the high priest, began the work of building again, and with them worked the prophets. Soon after, Tatnai the Persian governor on the west side of the river Jordan came to inspect the parts around Jerusalem. He was troubled because of the stories the enemies of the Jews told to him. He went to ask the elders in Jerusalem, and they told him of the proclamation that king Cyrus had made. Then Tatnai wrote to the new king of Persia, Darius. Darius made his wise men look through all the records of the kingdom to see if Cyrus had really commanded that the Temple should be rebuilt. Darius was a very kindhearted man. When he discovered that Cyrus had really sent out such a proclamation, he did all he could to help the people in Jerusalem. He sent orders to Tatnai to leave Zerubbabel and his people in peace to build the Temple. He even told him that part of the taxes from the province west of Jordan must be used for the work in Jerusalem.

So, twenty-one years after the work began, the Temple was completed. Zerubbabel and Joshua were still in charge, just as God's prophets, Zechariah and Haggai, had said they would be. The new Temple was not as richly decorated as Solomon's Temple had been. There was no Ark of the Covenant in the Holy of Holies any more, because it had been lost during all the fighting. It was never found again. In its place there was a white marble block. On that block the high priest sprinkled the blood of the sacrifice on the great Day of Atonement.

The Queue Who Loved
Her People

Esther 1 to 10

When Darius, king of Persia, died,
his son, Ahasuerus became king
in his place. Ahasuerus was not a
great man like his father. He was
too fond of feasting and pleasure.

In the third year of his reign,
Ahasuerus arranged a great feast
in his palace at Shushan. It lasted
for a hundred and eighty days—
nearly six months! All the princes
from the different provinces were
invited. The palace was beautifully decorated for the occasion.
No two drinking vessels were
alike, except that all were made
of gold. While the princes feasted
in the king's palace, a special feast
was held for the ladies in the
palace of the queen, who was
called Vashti.

On the seventh day of the feast,
when the king and his guests
had all had too much to drink,
Ahasuerus sent for queen Vashti
to come into the banqueting hall
and show her beauty to his guests.
It was the law of the land that no
lady was allowed to show her face
to any man except her husband.
Queen Vashti refused to come.
The king was very angry. He felt
that he had been put to shame in
front of his princes because his
wife would not obey him. He
called together his wise men to
tell him what to do. They said

that if he did not take firm action, the wives of all the other princes would become disobedient, too. He must send Vashti away at once, and make someone else queen in her place.

Then the king sent letters to all the provinces, commanding that the most beautiful young girls from all the villages and towns should be sent to Shushan, so that he could choose his new queen.

In the town of Shushan there lived a Jew called Mordecai. He had taken care of his orphan niece, Esther. She was a beautiful girl. Mordecai decided to take her to the palace. Perhaps she might be chosen as the next queen!

Esther was taken to Hegai, the king's chamberlain. She stayed under his care until one day Ahasuerus came to choose his new wife. And it was Esther he chose. Now she had a beautiful palace to live in, and all the riches she could wish for. But she could not see her beloved uncle, Mordecai, because she was the king's property, and his only. If she and her uncle wanted to tell one another anything, they had to send letters secretly by the palace servants.

Mordecai spent a lot of time at the palace gates where many of the men gathered to talk. One day he heard two men talking together. They were two of the king's chamberlains. They were planning to murder the king. At once Mordecai sent a message to Esther to tell her what was happening, and she warned the king. Both men were put to death, and the whole story of how Mordecai saved the king's life was written down in the royal history.

After this, Ahasuerus promoted one of his men, Haman the Agagite, to be the head over all the princes in the empire. Haman was the king's own right-hand man. All the people in and around the palace bowed before Haman, but one man would not. That man was Mordecai. As a faithful Jew, he would not bow before anyone except God. That made Haman angry, because he was a very proud man. He decided that Mordecai must be killed, and all the other Jews in the empire as well. He did not know that the queen herself was Jewish, because Mordecai had told Esther she must not tell anyone about this.

He went to the king with his complaint against the Jews. Haman promised that if he was allowed to have them all put to death, he would see to it that this terrible deed would cost the king nothing. He would pay the whole cost of it into the king's treasure house himself.

Ahasuerus did not understand what this was all about, but he trusted Haman. The king gave Haman permission to do what he wanted. So Haman sent out a proclamation, sealed with the king's own seal, into all parts of the land. The proclamation said that on the thirteenth day of the twelfth month, the month which they called Adar, all the Jews should be killed—men, women, and even little children. The proclamation said all who helped to kill them could take their riches for themselves.

When Mordecai heard this, he was terribly upset. In his mourning he tore his clothes, and put on sackcloth and rubbed ashes on his face.

Esther Appears Before the King

The queen had not been told about Haman's proclamation, but her servants came to tell her about the way Mordecai was mourning. She sent clothes to him to put on instead of the sackcloth, but he would not have them. When they were brought back, she asked one of the king's chamberlains, Hatach, to go to Mordecai to find the reason for his sorrow. Mordecai told him the whole terrible story. Mordecai asked Hatach to beg queen Esther to speak to the king and ask him to have mercy on the Jews.

Now Esther, although she was the queen, was not allowed to go into the king's presence unless he sent for her. Anyone who broke this law could be put to death immediately. Queen Esther was afraid to go to the king. She let Mordecai know about this, but he sent a message back to her: "You are a Jewess," he said. "Do not think that you will be safer in the palace than are the rest of your people. If you say nothing, then the Jews will be saved in another way, but you and your family

will be destroyed. And you don't know if perhaps God has brought you into the palace to save your people at just such a time as this."

When she received this message, Esther sent to Mordecai. She asked him to get together all the Jews in Shushan to fast and pray for her for three days. She and her servants would fast as well. On the third day she would go to the king to plead for her people. The king might have her killed, but she would not be afraid. Mordecai did exactly as she had said.

On the third day Esther put on her finest clothes, and went to the king. When she stood in the doorway of the throne room, she looked so beautiful that he fell in love with her all over again. He stretched out his golden scepter toward her as a mark of his favor, and asked her what he could do for her. Very cleverly she invited him to bring Haman with him to a special banquet that day in her own palace. When the feast came to an end, Ahasuerus again asked Esther what she wished. She answered that on the next day they should come to another banquet and then she would tell the king.

As Haman went out of the palace, he saw Mordecai sitting beside the gate. As usual, Mordecai did not stand up or bow to Haman. When Haman's wife, Zeresh, heard this, she told him to

have a gallows put up, seventy-five feet high, and to ask the king the next morning to have Mordecai hanged from it. Then he could go in and enjoy the queen't banquet. Immediately, he sent out his servants to put up the gallows.

That night, king Ahasuerus could not sleep. He sent for one of his learned men to read to him the story of his reign. When the reader came to the record of how Mordecai had discovered the plot of his chamberlains against him, and saved his life, Ahasuerus suddenly realized that he had never rewarded Mordecai for what he had done. He sent to find out if any of the princes was in the court at the time. There was. Haman was there, waiting for a chance to speak to the king about the hanging of Mordecai. When the king sent for him, Haman was excited. Now was his chance!

The king asked him a question: "What shall the king do for the man he wishes to honor?" Haman was thrilled. He was sure the king was speaking about him; wasn't he the king's favorite? In his greed, this is how he answered: "Let the royal robes be put on him, and let him be seated on the king's horse, and have the king's crown placed on his head. Let one of the king's greatest princes lead him through the street of Shushan and proclaim to the people that this is the man the king wishes to honor."

Then Haman received a shock. The king told him to go and do all this to Mordecai the Jew. And this he had to do. How bitter he was in his heart, but he had to hide all his anger and go in that same day with the king to queen Esther's banquet.

When the meal was over, king Ahasuerus asked Esther to tell him what her request was. All she asked for she could have, even up to half of his kingdom. The king loved her very much. Then she said: "O king, if I have found favor in your sight, spare my life and the lives of my people. For I, too, am a Jew, and it is proclaimed that we must all be killed."

"But who is the man, and where is he," asked the king, "who has dared to make a proclamation like this?" Then Esther pointed to Haman and said: "This wicked man is our enemy." Haman was terrified, especially when the angry king left his wine and went out into the garden. When he returned, one of his chamberlains told him about the gallows Haman had set up to hang Mordecai. Immediately the king told them to hang Haman from the gallows. So Haman died on the gallows he had made for Mordecai.

But the law which had been sent out for the killing of the Jews on the thirteenth day of the twelfth month was a law of the Medes and the Persians. It could not be changed. What was the king to do to save Esther's people? He made a new law, that all the Jews could defend themselves and their property if they were attacked. They could gather in groups and fight against their enemies. When the thirteenth day of Adar came, very few people attacked the Jews. Those who did were badly beaten, and many of them were killed. Instead of a day of death and sorrow for the Jews, it became a day of great rejoicing. Even to this day the Jews still keep this day as a feast day, which they call Purim. In the synagogues the rabbis read to the people the story of queen Esther, and of Mordecai who became a great prince in Shushan.

The People Learn God's Law Again

During the reign of Artaxerxes, the Jews in Jerusalem were having a very hard time. Not many had come to join them from other parts of the Persian empire. They were still being troubled by the Samaritans and other people who stole their cattle and robbed their lands. Some of the Jews were very poor and had borrowed money from richer people. Now they were unable to pay back what they owed so that they became slaves in their own land. Others had married the heathen people from round about, and God's Laws and worship were being forgotten. There was no complete wall around the city of Jerusalem so that the people there lived in constant danger of attack. Ninety long years after they had begun to come back from Babylon they still were not living in safety.

Then God sent to them Ezra, the scribe and Nehemiah, the governor to help them and lead them. Ezra came to teach them God's Law again. Nehemiah came to give them courage to finish building the walls of the city.

Ezra was a priest. He was allowed by king Artaxerxes to go from Babylon to help his people in Jerusalem. Artaxerxes was very friendly to the Jews. He helped them as Cyrus had done long before. Artaxerxes commanded that all the Jews who wanted to, could go with Ezra to Jerusalem. He sent with them great amounts of silver and gold from himself and his councillors. He even promised that if they needed anything for beautifying the Temple, they could ask for it from his own treasure house. All who served God in the Temple would be free from taxes. But all the people of Jerusalem and Judea must keep the Laws of God.

When Ezra came to Jerusalem, he found that most of the people had forgotten that there was a Law of God. He called the princes together, and spoke to them very seriously. He talked especially about the way the men of Judah had married heathen wives and broken God's commandments. A very solemn time of prayer was held. Ezra cried out to God to forgive them all and to keep them faithful and obedient to His Laws in the future. Then all the people mourned before God. They promised not to break His Laws again. They sent away from them their heathen wives, and their children of mixed blood. All the men who

had broken God's Laws by marrying in this way were separated from the true people of God.

After Ezra's coming, the Law was faithfully taught in the Temple. In every village and town, a synagogue was built. There, on every Sabbath day, the elders taught the people from the book of the Law.

Ezra became the man who, by God's calling, made the people of Judea God's people once more.

How the Walls of Jerusalem were Built

Nehemiah 1 to 7

While Ezra the priest was teaching the people of Jerusalem the Law of God, another man was leading them in the work of building up the city walls. This man was Nehemiah, who had been a very important officer in the palace of the king of Persia. He was the cupbearer of king Artaxerxes, and a very faithful Jew.

The news reached Nehemiah of the very unhappy condition of his people in Jerusalem. He heard that the city walls were broken down, that the gates had been burned, and that the people were living in great poverty. When this news came to him, Nehemiah mourned and fasted. He prayed that God would forgive His people for their sins, and show him how to help them. In the course of his duties, Nehemiah went in to serve the king. The king noticed how sad Nehemiah looked. He asked Nehemiah to tell him what was wrong. When he explained his troubles to the king, Artaxerxes asked how he could help. Nehemiah prayed, and then asked the king to give him permission to go to Jerusalem to his people there. He asked the king to send messages to the governors of the provinces along the way to help

him, and enable him to get safely to Jerusalem. The king and the queen gave him permission to go. They allowed him to go to Asaph, the controller of the royal forests, to obtain from him all the timber he would need for the building work in Jerusalem.

Then with a little party of horsemen, and a large party of Jews who wanted to go back to Jerusalem, Nehemiah began the journey of nearly one thousand miles through the desert.

Nehemiah's Work in Jerusalem

When Nehemiah reached Jerusalem he did not at first tell the people why he had come. For three days he remained there very quietly. Then one night with a few men he slipped out secretly to inspect the walls and gates of the city. When he had seen clearly the ruined condition of all the walls and gates he went back to where he was staying. The next day he went to the nobles and priests and rulers. He told them his plans for the rebuilding of the wall. He explained how God had answered his prayers, and how king Artaxerxes had promised to help. Then the people took heart, and said: "Let us begin with the work!"

Every family in the city had its part in the work. Each one had its section of the wall to do, or its gate to build. Each person worked very hard. It did not matter how noble the people were, or what kind of work they did, all joined in building the city wall. There was great enthusiasm. Everyone looked forward to the finishing of the work, and the safety of Jerusalem.

But there were some people who were very angry at what was happening. Sanballat the Horonite, and Tobiah the Ammonite, and Geshem the Arabian jeered at the people of Jerusalem. They tried to hinder the work. Sanballat laughed and said the Jews would never be able to make a wall out of the heaps of rubbish in Jerusalem. Tobiah said that if a fox leaned against their wall, it would fall over. But the Jews kept on.

This made the enemies so angry that they sent armed bands to attack the Jewish workers, and to try to stop the work. But Nehemiah had an answer for that. Half the people of the city built, and the other half carried arms, and were ready to fight off the attackers. When the enemies saw the preparedness of the people of Jerusalem, they were afraid to attack.

Then Sanballat and his friends worked out another scheme. They sent a letter to Nehemiah. They asked him to meet them in a little village on the plain of Ono, so that they could discuss their differences. Nehemiah was too clever for them, though. He knew that this was a trap. He also knew that they wanted to get him away from his own people and kill him. He sent back this message: "I am doing important work and cannot come away. Why should the work be stopped while I come down to you?" Four times they sent invitations to him, but they received the same answer every time. The fifth time they wrote that it was being said among the people living around about that Jerusalem's wall was being rebuilt so that the Jews could rebel against the Persian king. Nehemiah should come and discuss the matter with Sanballat so that they could end the rumors. But Nehemiah wrote back to him: "There is no truth in this. You have made up the story yourself."

Even some of the Jews inside the city were on the side of Sanballat and his men. They tried to make Nehemiah afraid. They told him to hide himself in the Temple, because his enemies were planning to assassinate him. Nehemiah just laughed at them: "Should I hide away in the Temple to save my life? I will not do it!"

After fifty-two days of hard work, the city wall was completed. The gates could be closed at last. Watchmen were set in all the watchtowers. The people were safe at last.

The Biggest Bible Class Ever Held

Nehemiah 8 to 13; Malachi 1 to 4
When the great work of rebuilding the walls of Jerusalem was complete, Nehemiah called all the people of the city and of the towns and villages round about to a great meeting. They met in the street which led to the gate where the water-carriers came in and out of the city. Men and women, even very young boys and girls, stood or sat in that street, because this was a very important day.

A great wooden pulpit had been especially made and set up in that street. Ezra the scribe stood on the pulpit. In his hands was a copy of the Book of God's Law. When he opened the Book, all the people stood up out of respect for the Word of God. Then Ezra blessed the Name of God, and all the people answered, "Amen," and bowed their heads and worshiped.

Sentence by sentence Ezra then read the Law to them. It took from early morning until the middle of the day. Every sentence had to be translated, because the Law was written in Hebrew and all the people now spoke Aramaic, the language of Palestine. There were other men standing alongside Ezra to help in the work of teaching the people.

Some of the listeners wept when they heard the Law. They realized how often they had broken God's commandments. But Nehemiah, and Ezra, and the Levites comforted the people. They told the people they should think of this day rather as a feast day and a time for rejoicing. So the people held a great feast. They sent food and drink to the poor who had none of their own.

On the next day the elders and priests and Levites held a meeting with Ezra so that he could explain the Law to them carefully. For seven days, one after the other, Ezra taught them the Law. Then they went to teach the rest of the people. When this week of teaching came to its end, the people

confessed their sins and the sins of their forefathers to God. Then they promised that they would not allow their children to marry into the heathen nations. They promised that they would keep God's Law and love Him with all their hearts. They would be careful to keep the Sabbath day, and to bring sacrifices and offerings of money to the Temple as commanded in the Law. All the promises were written down on a great parchment roll. All the princes, Levites and priests signed it in the name of the people.

Nehemiah felt that his work in Jerusalem was now completed. He returned to the palace of the king of Persia far away in Shushan to take up again his work as the royal cupbearer.

After a few years, though, he went back to Jerusalem, to see how his own people were getting along. What he found must have made him very sad. Many of the people were working on the Sabbath day, treading out grapes to make wine and bringing in sheaves of corn into the barns, and buying and selling just as on any other day. Their promise had been completely forgotten. Nehemiah was very angry with them, and said: "Why are you doing such wickedness on the Sabbath day? Do you not remember how our fathers brought God's wrath on them through this very sin?" Then Nehemiah made a new rule. Before dark when the Sabbath began, the city gates were closed. No one was allowed to bring in any load until after the Sabbath.

Because of this new rule, some of the traders had to spend the day outside the city walls. Nehemiah saw them from the wall. He gave them a serious warning that if they were found there again he would have them thrown into prison. They did not come back again on the Sabbath day.

A little while after the days of Ezra and Nehemiah, God sent His last prophet to Judah. The name of that prophet was Malachi. He taught the people many important things, but most important of all, he taught them about the Savior Whom God would send to them. This was what he had to tell about the coming of the Savior and his forerunner: "Behold, I send My messenger and he shall prepare the way before Me: and the Lord, Whom ye seek, shall suddenly come to His temple. . . . Behold, He is coming, says the Lord of hosts. . . . I will send you Elijah the prophet before the great and terrible day of the Lord. And he shall turn the heart of the fathers to the children, and the heart of the children to their fathers; lest I come and smite the earth with a curse."

And those are the closing words of the Old Testament.

THE NEW
TESTAMENT

God's Angels Bring Amazing News

Luke 1

About four hundred years after the time of Malachi the prophet, the Jewish people made up part of the Roman empire. There had been many wars in that part of the world. Their country had belonged for a time to the Greeks, and to the Egyptians. Now it was a province of Rome called Judea. Although it had a ruler of its own, Herod, it was under the control of the Roman emperor, or Caesar Augustus.

At that time there lived in Jerusalem a priest called Zacharias. His wife was called Elisabeth. They had no children, and they didn't expect to have any, because they were both old. One day Zacharias was carrying out his duties in the Temple. An angel appeared to Zacharias, standing at the right-hand side of the altar of incense. Zacharias was frightened. He had never seen an angel before. Then the angel spoke to him: "Do not be afraid, Zacharias. Your prayers for a child have been heard. Elisabeth your wife will bear you a son, and you must give him the name of John.

He will be great in God's sight. He will not drink wine or strong drink. His heart will be filled with the Holy Ghost from his birth. Because of his ministry, many of the children of Israel will be turned back to the Lord their God. He will go before the Lord in the spirit and power of Elijah to turn the hearts of the fathers and those that are disobedient to the wisdom of the just. As he does so, he will make ready a people prepared for the Lord."

Zacharias was amazed at those words. How could he and Elisa-beth have a son? They were both too old. He told the angel so, but the angel answered: "I am Gabriel. I stand in the presence of God and have been sent to bring you this message. But to prove that the message comes from God, this will be the sign. You will be unable to speak until the baby is born, because you have not believed my words."

When Zacharias came out of the holy place, he could not speak a word.

Six months after this the same angel, Gabriel, was sent by God to a young maiden in a little town called Nazareth. Her name was Mary. She was a cousin of Elisa-beth, the wife of Zacharias. Mary was soon going to marry a man called Joseph, a carpenter. Joseph was one of the descendants of David.

When the angel appeared in the room where Mary was sitting, he greeted her with these words: "Hail, favored one! The Lord is with you, and you are richly blessed above all women." When she saw him, Mary was frightened. She could not understand what he meant. But Gabriel comforted her with these words: "Do not be afraid, Mary. You have found favor in God's sight. You are going to have a Son. You must call Him Jesus. He will be great, and will be called the Son of the Most High. The Lord God will give Him the throne of His father David. He will reign over the house of Jacob forever. His kingdom will never come to an end."

But Mary could not understand how this could happen since she had not known a man. The angel explained: "The Holy Ghost will come upon you. The power of the Most High will overshadow you. Therefore the Holy One who is born will be called the Son of God." Then the angel went further by telling her that her cousin Elisabeth was going to have a baby, too. He would be born in three months' time.

Then Mary bowed her head and said: "Behold, I am the Lord's servant. Let it happen to me as He wishes." Then the angel went away from her.

Mary was very excited. At once she packed some clothes, and started on a long journey to go and see Elisabeth and tell her what had happened. When Mary arrived, Elisabeth said to her: "Blessed are you among women, and blessed is the Son who will be born to you! How is it that the mother of my Lord has come to visit me?"

Then Mary, filled with God's Spirit, sang a lovely song of praise and joy, which is still sung in many churches today. We call it the 'Magnificat.'

Three months later Elisabeth's son was born. When the infant was eight days old, they came to circumcise him. They were going

to call him Zacharias after his father, but his mother stopped them and said: "No! He must be called John." They said to her: "But there is no one in your family by that name!" Zacharias could not speak, so they tried to ask him in sign language what the name should be. Zacharias asked by signs for a writing tablet, and on it he wrote: "His name is John." As he wrote, his tongue was loosened, and he was able to speak once again. Not only did he speak, but he sang a song of praise to God, a song which, like Mary's, is still sung in churches today. It is called the 'Benedictus'.

This was the child who later became the greatest of God's prophets, John the Baptist.

Just a Baby in a Manger

Matthew 1; Luke 2

Soon after the birth of John the Baptist, an angel came to Joseph in a dream. Joseph was the carpenter from Nazareth who was going to marry Mary, the cousin of Elisabeth, John's mother. Joseph was a worried man, because he knew that Mary was going to have a child. He could not understand how this could have happened. But the angel brought him a comforting message from God. "Do not be upset, Joseph," he said. "The baby Mary is going to have is a special gift from God. It is God Who has brought that baby to life in her. She will have a Son. You must give Him the name of Jesus, which means 'Jehovah is salvation,' because He will save His people from their sins. All this is happening to fulfil the words of the prophets about the Savior God has promised to His people for many centuries now."

Not long afterward Joseph and Mary were married, and Joseph looked after her carefully. At this time the Roman emperor, Augustus, decided that a census should be taken in all his empire. He commanded Cyrenius, the governor of Syria, to see that this was done in Palestine. All the people were told to go to the nearest town. There the people were to tell to the special census officers their names and all about them. Joseph and Mary went from Nazareth to the little town of Bethlehem. It was very near the time for Mary's baby to be born. Because it was quite a long journey, nearly a hundred miles the way they had to go, Mary rode on the back of a donkey. When they reached the little town of Bethlehem after that very tiring journey, there were so many people there already that there was no room for Mary and Joseph in the inn. The only place that could be found for them was a stable. There Mary and Joseph had to spend the night. During that night Mary's baby was born. Because there was no bed for Him, they wrapped Him in swaddling clothes and laid Him down on the straw in a manger.

Out in the fields near Bethlehem was a little group of shepherds, looking after their flock of sheep. Suddenly a great light shone around them, and they saw standing by them, an angel from God. They were terrified, but the angel said to them: "Don't be afraid. I have come to bring you

wonderful news, which will fill you with joy. Tonight in the city of David, in Bethlehem, a Savior has been born for you. He is Christ the Lord. This is how you will know Him. You will find a little new-born Baby, wrapped in swaddling clothes, and lying in a manger."

And as he finished speaking, the shepherds saw around him a large number of angels, all shining bright. They were praising God, and this is what they sang: "Glory to God in the highest, and peace on earth to men with whom He is pleased!"

As the shepherds watched in amazement, the angels dis-

appeared. Once again the night was dark. The shepherds decided they must go at once into Bethlehem. They wanted to see this Baby, about whom God had sent the angel to tell them. When they came to the stable, they found Mary and Joseph and the Baby lying in a manger, just as the angel had said. Then they went out and told everyone they met of the wonderful thing that had happened.

When the Baby was eight days old, He was circumcised and given the name of Jesus, just as the angel had told Joseph.

It was a law among the Jews that after the first son was born in any family, the parents must go up to the Temple in Jerusalem and offer a sacrifice of thanksgiving to God. Because Joseph was a poor man, the sacrifice he took was two young pigeons.

When Joseph and Mary carried Jesus into the Temple, they met there an old man called Simeon. Simeon was a godly man who was longing for the coming of the Savior God had promised. God's Spirit had told him, in his heart, that he would not die until he had seen the Savior. On the day when Joseph and Mary took the little Jesus to the Temple, God's Spirit sent Simeon there, too. When the old man saw Jesus, he knew that He was the Savior. He took Jesus in his arms. Then he praised God and said: "Now, Lord, let Thy servant go in peace, as Thou hast promised; for my eyes have seen Thy salvation, which Thou hast prepared in the presence of all nations."

Joseph and Mary were amazed at what was being said about Jesus. Then Simeon prayed for God's blessing on them both. As he gave back the Baby, he said to Mary: "This Child is appointed for the fall and rise of many in Israel, and for a sign of God that will be opposed. A sword of sorrow will go even through your heart, but He will reveal the true nature of people's thoughts."

In the Temple that day there was also a very old lady called

Anna, who was a prophetess and brought God's messages to the people. She spent most of her time in the Temple, fasting and praying. When she saw the Baby in Mary's arms, she also praised God.

It was just a little Baby Who was born in Bethlehem. But God's angels and His Holy Spirit told many people in Bethlehem and in Jerusalem that He was the Savior about Whose coming all the prophets had spoken.

Wise Men Come to Worship

Matthew 2

Not long after Jesus was born in Bethlehem, wise men from the east arrived in Jerusalem. Like most of the wise men in those days, they spent much of their time following the stars. These men had seen one strange star, which seemed to move ahead of them toward the west. The Bible does not tell us how they found out, but they knew that this star would lead them to the one who was born King of the Jews.

When they arrived in Jerusalem they asked everyone they met where they could find the new-born King, for they had come to worship Him. No one could tell them, but the news soon reached the ears of king Herod. He was very

worried and so were many other people in Jerusalem. Herod quickly called together a meeting of the chief priests and the scribes. He asked them where the Scriptures said the Christ, the promised King of the Jews, would be born. They answered: "In Bethlehem in the land of Judah, as the prophet wrote it down, 'And you, Bethlehem, in the land of Judah, are by no means the least among the leaders of Judah, for out of you shall come forth a Ruler, who will shepherd My people, Israel.'"

When Herod heard that, he spoke to the wise men in private. He asked them to tell him when they had first seen the star which was leading them to the Christ. Then he sent them to Jerusalem and told them when they had found the Baby to come back and tell him, "so that I can also go and worship Him." That is what he said, but he did not really want to worship Christ at all. He had made an awful plan.

After they had spoken to the king, the wise men started on their journey to Bethlehem. As they journeyed, they found that the star was going on ahead of them once more. That made them very glad. They knew they were on the right road. The star led them until it stopped right above the place where the Child lay.

When the wise men went inside, they saw the Baby Jesus, with His mother, Mary. Immediately they threw themselves down and worshiped Him. Then they gave to Him the rich presents they had brought. There was gold, and frankincense, and myrrh. Wise men and rich men though they were, they knew that this Baby was the King of all.

That night they were warned in a dream. They must not go back to Herod as he had asked them to do. They must return to their own land by a different way.

When they had gone, an angel appeared to Joseph in a dream. The angel told Joseph that he must take Mary and the Baby and flee far away into Egypt as quickly as possible. So that very night Joseph took Mary and Jesus, and slipped out of Bethlehem under cover of the darkness. After a long and tiring journey they arrived in the land of Egypt. There they stayed until an angel brought them the news that king Herod had died. Then they went back, but not to Bethlehem. Instead they went to Nazareth, where Joseph and Mary lived before Jesus was born. The angel had warned Joseph to take his little family to Egypt for a very good reason. Herod had sent out his soldiers to murder all the little boys of two years old or less, who lived in Bethlehem or round about. He thought in that way the Baby born to be King would be killed, and his own throne would be kept safe. But Jesus was already away in Egypt.

The Little Boy Grows Up

Luke 2

Jesus of Nazareth grew up just as any other little boy did in Palestine in those days. We know very little about those early days in His life. In fact there is only one story in the Bible about His lifetime between being a baby and when He began to preach and teach at the age of about thirty.

Every year Joseph and Mary went up to Jerusalem to celebrate the Feast of the Passover. In the year that Jesus turned twelve, He went up with them. At the end of the feast, all the people who had come to Jerusalem from Nazareth began the long journey homeward together. Joseph and Mary thought that Jesus was with the rest of the boys and girls. At the end of the first day's traveling, they went to look for Him, but no one knew where He was.

Then Joseph and Mary turned back toward Jerusalem, looking for Jesus as they went. On the

third day they found Him, sitting in the Temple, listening to the Doctors of the Law and asking them questions.

Mary and Joseph were very upset by now. Mary went straight to Him and said: "Son, why have you treated us like this? Your father and I have looked for you all over. We were afraid." But Jesus answered: "How is it that you looked for Me and worried about Me? Do you not understand that I must be busy with the work My Father has given Me?" But they could not understand what He was telling them.

Then Jesus went back with Joseph and Mary to Nazareth and listened to them as a good son should listen to his parents.

Only a Voice

Matthew 3; Mark 1; Luke 3
Jesus of Nazareth did not leave His hometown nor begin to teach until He was about thirty years old. His cousin, John, began earlier to preach to people about their sins against God. John was six months older than Jesus, but he had never met his cousin. Before he began to teach, he lived in the wilderness, away from men, where he could think and pray. He even ate locusts and the wild honey he was able to find in hol-

low trees and in cracks in the rocks. His clothing was a cloak made of camel's hair, with a leather belt round his waist. Out there in the wilderness God spoke to John, and gave him a message to preach to the people of Judea.

When John began to preach, the people flocked from all parts of the land to listen. This is what he told them: "I am the voice of one crying in the wilderness, 'Prepare for the coming of the Lord. Make ready your hearts to receive Him. Repent of your sins, and seek the forgiveness of God'." And as they listened, many saw how wickedly they had lived, and grieved over it. Then they went to John where he was teaching alongside the river Jordan. There he baptized them when they turned away from their sins. That is why he was given the name of John the Baptist.

While they listened to John the Baptist, some of the people began to wonder. Who was this man? Could he perhaps be the Messiah Whom God had promised?

But John said to them, "I am only a voice crying in the wilderness. I am the messenger the prophet Isaiah wrote about long ago, who would come to prepare the way for the Messiah. After me comes One Who is mightier than I am. I am not even fit to stoop down and untie the laces of His sandals. I baptized you with water, but He will baptize you with the Holy Spirit."

One day when John was preaching to a large crowd beside the river Jordan, he looked up and saw Jesus coming toward him. The Spirit of God told him who this was, and he cried out, "Look! The Lamb of God Who takes away the sin of the world!"

But John was most surprised when Jesus came to him and asked to be baptized as well. He

protested, but Jesus told him this was all part of God's plan. So John baptized Jesus in the river Jordan. Then an amazing thing happened. As Jesus went up out of the water, the heavens were opened, and John saw the Spirit of God descending like a dove. Then a voice spoke from heaven. "This is My beloved Son, in Whom I am well pleased."

The Lord Jesus Defeats the Devil; and Chooses His Disciples

Matthew 4; Mark 1; Luke 4; John 1

After Jesus was baptized by John in the river Jordan, the Spirit of God led Him into the wilderness to enter into battle against the devil. For forty days and nights He ate nothing at all, and all that time the devil tempted Him. At the end of the forty days, He was very hungry. Then the devil attacked Him more fiercely than ever.

First, he came to the Lord and said to Him: "If Thou art the Son of God, command that these stones turn into loaves of bread." But the Lord answered him at once: "It is written in God's Word, 'Man shall not live on bread alone, but on every word that comes from the mouth of God.'"

Then the devil took Him into the holy city of Jerusalem. The devil took Jesus to the highest place of the Temple and said to Him: "If You *are* the Son of God, throw Yourself down; because, after all, it is written in God's Word, 'He shall give His angels charge concerning You, and they shall bear You up on their hands so that You do not strike Your foot against a stone.'" But Jesus said: "On the other hand, it is also written, 'You shall not tempt the Lord your God.'"

After that, the devil took Him away into a high mountain and showed Him all the world's kingdoms in their glory. Then he said: "I will give You all these things if only You will bow down and worship me." Then Jesus said: "Get away from Me, Satan! For it is written, 'You shall worship the Lord your God only'."

That was the end of the devil's attacks for the time being.

One day as He walked beside the Sea of Galilee, Jesus saw two fishermen casting a net into the sea to catch fish. They were brothers, and their names were Simon Peter and Andrew. Jesus called out to them: "Follow Me, and I will make you fishers of men." At once they left their nets, and went with Him.

A little further on He came upon two other brothers, James and John. They were in a boat with their father, Zebedee, busy mending the nets. Like the other brothers, James and John followed Jesus at once.

The next day in Galilee, Jesus met a man named Philip. When Jesus called him to follow, Philip came with the other four who were already disciples.

Philip wanted his friends to know about Jesus, too. Philip went off quickly to speak to a special friend called Nathanael. When he found him he said excitedly: "We have found the One of Whom Moses in the Law, and the prophets wrote, Jesus of Nazareth!"

But Nathanael answered: "Can anything good come out of Naza-reth?" Philip just answered: "Come and see!"

When Jesus saw Nathanael coming toward Him, he greeted him with these words, "Behold, a sincere Israelite, whose heart is altogether honest!" Nathanael answered in surprise: "But how do You know me?" But how much more surprised he was, when Jesus said: "I saw you before Philip called you, when you were sitting under the fig tree!" Then Nathanael could only say: "Rabbi, You are the Son of God, You are the King of Israel!"

That is how the Lord Jesus began to choose His disciples. There

were others—Simon the Zealot, Bartholomew, Jude, James the son of Alphaeus, Judas Iscariot, and Thaddeus. Altogether there were twelve men who went with Him during all the three years which He moved around preaching and healing and doing all kinds of miracles.

Water Turned into Wine at a Wedding

John 2 and 3

Jesus had very serious matters to speak about to the people of Galilee and Judea, but that did not mean that He did not have a good time. On the third day after Nathanael had come to Him to be one of His disciples, Jesus went with His new friends to a wedding feast to which He had been invited. The wedding was in the little village of Cana in Galilee. Mary, His mother, was there. The feast was a very happy one until they ran out of wine. How ashamed the hosts must have felt that there was not enough food and drink for everyone. But Mary had an idea. She went to Jesus and told Him that there was no wine.

At the entrance to the house there were six large stone water jars for the visitors to carry out the special ceremony of purifying themselves by washing their hands and their feet when they came in. Each of the jars held about twenty-five gallons of water. Jesus told the servants to fill them all to the brims with clean water. Then He told them to dip out some of the water and take it to the master of ceremonies.

When this man tasted it, he was surprised. He had been told that there was no wine, and now they brought him the best wine they had at the feast so far. He did not know where it had come from—but the servants knew! He went to the bridegroom to ask him what this meant. "At all feasts," he said, "they serve the best wine first, and afterward, when people have drunk quite a lot, they bring out what is not so good. But you have kept the best until last."

This was the first miracle done by our Lord Jesus; later He would do many more.

When the feast was over, Jesus went down to Capernaum with His family and His disciples and spent a few days there. Then He went to Jerusalem for the Passover Feast in the Temple there.

One night while Jesus was in Jerusalem, one of the Pharisees, a man called Nicodemus, came to see Him under cover of darkness. The Pharisees were a group of very strictly religious Jews. The Pharisees were proud of the careful way they kept the Law. Nicodemus was afraid of what the

other Pharisees would say about him if he went openly to Jesus, but he felt he must speak to Jesus.

"Master," he said, "we know that You are a teacher Who has come from God. No one could otherwise do the signs that You do." Jesus answered: "Truly, I tell you, that unless a person is born again, he cannot see the kingdom of God." Nicodemus did not understand what He meant, and that He was speaking about the new hearts we all need from God. "How can a person be born when he is old?" he asked. "How can anyone be born twice?" Jesus answered: "I tell you that unless you are born of water and God's Spirit, you cannot enter into the kingdom of God." By this He meant that we must be born of God's Spirit, otherwise we cannot become the children of God. He told Nicodemus that this was all very mysterious. Just as we cannot tell where the wind begins or where it is going, so we cannot tell how God's spirit gives the new birth. Nicodemus was still puzzled.

Then Jesus said to him: "As Moses lifted up the brass snake on a pole in the wilderness to save the people of Israel, so the Son of Man must also be lifted up so that all who believe in Him may have everlasting life. Because God so loved the world that He gave His only begotten Son, so that whoever believed in Him should not perish but have everlasting life. God did not send His Son into the world to condemn the world, but so that we could be saved. But those who will not come to the Son have condemned themselves already."

In this way Jesus was beginning to teach about how He would have to die on the cross to save His people from their sins.

The End of John the Baptist's Life

Matthew 14; Mark 6; Luke 3; John 3 and 4

When Jesus began to teach and to do miracles, many of John the Baptist's disciples left him and went to follow Jesus. John had expected this. He knew it must be so. Once he spoke to his disciples about Jesus and said to them: "He must increase, but I must decrease."

At that time the wife of king Herod Antipas, whose name was Herodias, was a very wicked woman. She hated to hear of this man going around teaching people about God. She persuaded Herod to have John arrested and thrown into prison. Herod himself was very interested in what John said, but Herodias hated him because he had said that it was not lawful for Herod to have her as his wife. She was really the wife

of his brother, Philip. She hated John so much that she wanted Herod to have him killed, but Herod was afraid to do that, because he knew that John was a holy and a good man Instead, he had John shut up in prison in the castle of Machaerus, away to the east of the Dead Sea. Some while afterward, though, on Herod's birthday, Herodias' daughter, Salome, came to dance for Herod. He enjoyed her dancing so much that he promised to give her anything she asked for as a reward. She went to ask her mother what she should ask for as her reward. That gave the terrible Herodias the chance she was waiting for. Back went Salome to Herod, and asked as her mother had told her: "Give me on a plate the head of John the Baptist." Herod was terribly upset, but because he had made a promise and did not want to break it in front of all his guests, he sent soldiers to John's cell to behead John and to bring his head to Salome.

So ended the life of the man Jesus Christ called the greatest of all the prophets.

The Stranger at the Well

One day when Jesus of Nazareth was traveling through the land of Samaria on His way from Judea to Galilee, He came to a city called Sychar. Just outside the city was a well which Jacob had made many centuries before. Because Jesus had traveled far and it was very hot. He sat down beside the well. It was now noon. While He sat there, a Samaritan woman came from the city to draw water. He asked her to give Him some water to drink. His disciples had gone into the city to buy food and He had no vessel with which to draw water out of the well.

Now, this surprised the Samaritan woman very much because He was clearly a Jew. The Jews ordinarily would have nothing to do with the Samaritans whom they looked upon as "unclean." She asked Him about it, and this was His answer: "If you knew Who was asking you for water, you would instead have asked Him,

and He would have given you the water of life." She said to Him: "But how could you? The well is deep, and you have nothing to draw water with. Where could you get the water of life you speak about?" She did not understand what He meant, but then He said: "Everyone who drinks water from this well will become thirsty again, but whoever drinks of the water that I give shall never thirst. The water that I give will become in him like a fountain overflowing to eternal life."

Then she said, still not understanding what He meant, "Sir, give me this water so that I will not get thirsty again, nor have to walk this long distance any more to draw water." Jesus' only answer was: "Go and get your husband and come here."

At that the Samaritan woman became very ashamed and said: "I have no husband." Jesus said to her: "You have told the truth. You have no husband. You have had five husbands, but the one you are living with now is not your husband. That is true." The woman said to Him: "Sir, I see that you are a prophet." Then she tried to change the subject. "Please tell me which of us are correct, the Jews or we Samaritans. You Jews say we must worship at Jerusalem in the Temple there, but our people believe we should worship here on Mount Gerizim." But Jesus answered:

"Woman, you do not know what you worship. The time is coming when God will be worshiped in many places other than this mountain or Jerusalem. God is a Spirit, and all who worship Him must do so in spirit and in truth and will be able to worship Him wherever they are."

Then she said: "I know that the Messiah is coming. When He comes He will teach us all things." Jesus said to her: "I who speak to you am He."

At this point the disciples came back from the city. They were surprised that Jesus was talking to this woman, but they did not say anything about it. In the meantime the woman left her waterpot and rushed into the city, and said excitedly to the men she knew, "Come and see a man who told me all the things that I have done. This is the Christ."

While this was happening, the disciples showed Jesus the food they had bought, and asked Him to eat. But He said: "I have food to eat that you do not know about." They wondered where He could have obtained food, but He said to them: "My food is to do the will of My Father Who sent Me, and to complete the work He has given Me. Do you not say, 'There are still four months and then comes the harvest'? I say to you. Open your eyes and look. The fields are already white for harvest." By that He meant that there were many people whose hearts were ready to receive the message of salvation. Already fruit was being reaped for eternal life.

For two days Jesus stayed on in Sychar, and many hearts were made glad because of what He told them. Then He continued on His journey to Galilee.

The Lord Jesus Heals in Capernaum; and There Is Trouble in Nazareth

John 4; Luke 4

Once in Galilee, Jesus made His way to Cana where He had turned water into wine. While He was there, a nobleman, one of the officers in king Herod's court, heard of Him. The nobleman went from Capernaum to speak to Him. He was worried because his son was lying at home, very ill. He asked Jesus to heal his son. "Please," he asked, "come down to Capernaum before my son dies." But Jesus said to him: "Go back home; your son lives." The officer believed what Jesus said, and started off home. On the way he met some of his slaves who were out looking for him. They told him that his son was getting better. When he heard this, the official asked them at what time the boy had begun to get better.

It was at the exact moment Jesus had said to him: "Your son lives."

Then that man believed in Jesus, and all his family believed in Jesus, too.

From Cana Jesus went on to Nazareth, where He had grown up. On the Sabbath day He went to the synagogue service in His usual way. But this time when it was time for the reading of the Bible, He took the scroll and began to read from the book of Isaiah. This is what he read: "The Spirit of the Lord is upon me, because He has anointed me to preach the gospel to the poor. He has sent me to heal the broken-hearted, to proclaim release to the captives and recovery of sight to the blind, to set at liberty those who are trodden down, to preach the acceptable year of the Lord." Then Jesus closed the scroll, and said, "Today this Scripture is being fulfilled in front of you all." Then He began to preach to them. All who listened were surprised at the grace of His words. They asked one another, "But isn't this Joseph's son?"

Jesus said to them: "No doubt you will say to Me the proverb, 'Physician, heal thyself, do here also what we hear you did in Capernaum.' But I say to you that no prophet is honored in his own land. And I remind you that in the days of Elijah, when there was a drought for three-and-a-half years, there were many widows

in Israel; but Elijah was not sent to any of them, but only to a widow in Zarephath in the land of Sidon. And there were many lepers in Israel during the lifetime of the prophet Elisha but none of them was cleansed of his leprosy, except Naaman the Syrian."

When they heard that, the people in the synagogue were very angry. They rushed forward and dragged Jesus out of the town to the brow of the hill on which the town was built. They wanted to throw Him down a cliff and kill Him, but miraculously He passed through the midst of them, and went safely away.

From Nazareth He went to Capernaum and taught the people there in the synagogue each Sabbath day.

A Net Full of Fish

Matthew 4; Mark 1; Luke 4 and 5
In the town of Capernaum, Jesus did some wonderful miracles and showed that His power was from God.

One day while He was speaking in the synagogue, a man in whose heart was an unclean spirit, began to shout at Him. "Leave us alone," the demon in him cried out. "What have we to do with You, Jesus of Nazareth? Have

You come to destroy us? I know that You are the Holy One of God."

Jesus spoke sharply to the demon and said: "Be silent, and come out of him." The demon threw the man down on the floor in a kind of fit. When the man woke up, he was normal, and the demon did not come back to his heart again. When the people saw what happened, they were amazed. What power Jesus had—just to speak, and the demon fled before Him! The fame of it spread through all the countryside.

All Jesus' teaching was with such authority that the people who listened to Him were amazed. He did not teach as the scribes did, with all manner of long-winded arguments. His words came with power and truth that no one could argue against. Day by day He did wonderful deeds in that little town. Simon Peter's mother-in-law was in bed one day

with a very bad fever. Jesus went into her room, took her by her hand and lifted her up. As He did so, the fever left her, and she was helpful to Jesus and the disciples. That evening at sunset, many that were sick, or possessed by demons, were brought to the street outside the house, and Jesus healed them.

Jesus was very tired after that. He went out to a quiet place in the desert to pray and to gain strength again from His Father in heaven.

A few days later as He walked along the sands beside the Sea of Galilee, a great crowd of people gathered around to hear Him preach the word of God. The crowd was so great, though, and pressed in so much around Him, that He could hardly speak. Nearby on the lake were two fishing boats that were not being used. He climbed into one of them, which belonged to Simon Peter, and used it as a pulpit. When He had finished speaking He told Simon Peter to row the boat out into deeper water, and let down his nets to catch many fish. The fisherman disciple was surprised, and said so. "We have fished all night and caught nothing. Still, because You told me to, I will let down the nets."

When Simon Peter and his fellow workers threw in their nets, the catch was so great that the nets began to break. Simon Peter called to the owner of the other ship nearby to come and help. Both ships began to settle in the water because of the weight of the fish.

When Simon Peter saw it, he threw himself down in front of Jesus and cried out: "Lord, depart from me! I am too sinful for You to have anything to do with me." James and John, the sons of Zebedee, Simon Peter's partners, did the same. But Jesus said to Simon: "Do not be afraid. From now on you will become fishers of men."

When they brought their boats to land, they left everything they had and followed Jesus.

Even the Lame and the Lepers were Healed!

Matthew 8 and 9; Mark 1 and 2;
Luke 5

After His visit to Capernaum, Jesus moved about from village to village in the rest of Galilee, teaching and healing the sick as He went. Crowds of people followed Him, to hear Him and to see what He did. The news had spread quickly of how wonderfully He had healed the sick of Capernaum.

One day a leper came to Him and begged Him to take away his terrible sickness. The rest of the people stood back. They were afraid the sickness might spread to them. But Jesus did not turn away. The leper worshiped Him and said: "Lord, if you are willing, you can make me clean." Jesus stretched out His hand and touched him, saying: "I am willing; be cleansed." And immediately the horrible white, dead patches of leprosy disappeared from him. Then Jesus told him not to spread the news but to go to the priest and offer to God a sacrifice of thanksgiving.

But the man could not keep quiet about the amazing thing that had happened to him. And the more he told people, the more they streamed along to listen to Jesus. People brought the sick and the demon-possessed to Him to be healed. So many came that Jesus could no longer go into the villages because of the crowd.

After several days, though, He managed to get back to Capernaum. While He was teaching in a house there one day, there were many Pharisees and doctors of the Law present. They had come from all the villages and towns round about Galilee. Some even came from Judea and Jerusalem. As usual, many sick people were brought to be healed, but there was no way of getting them into the house because of the crowd already inside.

A group of men had brought along one of their friends on a stretcher bed. He was unable to walk or even to move his arms. How could they get him to Jesus? They had an idea! Up onto the roof of the building they went, carrying their friend on his bed. There they removed some of the tiles from the roof. Then they let their friend down on his bed by means of ropes until he lay in front of Jesus. When Jesus saw the faith of those friends in Him, He said to the sick man: "Son, be of good cheer: your sins are forgiven!"

When the Pharisees heard that, they listened carefully. In their own minds they thought, "That is blasphemy! Only God can forgive sins. What right has this man to say such things?" But Jesus knew exactly what they were thinking. He said to them: "Why do you

think evil of Me in your hearts? Which is easier to say, Your sins are forgiven, or Get up from your bed and walk?" Then He turned again to the sick man and said: "But so that you may know that the Son of Man has the power to forgive sins, I say to you, Get up, take your bed, and go back to your home."

At once the man got up, took the stretcher bed he had been lying on, and went back home. He praised God all the way. Those who saw what the Lord did were all amazed, and even afraid. They said: "We have seen strange things here today." But the Pharisees hated Him.

The Man with the Withered Hand

Matthew 12; Mark 2 and 3;
Luke 6; John 5

While Jesus moved about the villages and towns of Galilee and Judea, healing the sick and teaching and doing good to all who were in trouble, the Pharisees and others who hated Him were trying all the time to find some way of destroying Him. They wanted to accuse Him of blasphemy when He told the paralyzed man in the house in Capernaum that his sins were forgiven and healed him. One of their cleverest plans was to

wheat field. The disciples were feeling hungry. As they went, they picked a few grains of wheat and ate them. When the Pharisees saw this, they said to Jesus: "Look, your disciples are doing what is against the Law on the Sabbath day." But He answered them: "Haven't you read what David did, when he and his followers were hungry? They went into the house of God, and took some of the sacred bread which only the priests are allowed to eat. And haven't you read in the Law that the priests break the Sabbath Law in the course of their work in the Temple and are innocent? I tell you there is Someone greater than the Temple here. If you had understood what the Scripture means where God says, 'I ask for compassion and not a sacrifice', you would not have condemned the innocent. For the Son of Man is Lord of the Sabbath."

But even that did not silence them. From the wheat fields He went on to the synagogue. When He arrived there, they brought to Him a man with a withered hand. Once again, trying to trap Him, they asked: "It is lawful to heal on the Sabbath?" But Jesus answered, "Which of you, if one of his sheep falls into a pit on the Sabbath day, will not go out and rescue it? How much more valuable is a man than a sheep! So then it is right and lawful to do

try to show that Jesus did not keep the Law and broke God's commandments. The favorite was to try to trick Him into breaking the Sabbath Law. This Law said: "Remember the Sabbath day to keep it holy." The Pharisees had made many additions to the Law. Some of the additions were quite ridiculous. The Pharisees were on the lookout all the time to see whether Jesus broke any of them.

One Sabbath day Jesus and His disciples were walking through a good on the Sabbath." Then he said to the man they had brought, "Stretch out your hand!" And as he stretched it out, it was healed and became useful just like his other.

But instead of rejoicing over what they had seen, the Pharisees planned how they might destroy Jesus.

The Cripple at the Pool

After this, Jesus went up to the Passover Feast in Jerusalem. This was His custom every year.

Near the Bethesda gate in the city wall of Jerusalem was a pool of water which had miraculous properties. At certain times the water was mysteriously stirred up by an angel from the Lord. The first sick person to step into the water after the stirring-up was immediately healed of his sickness. Around the pool lay many sick persons, waiting for the troubling of the water. One man had been ill for thirty-eight years. He was badly crippled and could not get down into the water quickly. He did not have any friends to take him down either.

When Jesus came to the place and saw him, He said to him: "Do you want to get well?" The

man answered: "Sir, there is no one to help me down into the pool. The others get there before me when the water is stirred up." Jesus said: "Take up your bed, and walk." And at once the man stood up, and was well!

Now again this happened on the Sabbath day. When the Pharisees saw the man who had been sick carrying his bed down the street, they told him angrily that

297

he was breaking the Law by doing this. All he answered was: "The man who made me well again, told me to take up my bed and go." Then they said: "Who was this man? Show him to us." But Jesus had slipped away in the crowd, and the man did not know who He was.

Later Jesus found the man in the Temple and said to him: "You are well now, but take care that you do not sin, or something worse will happen to you." The man then went away. When the Jews asked him now who had healed him, he was able to tell them that it was Jesus.

Once more they went to Jesus and accused Him of being a lawbreaker because he had healed the man on the Sabbath day. But Jesus said to them: "My Father has worked until now, and I work also." That made them very angry. He was not only breaking the Sabbath Law, but He was also saying that He was equal with God.

From then on, whatever Jesus did, the Pharisees tried to trap Him into doing wrong. They tried carefully to work out a way of having Him killed.

Jesus Calls Another Disciple and Explains the Principles of His Kingdom

*Matthew 5 to 9; Mark 2;
Luke 5 and 6*

One day when Jesus was in the city of Capernaum, He was walking down the street. He passed an office where the taxes were collected. In this office sat a tax collector called Matthew. Sometimes he was also called Levi. Jesus spoke to him, "Follow Me." Matthew stood up, left what he was doing, and without a moment's delay followed Jesus and became one of His disciples.

That night Jesus dined with Matthew in his house. Many tax gatherers and some sinful people came to the dinner. The tax collectors were hated and despised by the Jews. They were hated because they collected money from their own people to give to the Roman conquerors and because they often demanded more money than they should and put the difference in their own pockets.

When the scribes and Pharisees saw that Jesus was eating with such people as the despised tax collectors, they began to say to His disciples: "Why does He eat with tax gatherers and sinners?" When He heard this, Jesus turned to them and said: "It isn't healthy people who need a doctor, but

the sick. I did not come to call the righteous, but sinners. I go to these people because they know their need. You think that you need nothing."

One day Jesus climbed a little way up the slope of a mountain near the Sea of Galilee and sat down. He called to His disciples to come and sit close to Him. The rest of the people seated themselves in comfort a little way down the mountainside. There Jesus told them how people must all live who belong to the kingdom

of God. He explained to them the principles, or rules, of the kingdom. We call what He said there the "Sermon on the Mount." Here is a part of the most beautiful passages from the Sermon. The entire Sermon can be found in the fifth, sixth, and seventh chapters of Matthew in the Bible.

"Blessed are the poor in spirit: for theirs is the kingdom of heaven.

Blessed are they that mourn: for they shall be comforted.

Blessed are the meek: for they shall inherit the earth.

Blessed are they which do hunger and thirst after righteousness: for they shall be filled.

Blessed are the merciful: for they shall obtain mercy.

Blessed are the pure in heart: for they shall see God.

Blessed are the peacemakers: for they shall be called the children of God.

Blessed are they which are persecuted for righteousness' sake: for theirs is the kingdom of heaven.

Blessed are ye, when men shall revile you, and persecute you, and shall say all manner of evil against you falsely, for my sake. Rejoice, and be exceeding glad: for great is your reward in heaven: for so persecuted they the prophets which were before you.

Jesus also had some very important things to say about the way we treat those who behave as our enemies:

"Ye have heard that it hath been said, Thou shalt love thy neighbor, and hate thine enemy. But I say unto you, Love your enemies, bless them that curse you, and do good to them that hate you, and pray for them which despitefully use you, and persecute you; that ye may be the children of your Father which is in heaven.

It was in that Sermon also that He taught the disciples to pray what we call the "Lord's Prayer":

"Our Father Who art in heaven, Hallowed be Thy name. Thy kingdom come. Thy will be done in earth, as it is in heaven. Give us this day our daily bread. And forgive us our debts, as we forgive our debtors. And lead us not into temptation, but deliver us from evil: For thine is the kingdom, and the power, and the glory, for ever. Amen."

A Sick Man Healed; a Dead Boy Brought to Life; and a Sinful Woman Saved

Matthew 8; Luke 7

When Jesus went back to Capernaum, one of the first men who came to Him was a Roman centurion, an officer in charge of a hundred soldiers. Really, this man did not want to go to Jesus himself, but instead he sent some Jewish elders to ask Jesus to come and heal his slave. The poor slave was lying paralyzed and in very great pain.

The elders had great respect for the centurion. Unlike most of the Romans, he loved the Jewish people. He even had a synagogue built for them in Capernaum. The elders pleaded with Jesus to go to the centurion's home and do as he had asked.

Jesus started on His way with them. Before they reached the centurion's house they met a group of this officer's friends coming with a special message for Jesus. "Lord, do not trouble Thyself further. The centurion does

not feel himself worthy enough for You to come under his roof That is why he did not come to You. He was ashamed to trouble You. But he asks You only to speak the word. He knows that then his slave will be healed. He is a man with authority, but he has recognized that You have even greater authority. If he gives orders to his servants, they obey. He knows that Your orders will be obeyed also. Please give the order and his servant will be healed."

When Jesus heard this, he marvelled and said to the crowd following Him: "I have not found such faith, even among the people of Israel." And when the centurion's friends returned to his house they found the slave well once again. Jesus had heard the centurion's cry.

Soon afterward something even more wonderful took place. Jesus went to a town called Nain. As He approached the town, His little group met a sad procession coming toward them. It was a funeral procession. A dead man was being carried out to be buried. He was the only son of a widow, and she was weeping. When Jesus saw her, His heart was filled with sorrow for her. He went up to her and said: "Do not weep." Then He went and touched the stretcher on which the body was being carried and said: "Young man, I say to thee, arise." The young man sat up and began to speak. Jesus gave him back to his mother.

Then all the people who saw this were filled with fear and said among themselves: "A great prophet has arisen among us!" and, "God has visited His people." The news of what had happened spread very quickly through all the land.

One day a Pharisee, named Simon, invited Jesus to come and eat with him at his home.

As Jesus reclined beside the low table in the Pharisee's dining hall, a woman came into the room. This woman had been a very

303

wicked person. She had with her an alabaster jar of perfumed ointment. She wept over Jesus' feet and kissed them, and wiped them with her hair. Then she poured the perfume over them.

As Simon the Pharisee watched this, he thought to himself: "If this man were really a prophet, he would know what a terrible kind of person she is and would have nothing to do with her at all." But Jesus knew what he was thinking and said to him: "Simon, I have something to say to you." "Master, say it," replied the Pharisee.

Then Jesus told him a little story. "Two men owed money to a certain moneylender. The one owed him five hundred days' wages, the other only fifty days' wages, but neither of them was able to pay. Very kindly he let them both off. Which of them will love him more, do you think?" Simon answered: "I suppose the one who was let off the larger debt." Jesus said: "Your answer is correct." Then He turned to the woman and, looking at her, said to Simon: "Do you see this woman? When I came into this house, you did not even

offer Me water to wash My feet. She has washed them with her tears and wiped them with her hair. You gave Me no kiss of welcome, but she has not stopped kissing My feet. You did not anoint My head with oil, but she has covered My feet with sweet perfume. I tell you, Simon, that her sins which were many, are forgiven, for she loved much, but the one who is forgiven little, loves little." Then He said to the woman: "Your sins are forgiven." Those at table with Him looked at one another and asked: "Who can this be, who even forgives sins?"

But Jesus said again to the woman: "Your faith has saved you, go in peace."

A sick slave was made well again. A widow's son was brought back again from the dead. A sinful woman saved and made His loving servant. Could anyone fail to believe in Jesus? But there were some who still hated Him.

Tales Told by the Seaside

Matthew 13; Mark 4; Luke 8

The Lord Jesus often told stories to the crowds of people who flocked to listen to Him. The stories were a special kind. We call them parables or stories with a meaning. Jesus used them to teach the people truth from God's Word.

One day, when He was sitting beside the Sea of Galilee, a large crowd gathered around Him to listen to His teaching. There He told them what is perhaps the best known of all His stories, the Parable of the Sower.

"A sower went out one day," He said, "to sow seed in his plowed field. As he scattered his seed, some of it fell on the pathway next to the field, and the birds came and ate it up. Other seed fell on stony patches in the field, where the soil was shallow. That seed grew very quickly; but the young plants were not able to root well in the shallow soil. When the sun beat down on them, they withered away and died. Other seed fell among the thornbushes, and the thorns grew thickly and choked the young plants. But some of the seed fell on good soil. The young plants came up and gave a good crop. In some places there was a hundred times as much grain as had been planted. In other places there was sixty times as much and in others, thirty times. Let everyone that has ears listen to what I say."

Then Jesus explained to the disciples what the story of the sower meant. "The sower is one who sows the seed of God's Word among men. The seed that falls on the pathway beside the field is like the Word of God sown in human hearts and immediately snatched away by the devil. The seed that falls in stony places is like the Word sown in the hearts of people who are immediately full of joy, but they soon turn back to their old ways and do not grow in God's grace. Then the seed sown in thorny places is like God's Word being choked in people's hearts because they think more about riches and the things of the world and their interest in worldly pleasures. There are those in whose hearts the Word is sown and who honestly try to live by the Word. They produce fruit in their lives to God's glory, some thirty-fold, some sixty-fold, and some a hundred-fold."

Another story Jesus told was about a man who bought good seed and sowed it in his field. While his servants were asleep at night, his enemy came and spread a weed in the same field. When the seed sprouted, and the wheat came up, the servants were horrified to see the weeds there as well. They went to their master and asked him how this could have happened. He said to them that an enemy had done it. The servants wanted to get busy at once and root out all the weeds, but the master would not let them do it. If they tried to get rid of the weeds, they would tread down and kill too much of the wheat. Wheat and weeds must be allowed to grow together until the harvest time. Then the harvesters would be told to gather the weeds into bundles first and burn them. After

that the wheat would be gathered into his barn.

Jesus explained this story to the disciples. "The one who sowed the good seed," said Jesus, "is the Son of Man. The field is the world, and the good seed are those who belong to the kingdom of God. The bad seed and the weeds that grew from it, are the sons of the devil. The enemy who sowed them is the devil. The harvest time is the end of the age. The harvesters are God's angels. Just as the weeds in the story are gathered and burned, just so will it be at the end of the age. The Son of Man will send His angels into the world. They will gather out of His kingdom all who have been unrighteous. These will be thrown into everlasting fire and there will be weeping and gnashing of teeth. But the righteous, those faithful to the kingdom of God, will shine in their glory."

Jesus also described the kingdom of God as being like leaven, or yeast, which a woman took and mixed into dough made with three measures of flour. The leaven disappeared, but it made all the dough rise.

Those were stories He told to all the people who came to listen to Him, but there were some stories He told to the disciples only. He told them that the kingdom of heaven is like a treasure hidden in a field, which a man found and then sold everything he had and bought the field. In the same way, it is like a merchant looking for pearls who, when he finds one pearl of great value, goes and sells everything he has, so as to be able to buy the pearl.

The kingdom of heaven is also like a net cast into the sea, which was quickly filled with fish of all kinds. When it was brought up on the beach, they sorted out all the good fish and packed them in baskets to be used, but the bad fish they threw away. It will be like that at the end of the age. The wicked will be separated from the righteous. The wicked will be thrown into everlasting fire, and there will be weeping and gnashing of teeth.

"Peace, Be Still"

Matthew 8; Mark 4 and 5; Luke 8
When Jesus was very tired, He called upon the disciples to take Him by boat across to the other side of the Sea of Galilee where He could find some peace. It had been a long day of teaching, without a chance to rest or even to eat.

As soon as the boat launched out from the beach, Jesus lay down on the cushion in the back of the boat and fell asleep. Suddenly there was a great storm on the Sea. The little boat was tossed dangerously to and fro by the waves. The disciples were experienced fishermen, but even they were terrified at the fierceness of the storm. They went to Jesus and woke Him up and cried out: "Lord, save us. We are perishing!" Jesus said to them: "Why are you afraid, you men of little faith?" Then He spoke to the storm, "Peace, be still!" At once the wind subsided, and the waves calmed. The disciples were amazed! "What kind of a man is this," they asked, "that even the wind and the waves obey Him?"

When they arrived on the other side, they landed in the country of the Gadarenes. This was the country around the cities of Gadara and Gergasa. They had hardly landed when a man came running toward them. Oh, how terrible this man looked! He was demon possessed. Everybody was terrified by him, he was so fierce. He lived out in the caves in the hills that were normally used for graves. He was not allowed to come near the towns.

When this man saw Jesus and

the disciples coming, he came running toward Jesus and threw himself down on the ground in front of Him. Then Jesus said: "Come out of the man, unclean spirit!" But the man cried out: "What have I to do with Thee, Jesus, Son of the Most High God? I beg Thee not to torment me!" It was really not the man speaking, but the evil spirit. Then Jesus said to him: "What is your name?" and he answered: "My name is Legion, for we are many."

On the hillside nearby there was a big herd of pigs. The evil spirits in the man begged Jesus that when He cast them out, to let them go into the pigs. He agreed. At once the whole herd of pigs, about two thousand of them, rushed down the hillside right into the sea and were all drowned. The sick man sat there quietly, in his right mind, fully clothed and ready to go back to his real home.

But the man who had been called 'Legion' when the evil spirits were in him, felt differently about it. He became a missionary for Jesus in all that part of the world. He told people what mighty power the Lord had. All who saw him and heard him were amazed, because they knew what he had been like before.

A Little Girl Lives Again

Matthew 9 and 10; Mark 5; Luke 8 and 9

What wonderful works Jesus was able to do! He healed the sick and He even brought the dead to life again!

Once while Jesus was teaching in Capernaum, a ruler called Jairus pressed through the crowd to Him and cried out, "Lord, my daughter is dying, but come and lay Thy hand on her, and I know she will live again." Jesus at once began to follow the man toward

his home. On the way someone else came to Him, whose need was also very great. This time it was a woman who had been sick for twelve long years. She had heard of the wonderful power of Jesus. Now she crept up through the crowd following Him, and just touched the hem of His garment. As she did it, she felt the sickness going out of her. Though she had only touched His clothes, Jesus knew what had happened. He asked: "Who touched My clothes?" He looked around, and as His eyes fell on her, she trembled and was very frightened. She came and threw herself down in front of Him and told Him everything. Lovingly He spoke to her. "Daughter, your faith has made you well. Go in peace, and be healed of your sickness."

Now, while everyone was amazed over what had happened, some mesengers came from the home of Jairus. They said to him: "Your daughter is dead. Why do you trouble the Master now?" But Jesus heard what they said. This was His answer: "Do not be afraid, just believe." Then He told all the rest of the people not to follow Him any further. Only the disciples Peter, James and John must go with Him.

When the little party reached the home of Jairus, they found many people there weeping and sorrowing. Jesus turned them all out of the house, except Jairus and his wife. Then He took them and the three disciples into the room where the girl was lying. He took her by the hand and said to her· "Little girl, I say to you, wake up!" And at once she awoke, and got up, and walked. How her father and her mother and the disciples were amazed! Then Jesus told them to give her something to eat.

After this Jesus left Capernaum again, but wherever He went He healed the sick and taught all the people who gathered around Him. One day by the wayside, He found two blind men who sat there begging. They cried out to Him to have mercy on them. He asked them only one question, "Do you believe that I am able to give you back your sight?" When they said that they did, He gently touched their eyes. At once they could see.

Wherever He went, in the villages and towns, the people cried out to Him for help. The Pharisees hated Him for what He was doing. They said that He was healing the sick through the power of the devil.

Jesus was very sorry for all the suffering people who came to Him and who could not find help anywhere else. One day He said to His disciples: "Look how great the harvest is! There are not enough harvesters to help in the work. Pray to the Lord of the harvest, that He will send more harvesters to do the work."

Soon after this, Jesus called the twelve disciples to Him. He told them that He wanted them to go out two-by-two into all parts of the land, but not to the country of the Samaritans or to any part belonging to the Gentiles. They must go to the lost sheep of the house of Israel, and preach to them that the kingdom of heaven was at hand. He gave them power to heal the sick, cleanse lepers, raise the dead, and drive out evil spirits. They must not take any

money with them, but in each town to which they came they must seek out some good man, and ask if they could stay in his house till their work in that town was done. Wherever people refused to receive them, they must turn away, and God's curse would rest on them, their house, or their town. "Truly," said Jesus, "it will be easier for Sodom and Gomorrah in the Day of Judgment than for places like that. Behold, I send you out like sheep among wolves. They will treat you badly, and even drag you before the courts, and beat you. But do not worry about how you are to answer them. God will give you the words to use. It will not be you yourselves that speak, but the Spirit of the Father Himself."

So the disciples went out as the Lord had commanded them into all the villages and towns of Galilee and Judea.

Only Five Loaves and Two Fishes but They Fed Thousands

Matthew 14; Mark 6; Luke 9; John 6

After the disciples had completed their work of preaching throughout Galilee, they came back to the Lord Jesus. Then they went with Him to the little town of Bethsaida. They needed quiet and privacy after the hard work they had done, but crowds of people followed them. On the way there Jesus stopped on a hillside beside the Sea of Galilee to teach about the kingdom of God and to heal those who were sick.

By the time this was over it was quite late in the day. The people who had gathered to listen to Jesus had had no food. Jesus shocked the disciples by telling them to give the people food. Where could they possibly find enough food for about five thousand men, not even counting the women and children? Then Jesus said: "What food have you for them?" Andrew answered: "There is a boy here who has five barley loaves and two fishes, but what good are they when we have so many people to feed?"

But Jesus answered: "Get all the people to sit down." When all of them had sat down on the grass, Jesus took the loaves. When

He had given thanks to God, He broke the bread and handed the pieces to the disciples to give to the people. Then He did the same with the fish. The people, every single one of them, had as much as they could eat. When they were finished, the disciples picked up the pieces that were left. There were twelve baskets full left over!

When the people saw this wonderful sign of His power, they said: "Truly this must be the Great Prophet sent by God."

Then they wanted to make Him king, but Jesus slipped away and went up into the mountains alone to pray.

At evening, when the sun was setting, the disciples did as Jesus had told them. They got into a boat and started to row across the sea to Capernaum. But the wind became stronger, and the waves were rough so that the disciples were not able to row across to the other side before it became completely dark. When they had rowed about three or four miles, they saw Jesus walking on the sea and coming toward them. They were frightened. They were not sure who it was, and they did not know how it could happen that a person could walk on the water. But then Jesus called out: "It is I. Do not be afraid."

Peter, impetuous as usual, cried out: "Lord, if it is You, command me to come to You on the water." Jesus said: "Come!" and Peter got out of the boat and walked on the water toward Jesus. Then the roaring of the wind began to make him afraid again. Looking at the wild waves, he began to sink. Then he cried out: "Lord, save me!" Jesus stretched out His hand and took hold of him and said: "O man of little faith, why did you doubt?"

When they both stepped into the boat, the wind stopped. At once the boat was at the place

toward which they were rowing. At that the disciples worshiped Jesus and said to Him: "You are certainly God's Son!"

The exact place at which they landed was Gennesaret, a little village just south of Capernaum. When the people there saw who had arrived, they sent the news to all parts of the district. Soon Jesus was surrounded by a great crowd. Among those who came were a large number of people who had seen Him multiplying the loaves and the fishes the

afternoon before. They asked Him: "Master, when did You come here?" But He knew what was in their hearts, and gave them the answer they really deserved. "Truly, you have looked for Me, not because you saw signs which proved My authority, but because you ate of the food and your stomachs were filled. Do not labor for the food that perishes, but for the food that will give you eternal life, which the Son of Man shall give to you. On Him God the Father has set His seal."

At once they challenged Him. "Show us a sign to prove that God has sent you. Moses gave our fathers manna in the wilderness. What do you give us?"

Jesus answered: "It was not Moses who gave you that bread, but My Father in heaven. And now again it is My Father who gives you the true bread from heaven. I am the bread of life: whoever comes to Me shall not hunger, and whoever believes in Me shall never thirst."

They asked Him many questions about this. They tried to trap Him in what He said. Most of them turned away from Him and did not follow Him any more. Among the few who remained, were the twelve disciples. Jesus said sadly to them: "You do not want to go away as well, do you?" But Peter answered Him: "Lord, to whom shall we go? You have the words of eternal life."

Even one of the twelve, though, had an evil heart. This was Judas Iscariot, who one day would betray Jesus to His enemies for thirty pieces of silver.

The Answer to a Mother's Prayer

Matthew 15; Mark 7 and 8

When Jesus had spent a while in the neighborhood of Capernaum, He moved away with His disciples into the land of Tyre and Sidon. They lived on the coast of the Mediterranean Sea. This was not Jewish country, but Phoenicia, a part of what is now called Syria.

While Jesus and His disciples journeyed along one day, a Canaanite woman came to them and began to cry out to Jesus. "Have mercy on me, O Lord, Son of David. My daughter is cruelly possessed by a demon." But Jesus said nothing at all. The poor woman kept on crying out to Him. She made such a fuss that the disciples said to Him: "Please, Lord, send her away, because she is shouting after us." But He answered and said, in her hearing, something which must have sounded very unkind: "I was sent only to the lost sheep of the house of Israel." But she came and bowed down in front of Him and cried out: "Lord, help me!" Then He said to her: "It is not right to take the children's bread and throw it to the dogs." But the poor woman was so desperate that she said: "Yes, Lord, but even the dogs feed on the crumbs which fall from their master's table!" Jesus answered: "O woman, your faith is great indeed. Your cry is heard, and it will be as you wish." In that very moment her daughter was healed.

After a short time in the land of Tyre and Sidon, Jesus went back to the parts around the Sea of Galilee. Many people came again to hear Him, and to have their sicknesses healed by Him. The people who came were lame, and blind, and dumb. He healed them all. They glorified God for His mercy.

One day Jesus was in the part of the land east of the Sea of Galilee. The area was called Decapolis because there were ten towns there. This was near the town of Gadara where He had healed the demon-possessed man. The people brought to Him a man who was deaf, and spoke with difficulty. They begged Jesus to lay His hands on the man, and heal him. Jesus took him aside from the crowd, and put His fingers gently into the man's ears. Then He touched the man's tongue. With a deep sigh He then looked up to heaven, and said to the man: "Be opened!" At once the man could hear, and he was able to speak properly.

How amazed the crowds were. They said: "Look, He does all things well! He even makes the deaf to hear and the dumb to speak."

At Bethsaida, the people brought a blind man to Jesus. After taking the man aside privately, Jesus touched his eyes with saliva and then laid His hands gently on him. "Do you see anything?" He asked, and the man answered: "I see men, but they look like trees walking about." Then Jesus laid His hands on the man's eyes again. Now the man became able to see clearly. He was so glad that he wanted to tell everyone, but Jesus said that he must not even go into the town, nor tell anyone what had happened. Jesus wanted people to come to Him to hear His teaching and have their souls healed and not to think of Him only as a wonder-worker who could make their bodies well.

speak, said: "Thou art the Christ, the Son of the living God."

Then Jesus answered: "You are truly blessed, Simon son of Jonah, because flesh and blood did not reveal this to you, but My Father, Who is in heaven. I also say to you that you are Peter, and on this rock I will build My Church. The gates of Hell shall not have power over it." What He meant was that He would build His Church on the foundation of the faith that Peter had—faith that Jesus is the Christ Whom God has sent.

Glory Shines from Jesus' Face

Matthew 16; Mark 8 and 9; Luke 9
While Jesus was traveling about teaching and healing, He made a special point of explaining to His disciples who He was and what He had come to do. One day, while they were in the district of Caesarea-Philippi, at the foot of beautiful Mount Hermon, Jesus asked His disciples a question: "Who do people say that I, the Son of Man, am?" They answered: "Some say John the Baptist come to life again. Others say Elijah. Others again, Jeremiah or one of the prophets." Then Jesus said: "But who do you say that I am?" Simon Peter, always the first to

There were other things that Jesus taught His disciples which they just could not understand. He told them, for instance, what terrible things were going to happen to Him before long. "The Son of Man must go up to Jerusalem," He said, "and suffer many things at the hands of the elders and chief priests and scribes. They will hand Him over to the Gentiles, and He will be spat on and mocked and beaten, and killed. But on the third day He will rise again from the dead."

Peter was horrified to hear these things, and spoke sharply to Jesus: "God forbid it, Lord! This shall never happen to You."

But Jesus turned to him and said: "Get behind Me, Satan! You are a hindrance to Me, because you look at everything from man's point of view, and not God's." Jesus had come to save His people from their sins by dying for them on the Cross. If He was turned aside from that, there could be no salvation for us. That is why He spoke so sternly to Peter.

Then Jesus turned to the disciples and spoke very earnestly to them: "If anyone wishes to follow Me, he must deny himself and take up his cross and come after Me. For whoever tries to save his life, will lose it, and whoever gives up his life for My sake and the gospel's, will save it. What will it profit a man if he gains the whole world, and loses his own soul? What could a man give in exchange for his soul? Whoever is ashamed of Me and My words, of him will I also be ashamed when I come on the Day of Judgment, in great glory and with the holy angels."

A week later Jesus called Peter and James and John to go with Him to a quiet place at the top of a high mountain. While Jesus was praying there, the three disciples fell asleep. But suddenly they awoke and found the Lord Jesus transformed before them. His clothes had turned to a shining white, whiter than anyone on earth could possibly have made them. And with Him they saw Elijah and Moses talking about what was soon to happen to Him in Jerusalem. When it seemed as if Elijah and Moses were bidding Jesus farewell, Peter called out to Him, and said: "Master, it is good for us to be here. Let us make three tabernacles, one for You, and one for Moses, and one for Elijah." But as Peter spoke, a cloud began to form over the mountain top. The disciples were afraid. Then out of the cloud they heard a voice. The voice said: "This is My Son, My chosen One. Listen to Him!" When they looked

again, Jesus was alone. As they came down the mountain side, He told them that they must tell no one what they had seen until after He had risen from the dead.

When they reached the foot of the mountain once more, they found the rest of the disciples surrounded by a crowd of people. In the midst was a man who cried out to Jesus: "Please, Master, help me! My boy, my only son, is possessed by an evil spirit which makes him suddenly scream and go into a fit, foaming at the mouth. It throws him to the ground and hurts him terribly. I have asked Your disciples to help, but they could do nothing." Jesus exclaimed: "O unbelieving and perverted generation, how long must I bear with you! Bring here the boy."

While the boy was being brought to Jesus, the demon dashed him to the ground once more. He twisted and writhed about in a terrible convulsion. Jesus rebuked the evil spirit and at once the convulsion stopped. The boy lay so still that some thought he was dead. But Jesus took him by the hand, lifted him up, and gave him back to his father, completely well. All who watched were amazed at the greatness of God.

The disciples were puzzled, though. Why had they not been able to cast out the demon? Jesus

explained to them that this kind of evil spirit could only be driven out through fasting and prayer.

After this they continued their journey through Galilee. Jesus taught the people wherever they went. Several times He told the disciples how He would have to go up to Jerusalem and suffer and die there, but they did not understand. He had to bear the sorrowful knowledge alone.

Jesus Loves the Little Children

Matthew 17 and 18; Mark 9; Luke 9

When Jesus and His disciples reached the city of Capernaum once more, one of the tax collectors, who had the task of collecting the Temple tax, came to Peter and asked him if his Master did not pay tax. Peter said: "Yes," but he was not quite sure about it. Jesus knew what was going on in his mind. As soon as there was a chance, He asked Peter this question: "What do you think? Do the kings of the earth gather custom duties from their own children, or from strangers?" Peter answered: "From strangers." Then Jesus said to him: "That means that the children are exempt. But, so that we do not cause trouble, go down to the lake, and throw in a line. Take the first fish you catch, and open its mouth. There you will find a coin. It will be just enough for the tax. Take it to the tax collector for both of us."

Now while they walked along toward Capernaum, the disciples had been talking among themselves. In the quiet of the house where they were staying, Jesus asked them what they had been so busy discussing. But they were ashamed to tell Him that they had been arguing about which of them was the greatest, and who

323

would have the most important place in the Kingdom of Heaven. Jesus knew, though. He called them all to Him, and this is what He said: "If anyone wants to be first, let him look upon himself as the least of all, and be their servant."

Then Jesus took a little child in His arms, and said to them: "Everyone who receives one child like this in My Name, receives Me. And whoever receives Me is not receiving Me, but Him Who sent Me. Unless you are converted and become as humble as this little child, you shall not enter the Kingdom of Heaven. But see to it that you do not despise one of these little ones, because I tell you that the angels in heaven always see the face of My Father. Take care not to be stumbling blocks in the way of these little ones, because if you are, it would be better for you to have a mill-stone hung around your neck and be drowned in the depths of the sea."

Peter then had a question to ask Jesus: "Master, how many times must I forgive my brother if he harms me, up to seven times?" And Jesus said: "I do not say, up to seven times, but up to seventy times seven." He explained very carefully to Peter and the rest of the disciples how they should go about speaking to another believer who had done

them harm. He told them the parable, or story, of the unmerciful servant. He showed them that they should always be ready to forgive. This is the story: "There was once a king who was owed money by one of his servants. One day he decided that it was time they settled their accounts, and he had one man called in who owed him a very large amount of money. But the man had nothing with which to pay the debt, so the king commanded that he should be sold, with his wife and children. The servant fell on his knees and begged the king to have patience with him and he would pay everything. The king felt so sorry for him that he forgave him the whole debt. But the servant himself was not such a merciful man. He went out and found one of his fellow servants who owed him a very small sum of money. At once he demanded the payment of the debt, but the other man had nothing with which to pay, and begged him to have patience with him. Instead, the man had him thrown into prison until he could pay back what he owed. The news of this came very soon to the king's ears, and he was terribly angry. He sent at once for the man to whom he had shown mercy, and said to him, You wicked fellow! I forgave you your debt when you pleaded with me. Shouldn't you have had mercy on your fellow servant as well? But now you go to the torturers until you have paid back all you owe. This is how My Heavenly Father will treat you, if you do not each forgive your brother from the heart."

Jesus in Jerusalem for the Feast of Tabernacles

Matthew 8; Luke 9, 10 and 17;
John 7

Jesus went up to Jerusalem to join in the Feast of Tabernacles, but not openly, with the disciples. He sent them up on their own,

and then followed secretly later on. Shortly before Jesus and the disciples left Capernaum, a certain scribe went to Jesus, and said: "Teacher, I will follow Thee wherever Thou goest." But Jesus answered: "The foxes have holes, and the birds of the air have nests, but the Son of Man has nowhere to lay His head."

To another man, Jesus said: "Follow Me." The man had many excuses. "Let me first go and bury my father," he said. But Jesus said to him: "Allow the dead to bury their own dead; but you must go and tell people the news of the Kingdom of God." Another man said: "I will follow Thee, Lord, but I must first go and say good-by to the people at home." To him Jesus said: "No one who has once put his hand to the plough and looks back, is fit for the Kingdom of God."

Before the disciples had left Jesus to go up on their own to Jerusalem, they first accompanied Him through Samaria. This must have seemed strange to them, because the Jews hated the Samaritans and would have nothing to do with them. One day He sent some of the disciples ahead into a Samaritan village to find a place for them for the night, but the Samaritans refused to help them because they were going to Jerusalem. When James and John saw this, they asked Jesus if He wanted them to pray that fire should come down from heaven and destroy that village. But Jesus rebuked them and said: "You do not understand that the Son of Man has come not to destroy men's lives, but to save them." So they went on to another village where the people would give them a warmer welcome.

On the way from Samaria to Galilee the little party came upon a group of ten lepers. The lepers stood at a distance and cried out: "Jesus, Master, have mercy on us!" When Jesus saw them and heard their cry, He said to them: "Go and show yourselves to the

priests." As they went, they were cleansed of their terrible sickness. One of them, when he realized what had happened, turned back, loudly praising God, and threw himself down in front of Jesus. The leper thanked Jesus for what He had done. That man was a Samaritan. Jesus turned to the disciples and said: "Were there not ten men cleansed? But the nine, where are they? Were there no others to glorify God, except this foreigner?" Then He said to the Samaritan: "Rise and go your way, your faith has made you well."

After this, the disciples went on

to Jerusalem, while Jesus stayed behind for a few days. When He arrived in Jerusalem, the Feast of Tabernacles was already several days old. He went to the Temple and began to teach the crowds there. On the last day of the Festival, the custom was for the people to take offerings of water into the Temple as a reminder and a thanksgiving for the way God had given their forefathers water in the wilderness. On that day Jesus called out to the people: "If anyone is thirsty, let him come to Me and drink. Whoever believes in Me, from his innermost being will flow streams of living water." Many of the people were very troubled about this saying, but some were sure in their hearts that He was indeed the Christ. However, the chief priests and elders sent soldiers out to arrest Jesus. These men did not dare to touch Jesus. They went back and told the chief priests that they had never heard a man speak like this Man!

Whenever Jesus went to Jerusalem, He would spend a short time with three very dear friends, two sisters, Martha and Mary, and their brother, Lazarus. They lived in the little village of Bethany, on the Mount of Olives, just outside the city. Martha was very proud of her home. She took great care that Jesus was made as comfortable as possible whenever He came to visit. Her sister Mary was a different kind of person. She was content just to sit at Jesus' feet and listen to His teaching. Martha became very irritated about this. She was so busy with her preparations that she was annoyed to see Mary just sitting there. She went to Jesus and said: "Lord, do You not care that my sister has left me to do all the work alone? Please tell her to help me." But the Lord answered and said: "Martha, Martha, you are worried about too many things! But really only one thing is necessary. Mary has chosen the good part, and it cannot be taken away from her."

The Eyes of the Blind Are Opened

John 9 and Luke 10

One day, while Jesus was walking down one of the streets in Jerusalem, He saw a man who had been blind from birth. The disciples believed, as did all the Jews then, that all sickness or afflictions came as a direct result of someone's sin. They asked Jesus about this blind man: "Master, who sinned, this man, or his parents, that he should be born blind?" The answer must have surprised them: "It was neither this man nor his parents. This has hap-

pened so that the works of God might be displayed in him. We must do the works of God as long as it is day. The night is coming, when no one can work. While I am in the world, I am the light of the world."

When He had said this, He spat on the ground and made clay with the saliva. Then He touched the blind man's eyes with the clay. Jesus then told him to go and wash in the pool of Siloam. Friends led him away to the pool. When he came back he could see as well as anyone else. All the people who had known this man when he was a blind beggar were amazed.

"How could this possibly happen?" they asked. "How were your eyes opened?" He answered: "The man called Jesus made clay, and put it on my eyes, and told me to go and wash in the pool of Siloam. I did what He said, and now I can see."

Then they took him to the Pharisees, who asked him the same questions. But they were annoyed. It was the Sabbath day, and they said that Jesus could not have come from God, or else He would not have healed on the Sabbath!

Then the rulers spoke to the man who had been blind. "What do you say about the Man Who healed your eyes?" they asked him. He said: "He is a prophet." But they were still unwilling to believe that Jesus had really done this miracle. They even refused to listen to the man when he said that he never had been able to see before Jesus had opened his eyes. They called his parents and asked them about it, too. "Is this your son," they said, "who you say was born blind? Then how is it that now he can see?" His parents answered: "We know that this is our son, and that he was born blind. We do not know how it is that now he can see, or who opened his eyes. But he is old enough. Ask him yourselves!"

They called the man again, and said to him: "Give glory to God for what has happened. We know that this Man is a sinner." But he had the answer for them: "Whether He is a sinner, I do not know. But one thing I do know, once I was blind, now I can see." Then they said: "But what did He do to you? How did He open your eyes?" By now the man was getting angry. "I have told you already," he said, "but you will not listen. Why do you want to hear again? Do you want to become His disciples?"

That made them furious. They mocked him, and said: "You are His disciple, but we are Moses' disciples." But the man said to them: "Now that is a strange thing. This Man opened my eyes, yet you do not know where He is

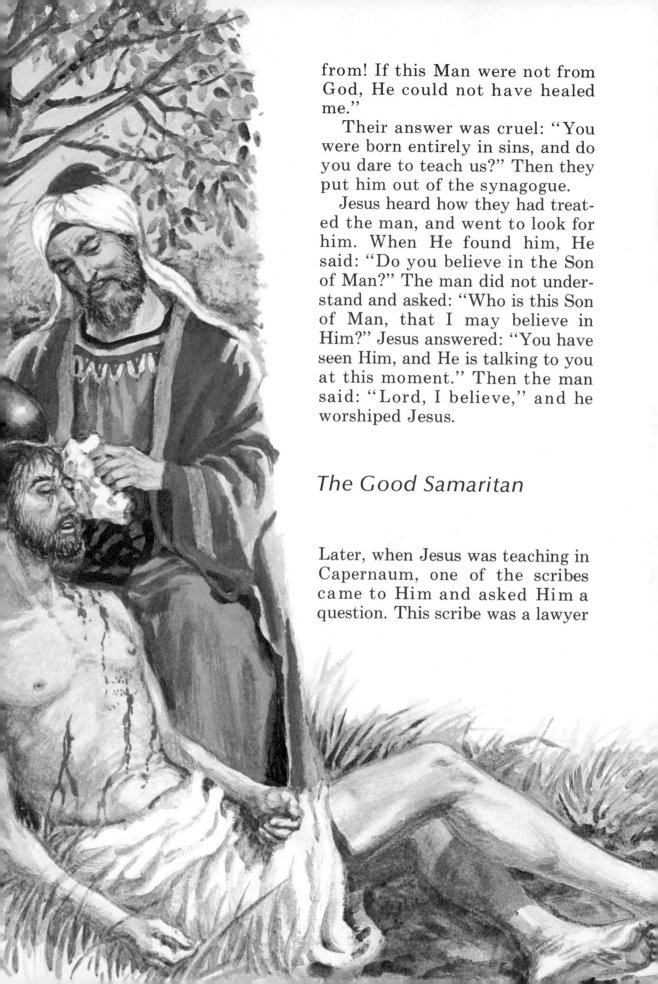

from! If this Man were not from God, He could not have healed me."

Their answer was cruel: "You were born entirely in sins, and do you dare to teach us?" Then they put him out of the synagogue.

Jesus heard how they had treated the man, and went to look for him. When He found him, He said: "Do you believe in the Son of Man?" The man did not understand and asked: "Who is this Son of Man, that I may believe in Him?" Jesus answered: "You have seen Him, and He is talking to you at this moment." Then the man said: "Lord, I believe," and he worshiped Jesus.

The Good Samaritan

Later, when Jesus was teaching in Capernaum, one of the scribes came to Him and asked Him a question. This scribe was a lawyer and an expert in the Law. This is the question he asked: "Master, which is the great commandment in the Law?" Jesus answered him, saying: "You shall love the Lord your God with all your heart and with all your soul and with all your mind. This is the first and great commandment, and the second is like it. You shall love your neighbor like yourself. The whole Law and all the writings of the prophets depend on these two commandments."

The lawyer knew that he had not kept the first commandment properly, so he tried to argue with the Lord Jesus about the second one: "But who is my neighbor?"

he asked. Then Jesus told him a story, a story which we now know as the Parable of the Good Samaritan.

"A certain man was traveling down from Jerusalem to Jericho. On the way he was attacked by robbers. They stripped him of his clothes and beat him and went off leaving him there half dead. Soon, a priest came along, also going to Jericho. When he saw the man lying there, he crossed over to the other side of the road and went on. Then a Levite came along and also crossed over to the other side and went on. But then a Samaritan came upon the man. When the Samaritan saw him, his heart was filled with pity. He stopped and bandaged the man's wounds, first putting a little wine and olive oil in them to help them get better. Then he lifted the man onto his own beast's back and took him to the nearest inn. He gave the innkeeper some money to take care of the man. The Samaritan promised that when he came back, if it had cost more to look after the man, he would pay the difference.

"Which of these three men, do you think, behaved like a neighbor to the man attacked by the robbers?"

Grudgingly the lawyer answered Jesus: "I suppose the one who pitied him and took care of him." Then Jesus said: "Go and behave in the same way."

That is how Jesus showed that to please God we must always be ready to help anyone who is in trouble or need.

Lazarus Lives Again

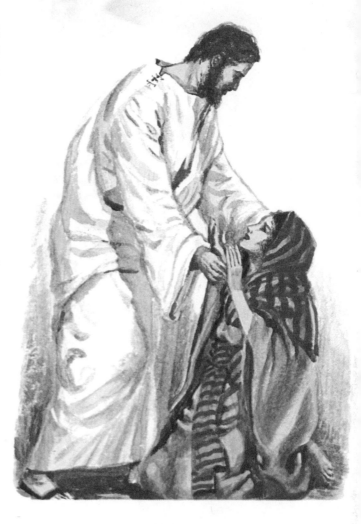

John 11

Martha and Mary and Lazarus, the very good friends of the Lord Jesus, lived in the little village of Bethany near Jerusalem. One day Lazarus fell very seriously ill. His sisters sent a messenger to find Jesus and tell Him the sad news.

Jesus loved these three, but when he received the news about Lazarus, He did a very strange thing. He stayed two days longer in the place where He was! On the third day He started off on the journey back from Galilee to Judea. The disciples were very worried at this, because they knew how much the Judeans hated Him. They knew how the Judeans were planning to kill Him. Jesus said to them: "Our friend Lazarus is sleeping, and I am going to Judea to wake him up." The disciples did not know what He meant. They said: "Lord, if he is asleep, that is good news. It means he is beginning to get better." But Jesus then put it plainly: "Lazarus is dead, but I am glad for your sakes that I was not there so that you may believe. Let us go to him."

When Jesus reached Bethany, Lazarus' body had already been in the tomb for four days. There were many people with Martha and Mary comforting them. When Martha heard that Jesus was near, she went out to meet Him, but Mary stayed behind in the house weeping.

When she came to Jesus, Martha said to Him: "Lord, if You had been here, my brother would not have died. But even now I know that God will give You whatever You ask from Him."

333

Jesus answered quietly: "Your brother will rise again." Martha said: "Yes, Lord, I know that he will rise again at the great resurrection on the last day."

Then Jesus replied: "I am the resurrection, and the life. Whoever believes in Me shall live, even if he dies, and whoever lives and believes in Me shall never die. Do you believe this?" And Martha said: "Yes, Lord, I do believe that You are the Christ, the Son of God, Who was promised by the Father."

When Martha had said this, she went away to call her sister Mary to come and speak to the Lord,

too. When she whispered the news of His coming to Mary, her sister stood up and quickly slipped out of the house. When the rest of the people saw this, they followed her. They thought she was going to the tomb to weep there.

When Mary reached Jesus, she threw herself down at His feet, and cried out: "Lord, if You had been here, my brother would not have died." When Jesus saw her weeping, and her other friends weeping too, He was very upset, and asked: "Where have you laid his body?" They said: "Lord, come and see!" And as He followed them, Jesus wept.

Many of the people, when they saw this, said: "See how much He loved Lazarus." But others were puzzled, and said: "Surely if this Man could open the eyes of the blind, He could also have prevented Lazarus from dying?"

By now Jesus was at the tomb, which was carved out of a rock, The tomb had a great stone lying against its mouth, to close it. Jesus said to the men standing by: "Take away the stone." But Martha was terribly upset at this. Lazarus had been in the grave for four days already! Jesus said to her: "Did I not tell you that if you believed, you would see the glory of God?"

So they took away the stone, and then Jesus began to pray: "Father, I thank You that You hear Me," He said. "I know that You hear Me, but I have prayed this for the sake of the people standing round about, that they may learn to believe that You really have sent Me." Then He cried out: "Lazarus, come forth!" And as He spoke, out of the tomb came Lazarus, bound hand and foot in bandages, and with his face wrapped in a cloth. Jesus told the men standing by to unwrap him and let him go home.

Many of the people standing by were amazed at Jesus' miraculous power. Many believed in Him, but others went to the Pharisees and told them about the things Jesus had done. The Pharisees decided at once to call a special council. They discussed what to do to put a stop to Christ's progress. Some of them even said: "This Man is doing many wonderful deeds. If we let Him go on like this, all the people will follow Him. There could even be a disturbance about it. Then the Romans will take away the few rights we still have left." But Caiaphas, the high priest, knew what they should do, and this is what he said: "It is better that one man should die rather than that the whole nation should be wiped out.

336

We must see to it that this Man is put out of the way." He did not realize it, but in his anger against Christ he was actually telling a great truth. Christ *had* come to die, so that many people, not only from among the Jews, but in all the world, should not have to die eternally.

From that time onward, the Jewish leaders were determined to put Jesus to death. And from then on, until the last week of His life, Jesus taught only in the small out-of-the-way wilderness village of Ephraim.

Tales That Teach

Matthew 19 and 20; Mark 10;
Luke 12 to 18

One day, when a great crowd had gathered to listen to Him, Jesus warned them what it would mean really to follow Him. "If anyone does not love Me more," He said, "than even his father and mother and wife and children and brothers and sisters, yes, even than his own life, he cannot be My disciple. Whoever is not willing to carry his own cross and come after Me, is not fit to be My disciple. I am telling you this beforehand, so that you know exactly what it means to follow Me. If you want to be My disciples, you must be ready to give up all for My sake."

Many of the tax gatherers and outcasts of the people were among the crowds who went to listen to Jesus. Sometimes He enjoyed a meal together with them, so that He could teach them. The Pharisees grumbled about this, and said: "This man goes about with sinners, and eats with them." Then Jesus told them several stories to show them how silly they were being. "Which one of you," He said, "who owns a hundred sheep and has lost one of them, will not leave the ninety-nine and go out and look for the other? When he finds it, he will carry it home across his shoulders, and then call his friends and

neighbors to rejoice with him because he has found it. In the same way there will be more joy in heaven over one sinner that repents than over ninety-nine righteous people who do not need to repent."

Then Jesus told them a story which is still very well known: the Parable of the Prodigal Son. "A certain man had two sons. The younger of them became tired of living at home. He went to his father and asked to be given the share of his father's riches that would one day be his. The father divided his wealth between the two sons. The younger son went to country a long way off. There he wasted all he had been given in pleasure and bad living. When he had spent everything, there was severe drought and famine in the land, and he was in great need. He went and found work with one of the people of the country far from home. He was sent out into the fields to feed pigs. Things went so badly for him that he longed even to eat the pigs' food, he was so hungry. Now all this made him begin to think. Back at home, even his father's servants would have all the food they needed. Here he was, a rich man's son, dying of hunger! He would go back to his father, and say to him: "Father, I have sinned against heaven, and against you, too. I am not fit to be called your son. Just

let me be as one of your servants."
After a long journey, he came in
sight of his home once more. Before he could actually reach home,
his father came running out to
meet him. The father then sent off
his slaves to bring out the best
robe and put it on him, and to put
a ring on his finger and sandals on
his feet. Then he told them also to
take the fattest calf and make
ready a great feast, so that all
could rejoice over the homecoming
of his son. 'For,' he said, 'this son
of mine was dead, and is alive
again. He was lost, and has been
found!' So the feasting began. But
the elder brother was annoyed
when he heard what was happening. He would not go in to the
feast, but called his father aside
and said to him: 'Look! I have
served you for many years. I have
listened to everything you told
me, but you have never held a
feast for me so that my friends
could come and enjoy it with me.
But now this son of yours has
come, who wasted all your riches
in wicked pleasures. For him you
have the fatted calf killed!' But his
father answered: 'My child, you
have always been with me, and all
that I have, is yours. But your
brother was dead and now he lives
again; he was lost, but now is
found.' "

In this story, Jesus was telling
that He had come to seek and to
save those that were lost.

The Rich Man and the Richer Beggar

Another story Jesus told was
about a rich man. The rich man
lived in great luxury, and feasted
every day. At the gate of his house
lay a poor beggar. The beggar's
body was covered with sores. He
longed to have even the crumbs
that fell from the rich man's table
to fill his empty stomach. It was
so bad for this poor man that even
the dogs came and licked his

sores. The beggar died, and the angels carried away his soul to Abraham's bosom. Shortly afterward the rich man died, and was buried. In the world of the dead he woke up to find himself in great torment. There he saw, a long way off, Abraham, and in his arms was Lazarus the beggar. Then he cried out to Abraham: "Father Abraham, have mercy on me and send Lazarus so that he may dip his finger in water and cool this tongue of mine, for I am in agony in this flame." But Abraham said: "Remember that in life you lived in luxury and comfort, while Lazarus suffered. Now he is being comforted, and you are suffering. Besides that, there is a great gap between you and us which cannot be crossed." Then the man cried out: "Father Abraham, I beg you to send him to my father's house. I have five brothers there. Warn them not to come to this place of torment also." But Abraham said: "They have the writings of Moses and the prophets. Let them pay attention to what they read there." But the man cried out in agony: "No, Father Abraham, but if someone goes to them from the dead, they will listen." Then Abraham ended the conversation with these words: "If they do not listen to Moses and the prophets, neither will their ways change if someone returns to them from the dead."

A rich young man came to Jesus one day and asked Him what he must do to gain eternal life. Jesus told him that, as a Jew, he must keep God's commandments. The young man said that he had always kept the Law since he was a child, but he felt that he still lacked something. Then Jesus said: "If you really want eternal life, sell all that you have and go and give to the poor. Then you will have treasure in Heaven. Come then and follow Me." That made the young man very sad. He was very much attached to all his possessions. He went away unhappy.

Jesus said to the disciples: "It is easier for a camel to go through the eye of a needle than for a rich man to enter the kingdom of God. But with God it is even possible for a rich man to be saved."

When Jesus taught the people, He used words they could understand easily. He did not want them to miss the lessons He was trying to bring to them. That was often the reason why He told them stories. Some of the stories were especially made up. Others were of incidents of which He knew, but all the stories carried important lessons for the people who heard them. One of them was the story of the unjust steward. There was once a rich man who paid another man to be his steward and look after his goods. It was reported to the rich man that this steward was wasting his property and not looking after it well. He sent for the steward and asked him about what he was hearing. "Give an account of your stewardship," he said, "because you cannot be steward any longer." The steward said to himself: "What shall I do now? I cannot dig, and I am ashamed to beg. I must do something, so that when I am turned out of the stewardship, I shall have friends to look after me." Then he called each of his master's debtors and reduced the amount each of them owed to the master. When the master heard of this, he praised the dishonest steward for his cleverness in gaining friends for himself by what he did. When Jesus had finished telling this story, He said to the disciples: "The children of this world are more cunning than the children of the light. If that man was clever enough to make sure he would have friends in his time of need, how much more clever you ought to be who are the children of righteousness! Take care that the people who have no care for the things of God do not put you to shame by their zeal."

Jesus was not praising the steward's dishonesty, but warning all His disciples to be more earnest about doing good than the ungodly were about doing evil. We cannot serve two masters. We must either serve God, or the prince of this world.

The Lord Jesus told other stories to warn people that they should take care not to think of themselves as better than others, but to be honest with themselves. One of them was the story of the Pharisee and the publican, or tax gatherer, who went to the Temple in Jerusalem to pray. The Pharisee stood and prayed: "God, I thank You that I am not like other people, swindlers, unjust, adulterers, or even like this tax gatherer. I fast twice a week and pay Temple tithes of all that I get." But the tax gatherer stood

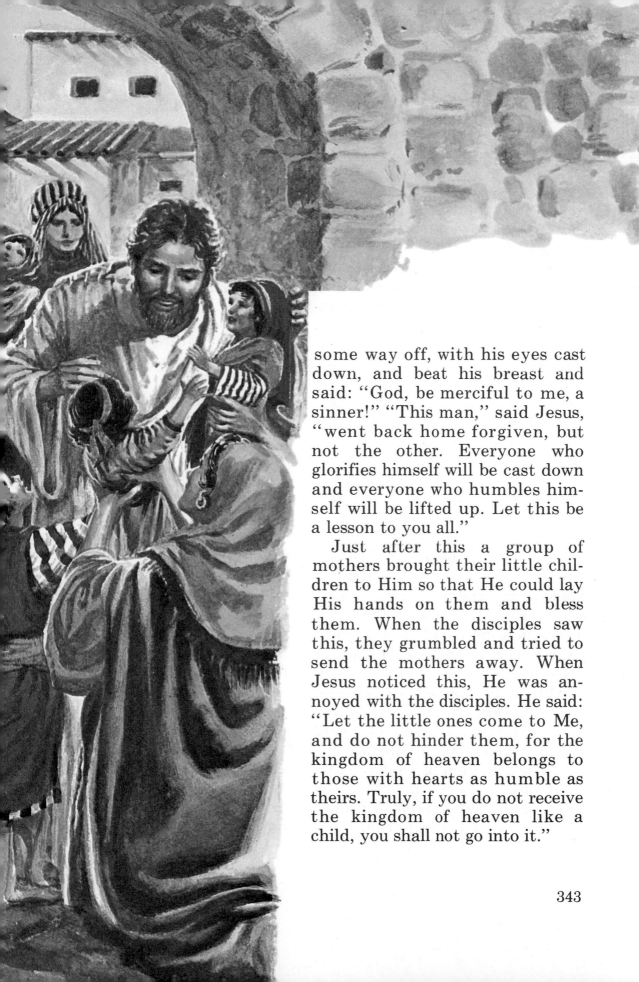

some way off, with his eyes cast down, and beat his breast and said: "God, be merciful to me, a sinner!" "This man," said Jesus, "went back home forgiven, but not the other. Everyone who glorifies himself will be cast down and everyone who humbles himself will be lifted up. Let this be a lesson to you all."

Just after this a group of mothers brought their little children to Him so that He could lay His hands on them and bless them. When the disciples saw this, they grumbled and tried to send the mothers away. When Jesus noticed this, He was annoyed with the disciples. He said: "Let the little ones come to Me, and do not hinder them, for the kingdom of heaven belongs to those with hearts as humble as theirs. Truly, if you do not receive the kingdom of heaven like a child, you shall not go into it."

Many of the people had questions to ask Him. One of them said: "Master, speak to my brother and tell him to divide the family inheritance with me." But Jesus answered: "Who appointed me to settle your petty squabbles? Be on your guard against greed. The real value of a man's life does not lie in the riches he possesses."

Then Jesus turned to His disciples, and said: "That is why I told you not to be anxious about your life, what you shall eat, nor for your body, what you shall put on. Life is more than food, and the body more than clothing. Think for a moment of the ravens. They do not sow nor reap, neither do they build storerooms to put away goods, but God feeds them. Are men not more important than birds? Think, too, of the lilies. They neither toil nor spin, but I tell you that Solomon in all his glory was never clothed like one of these. If God clothes the grass in the field like this, which is here today and gone tomorrow, how much more will He take care that you are clothed, O men of little faith! The people of the world worry about these things, but God knows all your needs. Trust in Him. Instead of being anxious about such things, seek first the kingdom of God and His righteousness. Then all your needs will be supplied. Do not be afraid, little flock. It is the Father's joy to give you the Kingdom. Give your riches to help the poor. Provide for yourselves instead treasure in heaven where no thief can snatch it away, nor moth destroy it. Where your treasure is, there will your heart be also."

The Lord Jesus Visits Jericho

Matthew 20; Mark 10; Luke 18 and 19

From the land of Ephraim, Jesus and His disciples began their sad journey up to Jerusalem. The road went through the city of Jericho. Near to that city Jesus again showed His power.

A poor blind beggar called Bartimaeus was sitting by the roadside. When he heard the crowd coming along the road, he asked what was happening. They told him that Jesus of Nazareth was passing by. At once the poor man began to cry out: "Jesus, Son of David, have mercy on me!" Those leading the crowd angrily told him to be still, but he cried out louder than ever. Then Jesus stopped, and told them to bring the blind man to Him. Then Jesus asked what he wanted done. The blind man answered: "Please, Lord, I am blind. I want to receive my sight." Jesus said to him: "Re-

ceive your sight. Your faith has made you well again."

Zacchaeus

That incident took place just before the party reached Jericho. In Jericho another great event was seen, a different kind of thing. This time a man's whole character was changed.

In Jericho lived a very rich man called Zacchaeus. He was the chief tax gatherer. He wanted very much to see Jesus, but he was short and could not see through the crowd. He had a clever idea, though. He climbed up into the branches of a sycamore tree and looked down from there to see the Lord Jesus. When Jesus reached the foot of that tree, He looked up and said: "Zacchaeus, come down quickly, because I must stay in your house today."

Though honest, Zacchaeus was a sinner. As he came down from the tree he said: "Lord, half of my possessions I give to the poor. If I have taken anything unjustly from a person, I will give him back four times as much." Jesus said to him: "Today salvation has come to this house. You have shown yourself to be a true son of Abraham. For the Son of Man has come to seek and to save that which was lost."

The Parable of the Pounds

As Jesus and His disciples drew nearer to Jerusalem, He knew that they expected Him to establish the kingdom of God. Jesus told a story to try to help them understand that He must first go away from this world for a time. The story was about a nobleman. The nobleman went to a far off country to receive a kingdom for himself and then returned home again. Before he left he called his ten servants, and gave to each of them a talent of money. They were to use the money to do business for him until he came back.

When the nobleman came back, having received the kingdom, he called the servants to whom he had given the money. He wanted to ask them how much they had gained by trading. The first reported that he had earned an extra ten pounds with his talent. When his master heard that, he said: "Well done, you good servant. Because you have been faithful in this little matter, I will make you the ruler over ten cities in my kingdom." The second reported that he had earned an extra five pounds. The master complimented him, too, and made him ruler over five cities. But the other man came and said: "Lord, here is your pound, which I have kept hidden in a cloth. I was afraid of you. I knew you were a hard man, so I did not risk possibly losing the money if I did business with it." Then his master said to him: "You have condemned yourself. Because you knew I was a hard man you

should have at least have placed my money in the bank where it could have earned interest." Then he said to those who stood by: "Take away the pound from him, and give it to the man who brought ten pounds." When they objected and said: "But, lord, that man has ten pounds already!" he said: "I say to you that to him that has shall be given, and from him that has not will be taken away even the little that he has. Now bring those that refused to have me as their king, and slay them all in front of me."

Jesus told His disciples this story to warn them that He must go away from them, but in His absence they must serve Him faithfully and fruitfully.

The Children Knew Their King

Matthew 21 and 26; Mark 11 and 14; Luke 19 and 22; John 12

Just outside Jerusalem where the Roman road from Jericho came into the city, was the little village of Bethphage. The village was on the slopes of the Mount of Olives. When the Lord and His party reached this place, He sent two disciples into the village on a special errand. As soon as they came into the village, He told them that they would find a donkey tied up with her colt alongside her. They must untie them, and bring them to the Lord. If anyone stopped them and asked them what they were doing, they should say that the Lord had need of the donkeys. All this was done to fulfil the words of the prophet Zechariah, who said: "Say to the daughter of Zion, 'See your King is coming to you, gentle, and mounted on a donkey.'"

The disciples brought the donkeys to the Lord. Then they spread their cloaks on the back of the donkey and set the Lord on her back. As He began slowly to move along the road into Jerusalem, the crowds that watched spread their cloaks in the way. Others cut down palm branches and spread them on the road in front of Him. As He went, they shouted out His praises: "Hosanna to the Son of David. Blessed is He Who comes in the Name of the Lord; Hosanna in the highest."

When the party reached the outskirts of Jerusalem, all the people who saw them and heard the shouts of praise, were puzzled, and asked: "Who is this?" Then the crowds shouted back to them: "This is the prophet Jesus, from Nazareth in Galilee." In the crowd were some of the Pharisees. They were very angry at what was happening. They went to Jesus and said to Him: "Master, rebuke your disciples." He answered: "I tell you this. If these people were to

be still, the very stones would cry out!"

Jesus went right on to the Temple in the middle of the city. There He found men, right in the courts of the House of Prayer, buying and selling doves and small animals for sacrifice. They were exchanging money for special Temple coins at very dishonest rates. And this was on the Sabbath day, too! Then Jesus was very angry. He said to the traders: "In the Scriptures it is written: My house shall be called a house of prayer, but you have made it a robbers' lair." He overturned the

tables of the money-changers. He drove out all the men who were dishonoring God's house with their crooked business. Then the blind and the lame flocked to Him, and He healed them in the Temple courtyard.

When they saw the wonders He was doing, even the little children gathered around and cried out: "Hosanna to the Son of David." The children knew their King, but the chief priests and the scribes were angry over what they saw and heard. They went to the Lord Jesus and said to Him crossly: "Don't You hear what they are saying?" Jesus answered: "Yes; but have you never read in

the Scriptures: Out of the mouths of babes and infants Thou hast prepared praise for Thyself?"

That night the Lord Jesus and His disciples went back to the little village of Bethany about two miles outside Jerusalem. They planned to spend the night for the last time with Martha and Mary and their brother Lazarus, the man Jesus had raised from the dead.

As Jesus and His disciples lay on low benches around the dinner-table, suddenly a woman came into the room with an alabaster jar of very expensive perfumed ointment. She poured it out on Jesus' head, and some on His feet as well, and wiped them with her own hair. Now some of the disciples were annoyed about this. They thought she was doing something very wasteful. One of them, Judas Iscariot, said: "Why was this ointment not sold, and the money given to the poor? It would have brought a high price." The truth was that Judas was not really interested in the poor. He was a thief and wanted to steal from the moneybag which the Lord had given him to look after.

Jesus said to him: "Leave her alone. She has done this to prepare Me beforehand for My burial. The poor are always with you. You will have many chances of helping them, but I shall not always be with you. Truly, I tell you that wherever this gospel is preached from now on, what this woman has done will be remembered to her honor."

Then Judas slipped out and went to the chief priests, and said to them: "What are you willing to give me to deliver Him into your hands?" And they paid him thirty pieces of silver. From then on, Judas looked for a suitable time to betray Jesus Christ into the hands of His enemies.

Jesus Visits the Temple for the Last Time

*Matthew 21; Mark 11;
Luke 20 and 21*

The next morning the Lord Jesus returned from Bethany to Jerusalem. On the way He saw a lone fig tree beside the road. There was no fruit on it. Then Jesus said: "Never bear any fruit again!" Now that seems a strange thing to do. The disciples thought so, too, especially when the leaves of the tree began to wither at once. Jesus explained why He had done this. "If you have faith in God, and do not doubt," He said, "you shall not only do what I have done to this fig tree, but if you say to this mountain: Be cast into the sea, that is what will happen. Whatever you ask for in prayer, really believing that God will give it, you shall receive."

Once again Jesus went up to the Temple. Again the priests and elders came to argue with Him. By this time the Pharisees and priests were doing their utmost to trap Jesus into saying something they could use as a reason for dragging Him before the courts and having Him condemned to death. They sent along some of their followers and some of the servants of Herod the tetrarch, to ask Him a question. "Tell us," they asked, "is it lawful to pay tax to the Roman Caesar, or not?" This was a tricky question. If He said it was right to pay tax, that would annoy the people who hated the Romans. If He said that it was not right, then He would be guilty of treason against the Roman rulers. But Jesus saw the trick. He asked them to bring Him a coin. He held it up in front of them and asked: "Whose likeness is on this coin?" They answered: "Caesar's." He said: "Then give to Caesar the things that belong to Caesar, and to God the things that are God's." The priests and Pharisees were speechless. They just did not know what to say.

The Lord Will Come Again

Matthew 24 and 25; Luke 21

As they left the Temple gates, Jesus pointed to the great Temple buildings, and said to His disciples: "Do you see the greatness of these buildings? I tell you that not one of these building-blocks will be left standing on another and not be thrown down." Then the disciples said to the Lord: "Tell us when these things will be, and what will be the sign of Thy coming, and of the end of the world?"

On the Mount of Olives, Jesus sat down and explained to His disciples what would happen in the ages to come. He spoke first of the destruction of the city of Jerusalem, and then of events that would take place before His return to judge all the world. He told of wars between the nations; of famine and earthquakes; of hatred for those that trusted in Him; of false prophets who would come and claim to be the Christ; and then when all these signs were over, of how He would come again in glory with His angels to make the whole world bow before him.

To explain what He meant, the Lord told His disciples the Parable of the Ten Young Maidens. He said: "In those days the Kingdom of Heaven will be like ten young maidens who took their lamps and went out to meet the bridegroom as he came to the marriage feast. Now five of the maidens were wise, and took spare oil with them for their lamps. The other five were foolish, and took none. The bridegroom was rather long in coming, and all the maidens began to dose off. But suddenly there was a shout: 'The bridegroom is approaching! Come out to meet him.' Then all of them got up and trimmed the wicks of their lamps but the foolish maidens found that their lamps were flickering out. There was no oil left in them. They asked the other girls

to give them some of their oil, but they refused because there would not be enough for them all. Instead they told the foolish maidens to go away and buy some oil quickly. While they were away, the bridegroom came, and the five wise maidens went in with him to the feast. Then the door was shut. When the other five maidens arrived back, they knocked on the door and asked to be let in, but the Lord answered that he did not know them. They had to turn away into the darkness of the night. "This is a warning to you," said the Lord, "to be watchful at all times, and ready, because you do not know the day and the hour when I will come again."

Jesus told the disciples that when He came again, He would come to judge between the godly and the ungodly. This is what it will be like: When the Son of Man comes in glory, attended by all the angels in Heaven, all the nations will be brought before Him. He will separate the good from the bad, just as a shepherd separates the sheep from the goats. Those who are His sheep He will set at His right hand. The others He will set at His left hand. Then He will say to those at His right hand: "Come you blessed of My Father, inherit the Kingdom He has prepared for you from the beginning of the world. For I was hungry, and you gave Me food. I was thirsty, and you gave Me to drink. I was a stranger, and you took Me in. I was naked, and you gave Me clothes. I was sick, and you visited Me. I was in prison, and you came to Me. . . . As you did it to one of these brothers who believe in Me, you did it also to Me." After that, He will say to those on His left hand: "Go away from Me, accursed ones, into the eternal fire which has been made ready for the devil and his angels." And He will say to them: "As much as you did not help one of the least of these brothers of Mine, who believe in Me, you did not do it to Me." And

these persons will go away into eternal punishment, but the righteous will have eternal life.

Now it was only three days to the Passover when Jesus would be betrayed and crucified.

The Last Supper

Matthew 26; Mark 14; Luke 22;
John 13 to 17

On the first day of the Feast of Unleavened Bread, the Passover Feast, the disciples came to the Lord Jesus. They asked Him where He wanted them to prepare for Him to eat the Passover. He gave them an answer which must have seemed very strange to them: "Go into the city and you will find a certain man there. Tell him that the Master says that His time is at hand and He wants to keep the Passover at his house with His disciples. The man will understand."

It was Peter and John who went into the city. As they walked along a certain street in Jerusalem, just as the Lord had told them, they met a man carrying a jar of water. They followed him to his home. When he turned in, they asked him where the guest chamber was where their Master was to eat the Passover. When he showed them, they prepared the room for the meal. Then they

waited until evening for the Lord to come. The Passover lamb had been killed and roasted and the bitter herbs prepared when the Lord arrived in the evening.

Before they began with the Passover meal, Jesus said to all the disciples: "I have longed to eat this Passover and to drink this cup with you before I suffer. But I say to you that I will not eat of this Passover, nor drink of the fruit of the vine with you again until the kingdom of God comes."

Then He stood in front of them and broke into fragments the bread for the meal. After saying a prayer of thanksgiving, He gave the pieces of bread to them, saying: "This is My body which is being given for you. Do this in remembrance of Me." Then He took a cup of wine. After He had given thanks to God for it, He gave it to them one by one, saying: "This cup is the new testament in My blood which is shed for you. Every time you drink of it, you must do it in remembrance of Me."

Then Jesus rose from the table. He took off His outer garment and picked up a towel and a basin of water. He began to wash the disciples' feet and dry them with the towel. When He came to Simon Peter, the disciple said to Him: "Lord, do You wash my feet? No, it cannot be!" But Jesus answered: "What I am doing, you cannot understand now, but you will understand later." Peter, as quick as ever, replied: "Lord, I will not allow You to wash my feet!" Then Jesus said to him: "If you do not allow Me to wash you, you have nothing to do with Me." Impetuous Peter took fright at that: "Lord, then wash not only my feet, but my hands and my head as well!" Jesus said to him: "You do not need more than that I should wash your feet, because those who have already washed need only to have their feet cleansed and then they will be altogether pure." Then to all the disciples He said: "And you are clean, but not all of you." When He said that, He was speaking of the one who would betray Him. Jesus knew who he was.

When He had washed their feet, Jesus lay down again beside the table, and said to them: "Do you understand what I have done to you? You call Me Master and Lord, and you are right, because I am. But if I, the Master and Lord, have washed your feet, you ought also to wash one another's feet. I have given you an example of how you ought to treat one another. I tell you truly. A slave is not greater than his master. Neither are those that are sent greater than the one who sent them. You have heard these things: blessed are you if you do as I have said."

As He sat there talking to them, Jesus suddenly became very sad, and said: "I tell you again, one of

you will betray Me. Just as the Scripture has said: 'He who eats my bread has lifted up his heel against Me.' I tell you this beforehand, so that when it happens, you may believe that I am really God, as I have said." But they didn't understand what He meant, so He said again: "One of you will betray Me."

Then they began to look at one another, and to wonder of whom He was speaking. One after the other, they asked: "Lord, is it I?" Jesus answered: "It is the one

to whom I shall give a morsel of bread after dipping it in the dish of sauce." When He had dipped the piece of bread, He gave it to Judas Iscariot. From that moment the devil took control of the spirit of Judas. The Lord said to him: "What you have to do, do quickly!" The rest of the disciples did not understand, but when Judas heard that, he left and went to tell the priests so that they could take Jesus and kill Him.

When Judas left, the Lord Jesus turned to His disciples and said: "Little children, I shall be with you only a little while longer. You will look for Me, but where I am going you cannot come." Simon Peter said: "But, Lord, why can I not follow You now? I will lay down my life for You." But the Lord said sadly to him: "Peter, I tell you that before the cock crows, you will deny Me three times." Then He turned to the rest of the disciples and said: "Before a new day dawns you will all have deserted Me. Not one of you will remain by My side, but I shall not be alone, for My Father will be with Me."

Then He gave a comforting message to the bewildered disciples: "Let not your hearts be troubled; you believe in God, keep trusting in Me also. I am going to prepare a place for you in My Father's house. I will come again to get you so that you can again be where I am. In the meantime, whatever you ask for from the Father in My Name will be given to you. I will not leave you as orphans. In the world you will have troubles, but be courageous. I have overcome the world."

After this He spent several hours quietly with the disciples, teaching them truth they would have to remember carefully when He had gone. Then He prayed a beautiful and majestic prayer for Himself and the disciples. The prayer is found in the Bible in John, chapter 17.

The Kiss of a Traitor

Matthew 26; Mark 14; Luke 22; John 18

At midnight, after the Lord had eaten the Last Supper with His disciples, He led them out across the brook Kidron to the foot of the Mount of Olives. There was a garden called Gethsemane. At the gateway, Jesus told the disciples to sit and wait for Him while He went into the garden to pray. He took Peter and James and John in with Him. When they were alone, He said to them: "My soul is deeply grieved, even to the point of death. Stay here and watch while I go a little deeper into the garden to pray." Then He went a little way further and threw Himself down on the

ground. He cried out to the Heavenly Father over and over again in agony: "My Father, if it is possible, let this cup pass from Me; yet let it happen not as I want, but as You do."

Going back to the three disciples, He found them not watching, but fast asleep. He said to Peter: "What, could you men not watch with Me even for one hour? You must keep watching and praying so that you do not come into temptation. The spirit is willing, but the flesh is weak." Then He went away and prayed a second time, saying: "My Father,

if this cup cannot pass away unless I drink it, Thy will be done." When He returned to the three disciples, they were asleep once again. He went back to pray a third time, using the same words. As He prayed His agony was so great that the sweat fell from Him like great drops of blood.

When He went back to them this time, He said: "Sleep on now, and take your rest. The time has come. The Son of Man is betrayed into the hands of sinners. Let us be going. The one who is to betray Me is nearby."

Even while He was speaking,

Judas Iscariot arrived. A large company of men with swords and sticks came with Judas. They had been sent by the chief priests and rulers of the people. Judas had arranged with these men that when they saw him greet someone with a kiss, they should immediately take that man prisoner.

When he saw Jesus, Judas stepped forward, saying: "Hail, Master," and kissed Him. Jesus looked at him, and said: "Friend, why have you come? Are you betraying the Son of Man with a kiss?" Then He said to the priests and soldiers who had come with Judas: "Have you come to take Me as if you were catching a thief, with sticks and swords? Did I not teach daily in the Temple, within your reach, and you did not touch Me? But this is your hour, and the hour of the prince of darkness. Take Me now, but let My disciples go in peace."

Now when the disciples saw what was going to happen, they fled, leaving Him alone in the hands of His enemies.

Those who had seized Him led Him away. They took Jesus to the high priest, Caiaphas, and his father-in-law, Annas. Annas had been high priest until the Romans deposed him, but he was still the most powerful man in the land. In the court of Caiaphas were gathered together all the priests and rulers who hated Jesus.

The priests had done their best to find witnesses who would be willing to produce false evidence against Jesus so that they could have Him sentenced to death. Finally, two came forward, who said: "This Man stated that He was able to destroy the Temple of God and build it again in three days." Then Caiaphas asked Jesus what He had to say to that. Jesus would not answer a word. Caiaphas was very angry, and tried to make Jesus speak, but He would

not. Then Caiaphas said: "Tell us, I demand in the Name of God, whether you are the Christ, the Son of God."

Jesus answered: "You have said it yourself. But I tell you this. You will still see the Son of Man sitting at the right hand of power, and coming on the clouds of heaven." Then the high priest tore his own robes and cried out: "He has blasphemed! We need no more witnesses. You have all heard what He said. What must be done with Him?" And they all shouted out: "He should be put to death!" Then they spat in His face, and beat Him with their fists, and slapped Him.

Now while this was happening, Peter stood by the fireside in the courtyard, listening to what was said. A servant girl came up to him, and said: "But you were with that Jesus of Galilee." Peter was frightened and said in front of all who were standing there: "I don't know what you're talking about!" A little later another servant girl saw him as he stood in the porch. She also said: "This fellow was with Jesus of Nazareth!" Peter swore, and said: "I don't know the Man!" After a while some of the men came up to him and said: "Surely you are one of His followers, too. Your accent gives you away. You are a Galilean." Then Peter began to curse and to swear and to say: "I do not know the Man." But as he spoke,

361

the cock crowed. Peter remembered how the Lord had said the night before that before the cock crowed he would have denied the Lord three times. And as Peter thought of this, the Lord turned and looked at him across the courtyard. Then Peter went out into the night, weeping bitterly.

Crowned But With Thorns

Matthew 27; Mark 15; Luke 23; John 18 and 19

The Jewish leaders had no power to sentence any prisoner without the consent of the Roman governor. When the 'trial' of the Lord Jesus by Caiaphas was over, they dragged Him away to the Roman governor, Pontius Pilate. By then Judas realized what a terrible thing he had done in betraying Jesus. He was dreadfully sorry, and went to the chief priests to give them back the money they had paid him. When he came to the Temple, he cried out to the priests: "I have done a terrible wrong in betraying innocent blood!" Cruelly they said: "What has that to do with us? You see to that yourself!" Judas tried to get them to take back the money. When they would not, he threw it down and went away and hanged himself.

While this terrible scene was taking place, the priestly party had reached the palace of Pontius Pilate with their prisoner, Jesus. When they arrived, Pilate challenged them: "What is your charge against this Man?" They answered him: "If He were not a wrongdoer, we would not have brought Him to you!" Then Pilate was angry and said: "Take Him, and judge Him according to your own law." The Jews then gave away the secret of what they were really trying to do. They said, "It is not lawful for us to put any man to death."

Pilate went back into the judgment hall. He called for Jesus to be brought to him privately. He said to Him: "Are you the King of the Jews, as these people say you claim to be? You have heard their accusations. What have you to say? What have you done?" Jesus answered: "My kingdom is not of this world. If My kingdom were of this world, then My disciples would have fought to save Me from My enemies. But My kingdom is of a different kind altogether." Pilate asked again: "Tell me, though, are you really a king?" Jesus said: "What you say is true. I am a king. I came into this world to make known the truth, and everyone who belongs to the truth listens to what I say and obeys Me." "Truth!" said Pilate. "What is truth?" Then he walked out to the Jews, and said to them: "I do not find any fault at all in your prisoner." He could not understand why they hated Jesus so bitterly, but they screamed with rage: "He has been stirring up the people in Jerusalem and right into Galilee."

That gave Pilate an idea. Galilee! This Man came from Galilee, and Galilee was under the control

of Herod the tetrarch. Herod was at the time in Jerusalem. He would send the prisoner to Herod for trial. This was the same Herod who had murdered John the Baptist. Pilate sent Jesus to him.

Now Herod was very glad to see Jesus. He asked Him many questions. Jesus would not say a word, although the priests were standing around and hurling all manner of accusations against Him. When he found he could get no answer, Herod allowed his guards to mock Jesus and beat Him. Herod then sent Jesus back to Pilate.

So Jesus stood again before Pilate, bound and weary and in pain. Before the governor could begin to question Him again, one of his servants brought a message from his wife: "Have nothing to do with that righteous Man. Last night I suffered greatly in a dream because of Him." That frightened Pilate more than ever. He tried in every way possible to have Jesus released.

It was the custom in those days that at the Passover season the governor would release one prisoner whom the people selected. At the time there was in prison a notorious rebel called Barabbas. It seemed unlikely that the people would select him for release because his record was a black one. Pilate hit on what he thought was a clever idea.

He turned to the crowd and said: "Whom do you want me to release for you? Barabbas, or Jesus, Who is called Christ?" He was horrified when he found that the priests and rulers had persuaded the crowd to ask for the release of Barabbas. He tried to argue with them, but they kept on shouting for Barabbas. Then he said to them: "What shall I do then with Jesus, Who is called Christ?" "Crucify Him, Crucify Him!" they screamed. Then he protested. "Why, what evil has He done?" he cried out. But they only shouted all the more: "Let Him be crucified!"

Then Pilate stood in full view of the crowd and took water and washed his hands, saying: "I am innocent of this Man's blood: see to it yourselves." Then he released Barabbas to them, and handed Jesus over to be crucified.

Then the Roman soldiers took Jesus, stripped His clothes from Him, and dressed Him in a scarlet robe. They made a wreath of thorns and placed it on His head as a crown. In His right hand they put a reed. Then they kneeled before Him as if He were their king. They mocked Him and jeered at Him. "Hail, King of the Jews!" they cried, and spit in His face. Then they took the reed and beat Him about the head so that the thorns pierced His brow and the blood ran down His face.

The Darkest Day in All History

Matthew 27; Mark 15; Luke 23; John 19

When the terrible and unjust trials were over, the soldiers of Pontius Pilate led Jesus Christ out to crucify Him. Through the streets of Jerusalem they led Him. They planned to crucify Him on the hill named Calvary, or Golgotha, the Place of a Skull. Jesus had to carry His own cross. When the weight of it became too much for Him and He fell to the ground, the soldiers made Simon the Cyrenian carry it the rest of the way.

Then they nailed Him by His hands and His feet to the cross. They raised the cross upright and planted it in the ground, so that His whole body hung from the cruel nails. Alongside Him were crucified two robbers, one at His right hand and one at His left. The two men cursed Him, but suddenly one said to Jesus: "Lord, remember me when You come into Your kingdom." And Jesus answered: "Truly, I say to you, this very day you will be with Me in Paradise." But the other robber still cursed Him.

There was a little group at the foot of the cross, weeping over what had been done to their Lord. His mother, Mary, was among them. Mary's sister, the mother of John and James was also there. Mary Magdalene, for whom He had done so much and who loved Him so greatly was there. Of the disciples, only John was there.

Jesus had been hanging on the cross since nine o'clock in the morning. Then, at about twelve o'clock, everything became dark. It remained like that for three long hours. Jesus never said a word.

Then, suddenly He cried out with a loud voice from the darkness: "My God, My God, why hast Thou forsaken Me?" These were the words which a prophet had told a thousand years before of

how terribly the Lord would suffer. Then Jesus said: "I am thirsty." Those standing by took a sponge soaked in sour wine and put it on the end of a reed and held it to His lips. When He received the wine, He said in triumph: "It is finished!" Then His head fell against His chest, and as He died, He said: "Father, into Thy hands I give My spirit." And as He died a great earthquake shook the place. The great curtain in front of the Holy Place in the Temple was torn in two from the top to the bottom.

The next day was to be a special Sabbath day for the Jews Their leaders asked the governor to take down the bodies from the crosses before evening. When the soldiers came to the body of the Lord Jesus, they thrust a spear into His side to make sure He was dead. Blood and water came out of the wound.

Joseph of Arimathea, a secret disciple of the Lord Jesus, and Nicodemus, who had asked Jesus questions about the Gospel, took the body, anointed it, bound it in the best linen, and then laid it in a new rock tomb. The tomb was in a garden belonging to Joseph of Arimathea. They rolled a great rock against the mouth of the tomb to close it.

Although the Lord Jesus was dead, the chief priests were still worried. They went to Pilate, and said to him: "Sir, this Man said when He was alive that on the third day He would rise again. Please give orders that the tomb be sealed and guarded until the third day. If this is not done, His disciples will come and steal away the body. They will tell everybody that He has risen from the dead. Then things will be worse than when He was still alive." Pilate said to them: "You have a Temple guard. Set your own men to guard the tomb as well as you know how."

So the Temple guards went to the tomb and sealed the rock door and kept watch until the three days were past.

The Brightest Dawn in All History

Matthew 28; Mark 16; Luke 24; John 20

When the Sabbath was over, as dawn broke on the first day of the week, Mary Magdalene, Mary the mother of James, and Salome took spices and ointments to anoint the body of Jesus. When they reached the tomb they found that an angel had come down from Heaven and had rolled back the rock from the door and now was sitting on it.

The guards were terrified. When the women saw the angel they were afraid, too. But he said to them: "Do not be afraid. I know you are looking for Jesus, Who was crucified. He is not here. He has risen from the dead, as He said He would. Come and see the place where His body lay. Then go quickly and tell His disciples that He has risen from the dead and goes before them into Galilee. They will see Him there."

The women went and told the disciples. Peter and John ran to the tomb. John reached the door first and bent down and looked in. There he saw the linen graveclothes lying just where the body had been, but John did not go in. Then Peter came and went right in. He saw the grave clothes lying there. He also saw in a different place the cloth which had been about Jesus' head, still folded as it had been. Then John went in. Both of them believed that Jesus really had risen again. Mary Magdalene stood there, weeping. As she turned away, she saw a man standing beside her. He said to her: "Woman, why are you weeping? What are you looking for?" Mary thought he was the gardener and said to him: "Sir, if you have carried away His body, tell me where you have laid Him, and I will take Him away." Then Jesus, for that was Who it was, said to her: "Mary." When she heard that, she turned and cried out: "Master!" Then she threw herself down and wanted to take hold of His feet and worship Him, but Jesus said to her: "Do not touch Me, for I have not yet ascended to My Father. Go to My brothers and say to them that I ascend to My Father and yours, and to My God and yours."

In the afternoon two of the disciples were going from Jerusalem to a village called Emmaus. As they went, they talked sadly about what had happened in the past few days. A stranger came up with them and began to join in their conversation. That stranger was really Jesus, although the disciples were not able to recognize Him. He asked them why they were so sad. They told him everything that had happened.

Then the stranger said to them: "O foolish men, so unwilling to

believe what the prophets have foretold! Was it not necessary for the Christ to suffer these things and to enter into His glory?"

When they came close to Emmaus, the village where they were going, they said to the stranger: "Stay with us for it is getting toward evening now and the day is nearly over." And He went in with them. As they all sat at the table, He took bread and blessed it. Then, breaking it, began to give it to them. Suddenly their eyes were opened and they recognized Jesus, their beloved Lord. In the same moment He vanished from their sight.

They rushed back to Jerusalem, and found their friends gathered in a room together. Excitedly they told of their experiences. Then suddenly, while they talked, there was Jesus standing with them! He greeted them with the words: "Peace be with you!" They were startled and thought for a moment they had seen a spirit, but Jesus said to them: "Why are you afraid and disturbed? Look at My hands and My feet. You can see I am your Lord. And a spirit does not have flesh and bones as you see Me to have." They were almost unable to believe what had happened because they were so full of joy. He asked them: "Have you anything here to eat?" They gave Him a piece of a broiled fish, and He ate it in front of them all. Then He said to them: "When I was still with you I told you that everything must happen which was foretold of Me in the Law of Moses and the Prophets and the Psalms. Now you know that it has happened as I said." Then He blessed them and vanished from their sight.

The Lord They Did Not Recognize

Matthew 28; Mark 16; Luke 24; John 20 and 21; Acts 1; 1 Corinthians 15

On the first Easter Day not all the disciples shared in the joy of knowing that their Lord was the victor over death and alive for evermore. Thomas was not with them that day, but during the week they met him and told him all that had happened to them. "We have seen the Lord," they said. But Thomas was so sorrowful over the death of the Lord that he would not believe what they told him. "Unless I see in His hands the marks of the nails, and put my finger into the holes, and put my hand into the wound in His side, I will not believe."

A whole week passed. On the first night of the new week the disciples were together again in the room in Jerusalem. This time Thomas was with them. The doors were locked so that the disciples would be safe inside. Suddenly Jesus stood in their midst and greeted them with the lovely words: "Peace be with you!" Then He turned to Thomas and said: "Thomas, put your finger into the holes in My hands, and place your hand in the wound in My side. Turn from your unbelief, and believe that I really am alive."

Thomas could only cry out: "My Lord and my God!" Jesus said to him: "You have seen Me, and so you have believed. Thomas, the blessed are those who do not need to see, but still believe!"

On the Resurrection morning Jesus and the angels had sent the women with a message to the disciples. They must go into Galilee. They would see Him there. One evening, while they waited, they decided to go out fishing on the lake. They spent the whole night out on the lake, but they did not catch a single fish. As the sun was rising, the little boat was close to the shore. The disciples were mak-ing a last effort to catch some fish. On the beach they saw a man standing, but they could not tell who it was. This man called out to them. It was really the Lord Jesus Himself. He said: "Sirs, have you caught anything?" They answered: "No, nothing at all." Then He said: "Cast in the net on the right side of the boat, and you will find fish." How surprised they were when the net was filled with so many fish that they could not haul it in! Then John realized who the man was. He said to Peter: "It is the Lord!" Peter was so excited that he jumped into the lake and swam to shore. The rest of the dis-

ciples rowed the boat to the shore, dragging the net full of fish behind.

Jesus later appeared where the eleven disciples were eating a meal together. There He gave them a great task which they must carry out in His Name. Those who believed through their teaching must also carry out this great task faithfully. "Go into all parts of the world and preach the Gospel to all people. Those that believe and are baptized shall be saved, but those who do not believe shall be damned." He made a wonderful promise to them also: "Lo, I am with you alway, even to the end of the world."

The last time Jesus showed Himself to His people was when He bid them farewell before returning into Heaven. He called them out to the Mount of Olives, near to the little village of Bethany. There He gave them His final message. They must go back to Jerusalem and wait there quietly until the Holy Ghost,

Whom He had promised to them, had come and filled them with power. Then they would become witnesses for Him. They would be preachers of the Gospel in Jerusalem and in all the provinces of Judea, in Samaria, and in every part of the known world.

He stretched out His arms and blessed them. As they watched, He rose slowly into the sky until a cloud hid Him from their sight. While they gazed up into the sky, two angels in white came to them and said: "Men of Galilee, why do you stand like this, gazing up into the sky? This same Jesus, Who has been taken away from you up into Heaven, will come again in the same way as you have seen Him go."

The Amazing Beginning of the Church

Acts 1 and 2

In the days after the Lord Jesus ascended into Heaven, the disciples

stayed together in Jerusalem, praying and worshiping and waiting for the coming of the Holy Ghost. While they were together in this way, it was soon clear that Peter would become one of their great leaders.

The tenth day after Jesus returned into Heaven was the Jewish festival of Pentecost. The name means 'The Fiftieth Day' because the festival was held on the fiftieth day after the Passover. On that day all the apostles of the Lord Jesus were together in one place. Suddenly there was a sound from Heaven like the roaring of a great wind. Then it was just as if tongues of fire settled on the heads of each of them. They were all filled with the Holy Spirit. They spoke in different languages as the Spirit gave them power. Very soon the news of this got abroad and crowds of people gathered to see what had happened.

Then Peter stepped forward, with the rest of the apostles and began to speak to the crowd in a loud voice so that all could hear. "Men of Judea, and all you who live in Jerusalem," he said, "this is what the prophet Joel foretold when he said, 'It shall take place in the last days, says God, that I will pour out My Spirit on men of all flesh. Your sons and your daughters shall prophesy, and your young men shall see visions, and your old men shall dream dreams. And every one that calls on the Name of the Lord shall be saved.' "

Then Peter told them of the Lord Jesus. Peter reminded them of the miracles Jesus had done in full view of them all, and how wickedly they had crucified Him but God raised Him from the dead. He explained to them how in the Psalms and in the Prophets it was foretold that the Christ, the Son of David, would rise again from the dead; and the disciples had seen the Risen Lord. They knew He was the Christ; and now as the Lord Himself had promised, the Holy Spirit had been poured out on His chosen ones.

When they heard this, the people were troubled and cried out to the disciples: "Men and brethren, what shall we do?" Peter said to them: "Repent, and be baptized, every one of you, in the Name of Jesus Christ, for the forgiveness of your sins. Then you, too, will receive the gift of the Holy Spirit. The promise is to you and to your children, and to those that are far off, as many as the Lord shall call."

The Cripple at the Temple Gate

Acts 3 and 4

In the early days of the church the apostles had wonderful powers given to them by God. One afternoon at about three o'clock, the time for evening service, Peter and John went up to the Temple. When they reached the gate of the Temple called the Beautiful Gate, they found sitting there a beggar who had been lame from birth. As the apostles came by, he asked them for a gift to help him. Peter and John stopped and fixed their gaze on him. Peter said to him: "Look at us." The man expected that they were going to give him some money. Instead, Peter said: "I have no silver or gold, but what I have I give to you. In the Name of Jesus Christ of Nazareth, stand up and

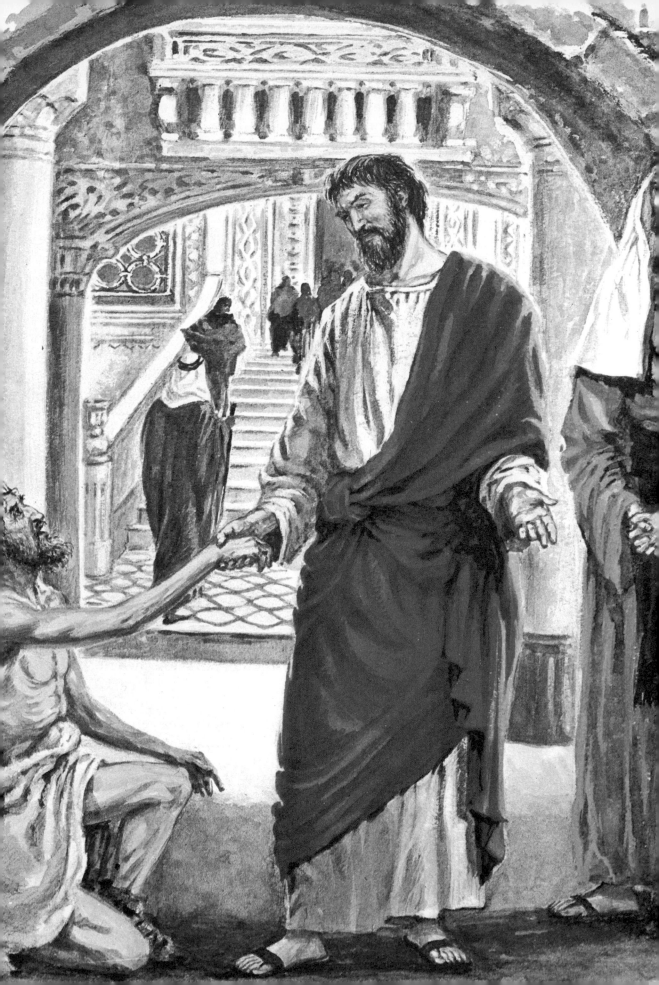

walk." Then Peter took him by the right hand, and lifted him up. The man's feet and ankle bones were strong in that very moment. The man leaped up, and walked with Peter and John into the Temple, praising God.

All the people there saw him. They were amazed, because they recognized him as the man who had sat at the Temple gate unable to walk. They crowded around to see. Then Peter began to speak to them. "Men of Israel," he said, "why are you amazed at this? And why do you look at us as if by our own power we have made this man well? By this act, the God of Abraham and of Isaac and of Jacob, the God of our fathers, has glorified His Son Jesus. This is the same Jesus Whom you delivered into the hands of the Gentiles and disowned in front of Pilate when the governor himself was willing to let Him go. You disowned the Holy and Righteous One and chose a murderer instead. You killed the Prince of Life. But God has raised Him from the dead, and we are witnesses of that fact. We have seen Him alive! It is through faith in His Name that this man has been healed."

While Peter was speaking, the Sadducees and priests and the ruler of the Temple came on the scene. They were angry to find the apostles teaching there. The Sadducees were especially angry be-cause the apostles taught that through Jesus there would be a Resurrection from the dead. The Sadducees did not believe in a life hereafter. To silence Peter and John they had them arrested and thrown into prison.

The next day, Annas and Caiaphas, the high priests, and other important officials who belonged to their family, came together in Jerusalem to try the two apostles. When Peter and John were brought into the room, they asked them: "By what power, or by what name, have you done this?"

Peter, filled with the Holy Ghost, answered them: "If we are being questioned about the good deed done to the crippled man and are being asked how he has received healing, we want you all to know. We want all the people of Israel to know. This man stands before you whole by the Name of Jesus Christ of Nazareth, Whom you crucified, but Whom God raised from the dead. This same Jesus is as the Psalmist said, the stone which was rejected by you, the builders. He has become the very cornerstone of the building. You will not find salvation anywhere else. There is no other name under heaven that has been given among men by which we must be saved."

The Temple leaders could find no reason for punishing the apostles. They were afraid of how

the people would react if they did. So they had to release Peter and John. Before they let them go, though, they threatened the two with terrible punishment if they did not stop speaking and teaching in Jesus' Name.

These two men were filled with a power the Temple rulers knew nothing about. They were filled with the power of the Holy Spirit. Straight back to the rest of the apostles they went. In the Upper Room, which had been their meeting-place since the Last Supper, they praised God and prayed for courage to keep on preaching the Gospel of salvation.

Stephen, Who Saw Jesus at the Gates of Heaven

Acts 6

Many of the first Christians who lived in Jerusalem were very poor. The richer Christians sold all that they had so that the money could be used to help the poor. Some of those Christians were Hebrews and some were Grecian Jews. There was a little unhappiness between them because it was felt that the Grecian Jewish widows were not being looked after properly. The twelve apostles were worried about this. They called a meeting of all the believers, and told them that it was impossible for them properly to look after this side of the work. They were appointed by the Lord to preach the Gospel, and other men must be found to take care of the poor and the sick.

The meeting agreed that this was necessary, and chose Stephen, and Philip, and five other men. They brought them to the apostles, who laid their hands on their heads and prayed for them. From then on these men took care of the needs of the poor, but Stephen and Philip also became great preachers of God's Word.

In Jerusalem there was a special synagogue where certain Jews from foreign places always worshiped together. Men from this synagogue tried to argue against the teaching of Stephen, but Stephen was so wonderfully guided by God's Spirit that he was able to answer all their arguments.

When their attempts failed, they found false witnesses who would lie about what Stephen had taught. These men said: "We have heard this Stephen say that Jesus of Nazareth will destroy this place and change all the customs which Moses gave to us."

The high priest then questioned him. "Is this true?" he asked.

Stephen answered in words which the Holy Spirit gave to him. He reminded them of how Moses had said many centuries ago that God would one day give them a great Prophet to speak to them in His Name. Now God had given them that Prophet, His own Son. Stephen reminded them that, just as their fathers had been hard of heart when they persecuted God's messengers before, they had by wicked hands taken and murdered the Holy Son of God.

When they heard that, the members of the Council were furious. But Stephen stood calmly in front of them. Looking up he saw Heaven opened in front of him, and the glory of God, and Jesus standing at God's right hand. Then he cried out: "Look, I see the heavens opened in front of me, and the Son of Man standing at the right hand of God."

The young man who took care of their coats, watched and agreed with all that the false witnesses did to Stephen. That day a terrible persecution began against all the Christians in and around Jerusalem. Saul stood at the head of it. He had Christian men and women dragged from their homes and thrown into prison. All those who could, except the apostles, fled to faraway parts of Judea and Samaria.

By the hands of Saul and those who were with him the church of Christ, where so many had lived in love and peace, was broken up. Its members were scattered far and wide.

But the men of the Council stopped their ears and would not listen. They rushed forward and dragged him away, out of the Council room and out to beyond the city walls. There the false witnesses took off their coats and gave them to a young man called Saul to keep. Then they began to stone Stephen, while he called out: "Lord Jesus, receive my spirit!" As he sank to his knees under the hail of stones, he cried out loudly: "Please, Lord, do not hold this sin against them." Then he fell asleep in death.

No harm came to the apostles in the city because they were kept hidden.

How the Good News Was Spread

Acts 8

Persecution did not silence the first Christians. Wherever they went, they preached the Gospel. Although the apostles had stayed behind in Jerusalem, after a while Philip went down to Samaria and began to preach there. God gave him the power to do many miracles, just as Stephen had done before. Great crowds of people listened to what he said, and believed. Unclean spirits were driven out of many unhappy people. Some that were paralyzed or crippled were healed.

Then an angel from the Lord told him to go southward to the desert road that leads from Jerusalem to Gaza. Along that road Philip met a chariot. In the chariot was seated an Abyssinian, one of the court officials of their great queen, Candace. This man was reading as he travelled along. He was a believer in the God of Israel and had been up to Jerusalem to worship in the Temple. Now he was reading from the book of Isaiah. He was reading the verses in Isaiah 53 which say, "He is brought as a lamb to the slaughter, and as a sheep before her shearers is dumb, so He opens not His mouth. In His humiliation His judgment was taken away and who shall declare His generation? For His life is taken from the earth." Philip asked the man if he understood what he was reading. "How can I," he asked, "unless some man will explain it to me? Of whom is the prophet speaking? Of himself, or about someone else?" Then Philip used the very verse he was reading, to tell him about the Lord Jesus

Christ, and that man believed. On the way they came to a stream. Right there and then the Abyssinian official asked Philip to baptize him.

When the baptism was over, the Spirit of God caught Philip away miraculously so that he disappeared from the traveler's sight. But the man continued on his way, praising God for what had happened.

On the Road to Damascus

Acts 9 and 22; Galatians 1

Saul, the young man who had looked after the coats of those who stoned Stephen to death, was enraged against the Christians. He wanted them to be persecuted not only in Jerusalem, but in all places where there were Jewish communities and where the Christians had come. He went to the high priest and asked for letters of authority so that he could go to Damascus to the synagogues there to arrest any Christians and bring them as prisoners to Jerusalem.

These letters were given to Saul by the high priest. Saul found a band of men and departed to Damascus. It was a long journey and took about ten days.

At last Saul came near to Damascus. The long journey was nearly over. Then suddenly, at midday, a light, far brighter than the sun shone from heaven round about Saul. He fell to the ground. Then he heard a voice saying to him: "Saul, Saul, why do you persecute Me?" Saul answered: "Who art Thou, Lord?" Then the voice spoke again: "I am Jesus, Whom you are persecuting: it is hard for you to fight against Me. Go now into Damascus, and you will be told there what you must do."

The men who were traveling with Saul stood there speechless. They were hearing a voice speaking, but not seeing anyone. When Saul got up from the ground, his eyes were open but he could see nothing. Others had to lead him by the hand until they came to the city of Damascus. For three days Saul was blind, and did not eat or drink.

In Damascus there lived a disciple of the Lord Jesus, called Ananias. In a vision the Lord said to him: "Ananias, go to the street called Straight, to the house of a man named Judas. A man of Tarsus is staying there, whose name is Saul. Ask for him when you get there. You see, he is praying, and in a vision he has seen a man named Ananias come and lay his hands on him so that he may be able to see again." Ananias answered: "But, Lord, I have heard many people tell about the harm this man has done to the believers in Jerusalem. And now he has authority from the high priest to persecute us in Damascus as well."

But the Lord said: "Ananias, go to him as I have told you, because he is My chosen servant to be a witness for Me to the Gentiles and before kings even, as well as to the children of Israel. I will show him how much he will have to suffer for My Name's sake."

So Ananias went to the house of Judas. He found Saul there as the Lord had told him. He laid his hands on the blind man, and said: "Brother Saul, the Lord Jesus, Who appeared to you while you were coming to Damascus, has sent me to you so that you may be given your sight again and receive the Holy Spirit." In that very moment something like scales fell from Saul's eyes. He was able to see again! Then he got up, and was baptized and became a follower of the Lord Jesus Christ. For three days he had eaten nothing. Now he feasted with Ananias and Judas as a Christian believer.

For several days longer Saul stayed with the disciples in Damascus. Every day he went into the synagogues and preached to the people the Gospel of Jesus Christ. He told them that Jesus is the Son of God. Those who heard were amazed. They knew how Saul had hated and harmed the Christians. They knew, too,

why he had come to Damascus. Each day his words were firmer and clearer. None could argue against him when he proved that Jesus is the Christ.

At first, many of the Christians would not have anything to do with him. They still remembered his terrible cruelty toward believers in earlier years, and were afraid. But Barnabas became his close friend. Barnabas told all the Christians how the Lord Jesus had met with Saul. He told them how Saul had preached fearlessly in Damascus. Soon Saul was accepted in all the congregations, and preached in all parts of Jerusalem.

The Gospel Is for All Nations

Acts 9 and 11

In Caesarea at that time there was stationed a Roman officer. He was a centurion who belonged to the Italian battalion of the Roman army. He was a believer in the God of Israel. The officer was a godly man, who was always kind to the Jews and spent much time in prayer.

One afternoon, while he was praying, he saw a vision of an angel who came to him, and said: "Cornelius, your prayers and your gifts to the poor have come to the notice of God in Heaven. Send some men now to Joppa, to the house of Simon the tanner, by the seashore. There they will find another man named Simon Peter. They must bring him to you in Caesarea." Cornelius sent three men off to Joppa at once.

At noon the next day, while these men were on their way from Caesarea, Peter went up on to the roof of the house of Simon the tanner to pray.

While he was there, he fell into a trance. He saw the heavens opened up and an object like a great sheet lowered down by its four corners to the ground. In this sheet were all kinds of animals and creeping things and birds. Then a voice said to Peter: "Arise, Peter, kill and eat." But Peter said: "No, Lord. I have never eaten anything which according to the Law is unholy or unclean." The voice answered: "What God has cleansed, you must no longer call unholy." This happened three times. Then, in the vision, the sheet was drawn back into heaven. Peter was puzzled about the meaning of what he had seen.

The men from Cornelius arrived and asked for Simon Peter. At the same time the Holy Spirit spoke to Peter, and said: "Three men are looking for you. Go down to them, for I have sent them to you Myself."

The next day Peter left with the men, to go to Caesarea. Cornelius was waiting. He explained about the angel who had come to him and told him to send for Peter. Now they had all gathered to hear what Peter had been commanded by the Lord to say.

This was the message the apostle gave to them: "Through all that has happened, I know now that God is not partial to the people of one nation only. In every nation those who fear God and keep His commandments are His blessed children. Now the glorious message about Jesus Christ, Whom God has sent, is not for the Jews only, but for people of all nations. You know of the life of Jesus Christ, how God anointed Him with power and how He went about doing good and healing all who were sick and tormented by the devil. You know, too, how He was crucified; but God raised Him up on the third day. We, and many of His disciples, saw Him after His resurrection, and even ate and drank with Him. Now, He has told us to go and preach to all people that He is the One Who will yet judge the living and the dead. He is the Messiah of Whom the prophets have told us. All who trust in Him will receive forgiveness of their sins."

While they were still listening to what Peter said, the Holy Spirit came into their hearts, and many believed in Jesus Christ.

All who believed were baptized in the Name of Jesus Christ,

and from then on the Gospel was preached to both Jews and Gentiles.

The First Missionaries

Acts 11 and 13

The Gospel of the Lord Jesus Christ was first preached in Jerusalem. The Gospel was preached there only until the persecution began in that city. As the Christians fled to other parts of the land, they carried the Gospel with them and told others about the Lord. Some went to Phoenicia, some to Cyprus, and some to Antioch. At first they spoke only to other Jews. There were some, though, who came to Antioch from other parts. They began to tell not only the Jews but Gentiles too, the wonderful truth about salvation through the Lord Jesus. Many of the Gentiles to whom they spoke put their trust in the Lord. The news about this soon reached the ears of the believers in Jerusalem. They sent Barnabas off to Antioch to see what was happening and to help if it was needed.

Barnabas decided that more workers were needed, so he went to Tarsus to find Saul. When he had found him there, he brought him to Antioch and the two of them spent a whole year teaching in that city. It is interesting that it was in Antioch that believers in the Lord Jesus were called Christians for the first time.

In Antioch there were now a number of strong leaders in the Church. There were Saul and Barnabas, and Simeon and Lucius, and Manaen, a young man who had been brought up with Herod the king! One day they were fasting and praying together, when the Holy Spirit brought them a special message. They must set apart Barnabas and Saul for the special work of carrying the Gospel into parts where its message had not yet been heard. Antioch was becoming the center for missionary work in the young Christian church.

After fasting and prayer, the leaders in the church laid their hands on Barnabas and Saul. These two then were sent out as the first missionaries. The two men traveled from Antioch in Syria to the port of Seleucia. There they set sail for the island of Cyprus. They landed at Salamis, and from there they journeyed through the whole land, visiting all the Jewish synagogues and preaching the Gospel.

When they reached the town of Paphos they found there a Jewish magician, a false prophet named Bar-jesus, or sometimes Elymas. He was with the proconsul, a man named Sergius Paulus. Now Sergius Paulus was a wise man and wanted very much to hear the Word of God, so he sent for Barnabas and Saul. After they had listened to what the two missionaries had to say, Elymas began to argue with them, and tried to turn Sergius Paulus against the faith.

Saul, now called Paul by many, looked Elymas straight in the eyes and said: "You are full of deceit and fraud, you enemy of good and son of the devil. When will you stop twisting the truths of God? The hand of the Lord is upon you, and you will be blind for a time." Immediately everything seemed to Elymas to turn misty and dark. He had to beg others to lead him by the hand because he could not see. When he saw that, the proconsul became a Christian.

After they had completed their work in Cyprus, Paul and Barnabas left by ship for Perga in Pamphylia, which is part of the country we now call Turkey. Paul and Barnabas went overland now to the town of Antioch. This was not the Syrian city from which they had come, but another town of the same name in the province of Pisidia. On the Sabbath they went into the synagogue for the service. After the reading of the Law and the Prophets, the synagogue officials invited them to speak if they had any message for the congregation.

At that, Paul spoke up and told them of the Lord Jesus Christ. He told how the prophets had promised that He would come to be the Savior, and how He had died and risen again. He told them that through faith in the Lord Jesus they would be forgiven their sins and become the children of God. They should be careful not to scoff, or the wrath of God would come upon them. Many of the listeners were impressed by Paul, and followed him and Barnabas to hear more of their teaching. The next Sabbath a very great crowd came to the synagogue to listen, but when the Jews saw this they began to contradict Paul and Barnabas and to blaspheme against the Lord. Then the two men took a bold stand and said: "It was necessary for the Gospel to be preached to you first, as Jews, but since you have rejected it, and judged yourselves unworthy of eternal life, we turn now to the Gentiles. This is the instruction given to us by the Lord, Who said: 'I have set you to be a light for the Gentiles, so that you may bring the word of salvation to the furthest parts of the earth'."

From there the apostles went to Iconium. Again they went into the synagogue to preach the Gospel. They spoke with such power that a great number of Jews and Gentiles became Christians. Once again, though, unbelieving Jews stirred up the Gentiles and aroused them against the apostles. The apostles stayed in Iconium for a long time. But there was division among the people. Eventually there was disorder against the new teaching. To avoid being stoned, Paul and Barnabas left the city and went to the cities of Lystra and Derbe in the provinces of Lycaonia.

At Lystra there was a man who had crippled feet and had never been able to walk. One day he was brought to listen to Paul preach. When Paul looked at him and saw that he believed, he cried out to him: "Stand up!" The man jumped to his feet and began to walk.

When the crowd saw what Paul had done, they began to shout in the Lycaonian language that the gods had become like men and come down to earth. They began to call Paul and Barnabas by the names of Hermes and Zeus, the names of their heathen gods. The priest of the temple of Zeus, which was just outside the city, even brought garlands to hang around the apostles' necks. He brought oxen to sacrifice to them! When Paul and Barnabas saw this, they rushed into the crowd and cried out: "Men, why are you doing this? We are human beings just like yourselves. We have come to preach the Gospel to you so that you may turn away from your vain worship to the living God Who made the heaven and the earth and the sea, and all that is in them."

Even after they had said these things it was still difficult for them to prevent the Lycaonians from sacrificing to them.

However, before long, Jews came from Pisidian Antioch, and Iconium, and stirred up the people against the apostles. They stoned Paul until they thought he was dead and dragged his body out of the city. But while the disciples stood around him, mourning, Paul rose up and went back with them into the city. The next day he and Barnabas left Lystra and went to Derbe. From there they went back to Lystra, to Iconium and to Pisidian Antioch, stopping in each place to teach the believers there and encourage them in the faith.

When Paul and Barnabas returned to Antioch they found an argument raging between the disciples there. Some believers said the Gentiles had to accept the Jewish laws. Others said it was not necessary. So the church decided to send Paul and Barnabas to Jerusalem to discuss the problem with the elders there.

After the matter had been carefully discussed, it was decided to let the Gentile believers know that they need not keep the Jewish laws and ceremonies.

Paul and Barnabas were accompanied in Antioch by two believers, Judas and Silas. They stayed a while and then decided to go on a tour of the places where they had preached before, so that they could help the young churches there. Barnabas wanted to take along a young man by the name of John Mark, but Paul did not agree because John Mark had left them the last time they visited Pamphylia and had gone back to Jerusalem. There was such an argument over this, that in the end Barnabas took John Mark with him to Cyprus and separated for a time from Paul. Paul then chose Silas to be his companion. They went to all the churches in Syria and Cilicia.

On the way they visited the cities of Derbe and Lystra. At Lystra there lived a young believer named Timothy. Paul asked him to go with him on his missionary travels.

At Troas, Paul saw a vision of a man from Macedonia crying out to him to come and help them. They felt this to be a sign from the Holy Spirit which could not be ignored. So they went on to the great Macedonian city of Philippi.

Paul Preaches in Athens

Acts 17

After Paul and Silas had left Philippi in Macedonia they traveled to the city of Thessalonica. There was a Jewish synagogue in that city. According to his usual practice, Paul went to the synagogue. For three Sabbath days he reasoned with the Jews from the Scriptures, explaining how it was taught that the Christ had to suffer and die, and rise

again from the dead. Then he told them that Jesus was the promised Christ. Some of the listeners believed and joined Paul and Silas, as did also some of the God-fearing Greeks.

As so often happened, though, the Jewish leaders did their best to stop the preaching. After trouble with the authorities, Paul and Silas left the city and went to Berea.

At Berea, Paul began his teaching as usual in the synagogue. Now the people there were nobler than in Thessalonica. They heard Paul with eagerness, and carefully studied their Bibles to see whether his teaching was correct. Because of this, many of them believed, and a number of the leading Greeks did so as well. When the Jews of Thessalonica heard of this, they sent men to Berea to cause trouble there, too. To avoid trouble, Paul left for the coast and went by ship southward to Athens. Silas and Timothy remained for the time being in Berea, quietly, encouraging the believers there. They would join Paul later.

While Paul waited in Athens, he was horrified to see the idol worship that was being carried on everywhere. In the synagogue he reasoned with the Jews and the Greek believers in the living God. Every day in the market place he preached to all who would listen.

Because there was such interest, he went to the Areopagus, a rocky hill on which stood the temple of the Greek god of war. The hill overlooked the market place. The people asked him to explain the new teaching he was proclaiming. They said: "We are hearing strange things about your doctrine."

Paul stood up and said to them: "Men of Athens, I notice that you are a very religious people. You have even, I see, built an altar for 'The Unknown God', so that you are sure not to leave out any of the gods which you feel ought to be worshiped. Now the God unknown to you, the real God, is the One I am proclaiming. He is the God of heaven and earth, Who has made the world and all things in it. He does not dwell in man-made temples, and does not need our gifts, seeing He is the giver of life and breath to all. It is He Who has made of one blood all the nations that live on earth, and has settled their times and where they are to live. Therefore all should seek God, to serve Him and worship Him, though He is not far from any of us. As your own poets have said: 'In Him we live and move and have our being.' If we are then His creation, we ought not to think that He is like gold or silver or stone, nor like an image made by the art and thought of man. God has overlook-ed men's ignorance in the past, but now He is calling on all in the whole world to repent. He has fixed a day for the judgment of the world in righteousness. And the Judge will be this Man Whose appointment He has sealed by raising Him from the dead."

When they heard Paul mention the resurrection of the dead, some of the councillors sneered and said: "We shall hear you at some other time on this subject."

So Paul left them, but a few who had heard him believed and became Christians.

The Church in Corinth

Acts 18

When he left Athens, Paul went to another of the great Greek cities, Corinth. In that city he came across a Jew named Aquila, who had come from Italy with his wife, Priscilla, not long before. At that time the Emperor Claudius had driven all Jews out of Rome. Aquila and Priscilla had sought safety in Greece. Paul went to stay with them because they were tentmakers by trade. Paul was also a tentmaker and they could carry on their work together. Each Sabbath, Paul taught in the synagogue and persuaded both Jews

and Greeks of the truth of the Gospel.

When Silas and Timothy arrived, Paul left his tent making and spent all his time preaching and trying to prove to the Jews that Jesus was the Christ. But they would not listen to him. They cursed him for what he said. He turned from them, saying: "Your blood be on your own heads. From now on I shall go to the Gentiles."

In a vision God encouraged Paul and told him: "Do not be afraid. Go on speaking. I am with you, and no one will hurt you or attack you, for I have many people in this city."

For eighteen months Paul preached the Gospel without being disturbed at all. Then when Gallio became proconsul of the province of Achaia, the Jews conspired against Paul and had him brought before Gallio. "This man," they said, "persuades people to worship God in a way that is against our Law."

Just as Paul was about to defend himself, Gallio interrupted. "If this were a matter of serious crime," he said, "I should deal with it. But if you wish to argue here about words and religious laws, I will have nothing to do with you."

For a while longer Paul remained in Corinth. Then he began his missionary journeys again. This time Priscilla and Aquila went with him. First they went to Cenchrea, and then to Ephesus. There he left his companions. Before he went on, though, he first taught for a short while in the synagogue. When they asked him to stay, he decided not to, but promised to come back later if it was the will of God.

Taking a ship from Ephesus, he returned to Caesarea near Jerusalem. After a short stay he went up to Jerusalem to greet the church there. Then he traveled to Antioch, to the church which had sent him out as a missionary.

Riots and Righteousness in Ephesus

Acts 18 to 20

In Antioch Paul spent some time preaching, but also resting and preparing himself for a new missionary tour. Then he left for the provinces of Galatia and Phrygia. There he visited all the new churches and taught the disciples. He especially encouraged the leaders who had to stand up to much opposition from unbelievers.

After this Paul went to the synagogue where he taught regularly for a period of three months. At first he was listened to with interest, but then some people argued against him and made a disturbance about his teaching. Then Paul withdrew from the synagogue. He took those who trusted in the Lord Jesus with him. Then he began to teach in the hall of a philosopher called Tyrannus. For two years he taught there, so that all who lived in the province of Asia, both Jews and Greeks, were able to hear the

Lord's Word. God gave Paul wonderful powers at this time so that even handkerchiefs or aprons which he had touched were brought to the sick and they were healed and evil spirits went out of them!

Paul's power was so amazing that some false teachers in the area tried to copy what Paul was doing. Traveling Jewish exorcists, who claimed to be able to drive out evil spirits, tried to name the Name of the Lord Jesus over unhappy demon-possessed people and said: "We charge you to go out, in the name of Jesus whom Paul preaches."

The seven sons of Sceva, a Jewish priest, were doing this, but

came to Paul and told him what they had been doing. They brought their books of magic and piled them up and set them on fire. The value of those books was fifty thousand pieces of silver. Many people put their trust in the Lord Jesus Christ because of what had happened to the magicians of Ephesus.

At this time it was Paul's plan to go into the provinces of Macedonia and Achaia and from there to Jerusalem. After that he would go to Rome. Before he left, however, he sent two of his helpers, Timothy and Erastus into Macedonia to prepare the churches there for his coming.

Soon after they had left, the situation in Ephesus took an unpleasant turn. Many of the magicians had given up their practice. The people had begun to understand how worthless the ways of the magicians were. Much of their magic had been connected with the worship of a goddess named Diana, or Artemis in Greek. The silversmiths of the city had done a roaring trade making small silver idols of the goddess. But now their business was falling off badly. One of them, Demetrius, called together the rest of the silversmiths to discuss their position. "Men, you know that our prosperity, and the prosperity of the city depends on this trade of ours. Now this Paul has come here and persuaded many of the

they were horrified one day when one of the evil spirits turned upon them. As they spoke, the evil spirit cried out: "Jesus I know, and Paul I know, but who are you?" Then the demon-possessed man attacked them and knocked two of them down. They all fled from the house with their clothes torn off and with many wounds on their bodies.

This news soon got about Ephesus, and all who practiced magic became afraid of what might happen to them. Many people, not only in Ephesus, but in most of the province of Asia, that gods made with hands are not gods at all. There is danger now that our trade will collapse altogether, and that even the Temple of the Goddess Diana will be dishonored."

When they heard this, the silversmiths were very angry and shouted out: "Great is Diana of the Ephesians!" They then rushed into the streets, stirring up the people of the town against the Christians. In the square there was a great deal of pushing and shouting and confusion. Not all the people knew what the fuss was about, but for two hours they continued shouting: "Great is Diana of the Ephesians!"

Eventually the town clerk managed to quiet them down and speak to them. This is what he said: "Men of Ephesus, is there any person, after all, who does not know that the city of Ephesus is the guardian of the Temple of Diana, and of the image that fell down from Jupiter? So what is the need for this commotion? If Demetrius and his companions have a complaint against anyone, there are courts and magistrates before whom they can be brought. And if you want anything more to be done, there is the city assembly. But this riotous behaviour must not continue, or else the provincial authorities will call us to account for it." After this he sent the crowd away.

When the uproar had settled down, Paul said good-by to the disciples and left for Macedonia, as he had planned to do before the trouble had begun.

Paul's Last Journey to Jerusalem

Acts 20 to 21

Nowadays Macedonia is a part of Greece, but in the time of Paul's ministry it was a separate Roman province. After the troubles in Ephesus, Paul left the province of Asia and went by ship across to Macedonia. He visited all the

churches in those parts, in Philippi and Thessalonica and Berea, and other towns. He preached and encouraged the disciples. Then he journeyed southward by road to the province of Greece. There he spent about three months. Paul planned to go back to Syria to the church in Antioch which had sent him out as a missionary, but he had to change his plans because he discovered that the Jews were once more lying in wait for him. Back through Macedonia he went. This time a number of Macedonian Christians went with him as he preached from town to town. They travelled across Macedonia and at Philippi they embarked on a ship to take them across to Troas in the province of Asia. The voyage took them five days. They spent seven days in Troas.

On the first day of the week, the disciples in Troas gathered for the breaking of bread (some would call this a Communion Service). Paul preached to them that night. He spoke until midnight.

Now they were all together in the upper room of a house. Some of the listeners sat on the window ledges because the room was so crowded. In one window sat a young man called Eutychus. During the sermon he fell asleep. Suddenly he slumped forward and fell out of the window. When some of Paul's listeners got to him, he

was dead. Paul went down quickly to him. He threw himself down on Eutychus, and took him in his arms and said: "Do not be distressed. His life is still in him." Then the young man came to life and they were greatly comforted. Paul went back to his meeting and preached until daybreak. Then he departed.

Early in the morning Paul started off on the first stage of his journey to Jerusalem. He wanted to be there for the festival of Pentecost. At Assos he met the rest of his party and went on board with them. After a few days sailing, they arrived at Miletus where they stayed over for a few days. Paul sent for the elders of the church in Ephesus. When they came, he gave them a very solemn message. "You know," he said, "how since the first day I set foot in Asia, I have served the Lord in all humility, even with tears and suffering because of what the Jews have done against me. I have not kept back from you any of the teaching God sent me to give. I have preached both publicly and privately, from house to house, telling both Jews and Greeks to repent and believe in our Lord Jesus Christ. Now the Holy Spirit has made it clear to me that I must go to Jerusalem. I do not know what will happen to me there, but the Holy Spirit keeps telling me that imprisonment and all manner of sufferings lie ahead of me. I do not look upon my life as a thing to be clung to. What matters most is the faithful performance of the ministry to which the Lord has called me, to proclaim the Gospel of the grace of God. I warn you to take care of yourselves and of the whole flock over which the Holy Spirit has made you shepherds, because after my going ferocious wolves will get in among you to destroy the flock. False teachers will appear in

your own ranks and will draw disciples away from the truth. So keep on the alert always, and remember that for three years I did not cease to advise and teach you, even with tears. Now I commend you to God's keeping. I have coveted none of your possessions. You know that my own hands ministered to my needs and the needs of all my party. By my example, I have shown you that by working hard you must help the weak, and always remember that the Lord Jesus Himself said: "It is more blessed to give than to receive."

From Miletus the ship set sail past the islands of Coos and Rhodes, and then across the open sea past Cyprus, until it came to the Syrian port of Tyre. Paul and his party remained at Tyre for seven days, staying with the disciples there. They had been warned by the Holy Spirit that Paul was going into great danger. They pleaded with him not to continue his journey to Jerusalem.

From Tyre, Paul's ship went on to Ptolemais. After greeting the Christian brethren there, they stayed with them for a day. Then the next day they sailed on to Caesarea where they left the ship to continue their journey overland to Jerusalem.

At Caesarea, Paul and his party stayed in the house of Philip the evangelist. He was one of the seven chosen to look after the needs of widows and the poor and the sick in the church at Jerusalem. While they were there, a prophet named Agabus came down from Judea to see Paul. Walking up to Paul's party, he took Paul's belt and used it to bind his own feet and hands, and then said: "This is what the Holy Spirit says: 'In the same way as I have bound my hands and feet, the Jews in Jerusalem will bind the man that owns this belt, and hand him over to the Romans.'"

Now when they heard that, Paul's friends and all the Christians who had gathered at Philip's house were most upset and begged Paul not to go to Jerusalem. But he said to them: "What are you trying to do, weeping and breaking my heart? I am ready not only to be bound, but even to die at Jerusalem for the sake of the Lord Jesus Christ."

When they found they could not make him change his mind, they said: "The Lord's will be done."

From the
Castle Steps

Acts 21 and 22

After Paul had been back in Jerusalem for a week, he was seen there by some of the Jews who had previously caused so much trouble in the province of Asia. He had gone every day to the Temple to worship. At once these troublesome people caused an outcry, and stirred up the people against Paul. They caught hold of him and cried out: "Men of Israel, help! This is the man who is turning everyone against the Law of Moses and against the worship that is carried on here. Now he has even brought Gentiles into the Temple and defiled it!" They had seen him before in the street with Trophimus, an Ephesian, and thought that Paul had brought him into the Temple.

The Jews who had accused Paul dragged him out of the Temple, beating him as they went. The news quickly reached the captain of the Roman guard that there was likely to be a riot. He quickly called together a number of officers and soldiers and ran down to put a stop to the trouble. As soon as the Jews saw the Roman soldiers, they stopped hitting Paul. The Romans took him prisoner instead.

Just as Paul was being taken through the doorway of the barracks, he spoke to the captain of the guard and asked for permission to speak to the crowd before he was imprisoned.

"Brethren and fathers," he called out, "hear my defense. I am a Jew, brought up in Tarsus in the province of Cilicia, it is true, but as strictly a Jew as any man could be." Then he told them how he had persecuted Christians and how God had spoken to him on the road to Damascus. He told them of his blindness and how through God's power Ananias had healed him again.

"Soon after my sight was restored I came back to Jerusalem. One day while I was in the Temple praying, I fell into a trance and heard the Lord warning me to leave Jerusalem quickly, because the people would not listen to what I had to tell about Him. The Lord said: 'Go! I am sending you far away to the Gentiles.'"

The crowd had been quiet up to this point, but when they heard Paul speak of going to the Gentiles, they became enraged again. "Away with him!" they shouted. "Such a fellow ought not to be allowed to live!"

The captain of the guard felt that Paul should be taken to a safer place, so he ordered him to be brought inside the barracks.

But the barracks was not really so much safer! The soldiers stretched Paul out and fastened him down with leather thongs so that they could scourge him. When Paul realized what they were doing, he said to the centurion in charge: "Is it lawful for you to scourge a man who is a Roman citizen and has not been found guilty of any crime?" When the centurion heard that, he went at once to the captain of the guard and said: "What are you doing now? This man is a Roman!" The captain went quickly to Paul and asked him if this was true. When Paul said it was, the captain was afraid. He decided that Paul must be released at once and a proper hearing must be held of all the complaints against him. However, for Paul's own safety he must remain in the barracks until the time chosen for the hearing.

Serving the Savior in Prison

Acts 22 to 24

Forty of the Jews got together and worked out a plan to kill Paul. But the captain heard of the plot. The captain wanted to see that Paul had fair treatment. He sent Paul under guard to the Roman governor Felix, in Caesarea, about fifty miles away.

After inquiry from which province Paul had come, in order to make sure that he had the right to deal with the case, Felix instructed that he should be imprisoned in Herod's palace until his accusers arrived.

Five days later Ananias, the high priest arrived with some of the elders and a lawyer called Tertullus. They put forward their evidence against Paul. Tertullus made a long speech to the governor in which he spoke of Paul as a perfect pest, a man who had caused trouble among the Jews in all parts of the empire, and a ringleader in the sect of the Nazarenes. He even accused Paul of having tried to defile the Temple by bringing heathen men into its courts. The elders all showed their strong agreement with what Tertullus had said.

Then the governor gave Paul the chance to speak. Paul said, "You will be able to understand the defense I put forward. It is only twelve days since I went to Jerusalem. In that time I have caused no trouble, either in the Temple or elsewhere in the city, and I have not quarrelled with anyone. I confess to you that I do worship God as a Christian, a way which they call false, but I still place the fullest confidence in the Law of Moses and in the writings of the prophets. I believe exactly as these men do that there is to be a resurrection both of the righteous and of the wicked. These men found me worshiping in the Temple. But there were men there from the province of Asia, who stirred up trouble against me. These men are the ones who ought to be here today as my accusers, if they have anything to say against me. But those who are here, let them say of what crime they found me guilty when I appeared before the Council in Jerusalem! Unless, of course, it was because I said I believed in the resurrection of the dead!"

Felix was unwilling now to carry on with the case. He understood a little about the Christian faith. He put the Jewish leaders off by saying that he would examine the case more fully when Claudius Lysias, the captain of the guard, came to Caesarea from Jerusalem. Then he told one of the centurions to take care of Paul, giving him some liberty and allowing his friends to visit him and take care of him.

A few days later Felix and his wife, Drusilla, who was a Jewess, sent for Paul to listen to what he had to tell about the Lord Jesus Christ. However, Felix was a dishonest man and was hoping that Paul would pay him a bribe to let him go free. He sent often for Paul and talked to him about the Christian faith, but he was not really interested in anything except the money he thought Paul might give him.

After two years Porcius Festus was appointed governor in the place of Felix. Because Felix wanted to leave a good impression in the minds of the Jews, he left Paul a prisoner for Festus to deal with.

The King Who Heard But Did Not Heed

Acts 25 and 26

Soon after Festus arrived in Caesarea, he decided to go up to Jerusalem to meet the Jewish leaders. One of the first matters those leaders wanted to discuss with him was the fate of Paul. They asked for him to be brought to Jerusalem to be put on trial there. They still had it in mind to lay an ambush for the party and to kill Paul.

Festus said he would soon be returning to Caesarea. They must send their leaders with Paul, and if he had done anything wrong, they could bring their evidence against him there.

About ten days later the case began in Caesarea. The Jews who had come from Jerusalem brought many serious charges against Paul. They could prove none of them. Then Paul stood up and said: "I have done nothing wrong against the Jewish Law nor against Caesar." Festus asked him if he was willing to go to Jerusalem and stand trial before him there, but Paul said: "I am standing before the Roman tribunal now, and that is where I ought to be tried. I have done no wrong to the Jews as you know already. If I have done anything that deserves the death penalty, I am willing to die. But if none of the charges is true which these men bring against me, no one can hand me over to them. As a Roman citizen, I appeal to Caesar."

Festus discussed the matter with his advisers and then gave his verdict: "You have appealed to Caesar; to Caesar you shall go."

A little after this, Herod Agrippa, the king of Judea, and his wife Bernice arrived in Caesarea to welcome Festus, the new Roman governor. While there, Festus told them about Paul.

Agrippa was curious about the whole matter. "I should like to hear the man myself," he said. The meeting was arranged for the next day. In the morning, Agrippa and Bernice went into the audience hall and took their seats on the royal thrones in the midst of great pomp and ceremony.

Festus then sent for Paul to be brought in. "The Jewish rulers have demanded that this man be put to death, but I have not found him to be guilty of any serious crime. Now he has appealed to Caesar Augustus, and I must send him to Rome. But I do not know what to write in my report that must go to Caesar. For that reason I have brought him in front of you. You may examine him so that I may have something to put in writing."

Then King Agrippa told Paul to

explain his position. This is what Paul said: "King Agrippa, I feel fortunate in being asked to explain my views to you, because I know how well you understand the Jewish customs and laws which I am accused of breaking. The Jews know of my background. They know that from my childhood I have kept the Law, and lived as a Pharisee, a member of the strictest party in our Jewish faith. And now I stand on trial because of what I believe in connection with the promise God made to our forefathers, of One He would send to be our Savior. It is the fulfilment of this that our twelve tribes long for. They worship fervently day after day. Because of this I am accused by the Jews and made to seem like a criminal! Why is it thought unbelievable by any of you that God should raise the dead?"

Then he continued and told of how he persecuted the Christians and how he was stricken down on the road to Damascus.

Then Agrippa said: "Paul, you have almost persuaded me to be a Christian!" Paul answered: "I wish to God that not only you, but all who listen to me here might become as I am, except for these chains!"

Then the king and queen, and the Roman governor, and the people sitting with them arose to leave the hall. Privately they talked about the matter and agreed that Paul had done nothing that deserved either death or imprisonment. And, as Agrippa said to Festus: "We could have set this man free if he had not appealed to Caesar."

A Storm at Sea

Acts 27 to 28

After Paul had been in prison for two years, without his case having been properly heard, it was decided that he and some other prisoners should now be taken to Rome. Under the guard of a centurion called Julius, of the Augustan Legion, they were taken on board an Adramyttium ship which was about to sail by the seaports of the province of Asia. From Caesarea they sailed northward up the coast to Sidon. There Julius the centurion very kindly allowed Paul to visit his Christian friends and be cared for by them.

After leaving Sidon they sailed across the Phoenician Sea. Then they skirted the coast of the island of Cyprus to have shelter from the heavy winds. Passing the north end of Cyprus, they came to the port of Myra in Lycia. There they transferred to a ship from Alexandria which was going to Italy. After passing between Rhodes and the mainland, they planned to sail south of Achaia (Greece) and directly across to Italy. At first they made slow progress. Then the winds were contrary, and they found difficulty in keeping to their course. It was decided to sail around the southern side of Crete, so as to be sheltered from the fierce winds which could make navigation dangerous at that time of the year.

With great difficulty they reached a place called Fair Havens, near the town of Lasea. Here Paul warned them that to go on at that time of the year would be very dangerous. But the centurion chose instead to take the advice of the pilot and the ship's owner. Because the harbor was not suitable for wintering, they decided to try to reach the harbor of Phoenix near the western end of Crete. There would be enough protection there and they could spend the worst part of the winter.

When a soft wind arose, they felt the time had come to set sail for their winter quarters, so they weighed anchor and sailed along toward Phoenix. They kept close inshore for safety's sake. Soon afterward, though, a violent wind burst upon them from the direction of the island. It was so fierce that they could not tack back toward the island, but simply had to let the ship drift before the wind.

For days they saw neither sun nor stars, and the storm raged. Finally, they gave up all hope of ever safely reaching land. There was very little food left. If they did not die by drowning it seemed as if they might starve to death.

Paul then spoke to the captain and said: "Although the ship will be lost, there will not be any loss of life. This very night an angel of the God I serve appeared to me and said to me: 'Do not be afraid, Paul. You must appear before Caesar, and all the men who are with you will be safe as well.' So I say to you, Keep up your courage, because I trust in God that it will turn out exactly as I have been told. But we will run aground on a certain island."

When the fourteenth night of their voyage had come, they were being driven hither and thither in the Adriatic Sea. About midnight the sailors reported that they were approaching land. Taking soundings, they found that they were driving rapidly toward the land. Fearing that they might end up on the rocks, the sailors threw out four anchors from the stern. The sailors wished that the night would end so that they could see better what was going on.

Just before dawn, Paul encouraged them all to take a little food,

because of the fast they had had, and because of what lay just ahead of them. "Do not be afraid," he said. "Not a hair on your heads will be harmed." When he had said this, he took bread himself, and gave thanks to God in front of them all. Then he began to eat, and the rest of them followed his example.

When it became light, they saw a safe-looking beach and decided to try to direct the ship to it if they could. However, the ship struck a reef where two currents met, and ran aground. The prow was stuck in the rocks, and the waves began to break up the stern.

The soldiers thought that they should kill the prisoners in case they swam ashore and escaped. However, the centurion prevented them from doing this. Those who could swim were told to jump overboard first and get to land. The rest were to follow on planks or anything else that would float.

All arrived safely on shore. When they were able to look around, they found that they were on the island of Malta.

The Good News Reaches Rome

Acts 28

The people of Malta were very kind to Paul and all the others from the wreck. Publius, the leading man of the island, entertained them for three days. The father of this man was very sick with fever and dysentery. Paul went to see him. After Paul had laid his hands on the old man and prayed for him, he was healed.

When the news of this got abroad, many other people who suffered from one illness or another were brought to Paul. They, too, were cured.

From Malta they sailed to the port of Syracuse in Sicily. Then they sailed to Rhegium at the mouth of the narrows between Sicily and Italy. From Rhegium a south wind carried them right across the Etruscan Sea to Puteoli, where they disembarked.

When they finally arrived in Rome, the centurion handed over the prisoners to the captain of the guard. Paul was allowed to live in a house of his own with only one soldier to guard him.

For two years Paul remained in that house, and though he was a prisoner, he lived in safety. The Word of God was taught in Rome.

The Throne of God

Revelation 1 to 5

The last of the apostles was John, the son of Zebedee. When he was an old man, the Roman emperor, Domitian, banished him to the lonely island of Patmos in the Aegean Sea, about twenty-five miles off the coast of Asia.

One day while John was on that barren little island, earnestly worshiping, and held in the power of God's Spirit, he suddenly heard behind him a great voice speaking like the sound of a war trumpet. The voice said: "I am the Alpha and the Omega, the First and the Last." It was the Lord Jesus speaking. He went on to say: "You must write down quickly what you see in this vision, and send the writing to the seven churches in Asia."

John turned to see who was speaking to him. There he saw seven golden lampstands. In the midst of the lampstands stood One Whom John knew to be the Lord Jesus Christ, the Son of Man. But He looked more glorious than John had seen Him before.

When John saw Him, he threw himself down in fear and adoration. The Lord laid His right hand on him and said: "Do not be afraid! Write down the things you have seen, and all about what is happening and what will still happen. The seven stars in My right hand are the leaders of the seven churches. The seven golden lampstands are the churches themselves." Then the Lord gave to John a special message for each of the seven churches. John had to write the messages in the form of letters, but the words in them were all from the Lord Himself. The seven churches were in Ephesus, Smyrna, Pergamum, Thyatira, Sardis, Philadelphia and Laodicea.

After this John saw a door opened into Heaven. A great voice like a trumpet called on him to come and he would be told some of the things which must happen in the future. Immediately he was in the power of the Holy Spirit, and was able to see some of the glories of Heaven. In front of him stood a throne. On the throne sat a Being so full of glory that John could not look directly at Him. Around the throne was a great ring like a rainbow, colored green like an emerald. Arranged around the Throne were twenty-four other thrones. On each of them sat an elder, clothed in white, and with a golden crown on his head. From the Great Throne came flashes of lightning, and rumblings like thunder, and the sound of many voices. In front of the Throne were seven blazing torches and the floor was a sea of transparent glass, shining like crystal. Around the Throne, at the center of each side of the Throne stood four living creatures, full of eyes in front and behind. One looked like a lion, one like an ox, one like a man, and one like an eagle. Each of them had three pairs of wings. They kept on saying, without stopping, "Holy, holy, holy, Lord God Almighty, Who was, and is, and is to come."

Then John saw between the Throne and the four living creatures, a Lamb standing, as if slain. He knew that the Lamb was the Lord Jesus Christ. The Lamb came and took the scroll out of the hand of the One that sat on the throne. As He stepped forward again, the four living creatures and the twenty-four elders worshiped before Him.

The City of God

John's vision on the island of Patmos was a long one. The Lord Jesus told him much about things that were still to happen. Some of them have not even happened yet, so it is important to study the book of Revelation in which they are written.

One part of the vision was of all God's people gathered together in glory. He saw a great host of people, so many that no one could count them, gathered from all nations on earth. They stood in front of the Throne of God and in front of the Lamb. Clothed in white robes, and with palm branches in their hands, they cried out in a loud voice: "Salvation belongs to our God Who is seated on the Throne, and to the Lamb!" As they shouted out this mighty shout, all the angels and the elders and the living creatures threw themselves down around the Throne, worshiping.

Then one of the elders asked John a question: "Who are these people clothed in white robes? and where do they come from?" John answered: "Sir, you know." Then the elder said: "These are persons who have come out of great persecution, and have washed their robes and made them white in the blood of the Lamb. That is why

412

they stand here in the presence of God and serve Him day and night in His Temple. He will protect them and spread His tent over them forever. They will never again be hungry or thirsty. The sun will not scorch them. The Lamb in the center of the Heavenly Throne will be their Shepherd. He will guide them to fountains of living water. God will wipe away all tears from their eyes."

A while later, John saw the city of God, where all will live who love the Lamb. A great voice cried out to him, and said: "Look! The dwelling place of God is with men. They shall be His people, and He will live in the midst of them. They will not know the meaning of sorrow any more, nor pain, nor death. All these things have passed away." Then God spoke from the throne: "See, I make all things new. To him that is thirsty, I will give from the fountain of the Water of Life. Those who win the victory over sin and Satan will inherit all things. I will be their God, and they will be My sons."

Then an angel of God came and carried John away in spirit to a high mountain. The angel showed John the city of God, the New Jerusalem, which came down out of Heaven. In Revelation 21 there is a beautiful description of this city.

After this John saw a crystal-clear river of the Water of Life, flowing from the Throne of God

and the Lamb, and passing through the city of God. Beside the river grew the Tree of Life. The tree bore twelve different kinds of fruit, one for each month of the year. The leaves of that tree were for the healing of the nations. In that city was no darkness at all. No light of any kind was needed, for the Lord God Himself will give light to all His people there forever.

When John saw and heard these glorious things, he fell down at the feet of the angel who had shown them to him to worship him. The angel said to him: "You must not do that! I am a servant of God like you are, and like the prophets, and like all who obey the teaching of this book. Worship God, and Him only!"

Then He said: "Do not hide away the teaching of this book, but tell it to all believers. The time for its fulfilment is near."

After this, the Lord Jesus Himself ended John's vision by saying to him: "I, Jesus, have sent My angel to tell you about these things so that My people in the churches may hear about them. I am the Root and Offspring of David. I am the Bright and Morning Star. The Spirit and the Bride say: Come! And let him that listens to this teaching say: Come! Let everyone that is thirsty in soul come and take freely of the Water of Life. . . . He Who tells you of the certainty of these things, says: Look! I will come swiftly. Amen."

MILL FOR GRINDING GRAIN

GRINDING TOOLS

PLOW

SCALES